T0247886

ANGLO-CHINESE DIPLOMACY
1906–1920

ANGLO-CHINESE DIPLOMACY

in the careers of
Sir John Jordan and Yüan Shih-k'ai

1906-1920

CHAN LAU KIT-CHING

HONG KONG UNIVERSITY PRESS
1978

Printed in Hong Kong by

LIBRA PRESS LTD.

56 Wong Chuk Hang Road 5D, Aberdeen

CONTENTS

PREFACE

YÜAN SHIH-K'AI (1859–1916) has inspired much historical discussion, writing, and scholarship. One recurrent theme is that he was respected, admired, and even fervently supported by the foreigners in China. In short, from the turn of the century Yüan was regarded as the strong man to whom foreign missionaries, as in the Boxer Uprising, looked for protection, and on whom foreign merchants and governments depended for the peace and stability which they recognized as vital for their economic prosperity in China.

Chinese Communist and Nationalist historians have denounced this foreign attitude to Yüan. They see it as a major contribution to his political influence, which brought about the decade of warlordism following his death and China's ensuing political tumults. To the Communist writers the harm was only undone in 1949 when the Communists took over control in China. The Nationalists, on the other hand, still feel themselves experiencing bitter consequences of Yüan's influence. Impartial historians have generally agreed on the crucial importance of foreign backing in Yüan's political career.

This book attempts to explain this aspect of Yüan Shih-k'ai's political power by analysing the relationship between him and Sir John Newell Jordan, British minister at Peking from 1906 to 1920. To say that Jordan was an important foreigner, when he was representing a nation which at least until Yüan's death was still regarded as the most influential power in China, is an understatement. The interaction between Jordan and Yüan mirrors not only Anglo-Chinese relations but also international diplomacy in China during this fascinating period.

That this study should in the main be undertaken from the point of view of Jordan, is largely determined by the available source materials. Jordan's opinions, attitudes and emotions emerge clearly from his telegrams and dispatches to the Foreign Office and to the consular staff in China, and from his private correspondence. The same, however, are not available for Yüan. Accessible materials attributed to him are mostly official statements and public announcements which are no guarantee, to say the least, of genuine feelings and intentions.

The story begins in the year 1906 when Jordan arrived in China as British minister, and Yüan Shih-k'ai was governor-general of Chihli, the

Anglo-Chinese Diplomacy 1906–1920

capital province of China. The first chapter deals with the period from
1906 to the outbreak of the 1911 Revolution, when Jordan's views on
Chinese politics in general and Yüan Shih-k'ai in particular were formed.
The second chapter concentrates on Jordan's strenuous efforts after the
1911 Revolution to have Yüan Shih-k'ai accepted as the *de facto* ruler
within the framework of continued Manchu sovereignty. Jordan failed.
The retention of the Manchu dynasty, in whatever reduced or humiliated
form, was anathema to the revolutionaries and their collaborators whose
control grew rapidly with the outbreak of the revolution. Chapter three
is concerned with the years 1912–1915, undoubtedly Jordan's most
rewarding time as British representative in China. The last chapter, in
contrast, follows Jordan's anxiety as he watched the progress of Yüan's
monarchical movement, which ended in tragic failure and with Yüan's
death in June 1916.

In 1920, however, Jordan did not leave China in despair. He had
recovered from the events of 1916 and, despite the divided state of China
at the time of his departure, his goodwill towards the Chinese continued.
For instance, even in his retirement as a member of the British delegation
sent to the Washington Conference, he was devoting himself to what he
regarded as a good cause for China—as he had done in supporting Yüan
Shih-k'ai as the most dependable man to safeguard the interests of both
China and Britain.

I dedicate this book, unworthy though it is, to Professor W. G.
Beasley, School of Oriental and African Studies, University of London,
and Dr I. H. Nish, London School of Economics and Political Science,
who have been sources of strength, support, and inspiration in my
academic life, and to whom I am deeply grateful. Dr Peter Lowe of the
University of Manchester has patiently read through the manuscript
and given much good advice. Thanks are also due to Miss Natalie
Graham for her diligent editing of the manuscript.

K.C.L.C.

ABBREVIATIONS

CCST : Shen Yün-lung (ed.) 沈雲龍, *Chin-tai Chung-kuo shih-liao ts'ung-k'an* 近代中國史料叢刊 [Collection of materials relating to modern Chinese history], Taipei, 1966–.

Cheng-chih shih : Li Chien-nung 李劍農, *Chung-kuo chin pai nien cheng-chih shih* 中國近百年政治史 [Political history of China in the past century], 2 vols., Taiwan, 1957.

CHST : Wu Hsiang-hsiang (ed.) 吳相湘, *Chung-kuo hsien-tai shih-liao ts'ung-shu* 中國現代史料叢書 [Collection of materials relating to contemporary Chinese history], Taipei, 1962– .

CHT : Wu Hsiang-hsiang (ed.), *Chung-kuo hsien-tai shih ts'ung-k'an* 中國現代史叢刊 [Collection on Chinese contemporary history], 6 vols., Taipei, 1960–64.

HHKM : Ch'ai Te-keng 柴德賡 etc. (ed.), *Hsin-hai ke-ming* 辛亥革命 [The 1911 Revolution], 8 vols., Shanghai, 1957.

NGB : Japanese Foreign Ministry, *Nihon gaiko bunsho* 日本外交文書 [Documents relating to Japan's foreign relations].

Treaties : J. V. A. MacMurray, *Treaties and agreements with and concerning China*, 2 vols., New York, 1921.

YSH : Shen Yün-lung (ed.), *Yüan Shih-k'ai shih-liao hui-k'an* 袁世凱史料彙刊 [Collection of materials relating to Yüan Shih-k'ai], 17 titles, Taipei, 1966.

CHAPTER I

BRITISH POLICY TOWARDS CHINA AND JORDAN'S CAREER BEFORE 1906

FROM the Opium War until the early twentieth century Britain's policy in China aimed at maximum economic benefit with minimum political involvement. However, on many occasions either her economic activities were endangered, or Britain was unwilling to undertake greater political involvement in order to protect her interests. There were times when troubles were caused by China, but they often resulted from international rivalry to control and influence her.

Whatever the situation, Britain always took the same cautious consideration. Thus, after much indecision, Britain actively intervened on the side of the Manchus towards the end of the T'ai-p'ing Rebellion, 1850–1864, at the same time trying to minimize the scale of intervention. This intervention is attributed by J. S. Gregory to 'a simple issue of commercial advantage'. By 1862 it had become obvious that only direct foreign involvement could ensure 'a Manchu victory' which was important to Britain 'in defence of the treaty rights she had exacted from the Manchu government since 1842 and of the trading interests which had developed and, it was believed, would develop under their sanction'.[1]

For the rest of the nineteenth century Britain's aim in China was thwarted many times by the so-called 'missionary problem'. Anti-Christian and anti-missionary violence incited by Chinese xenophobia threatened the British economic position on both immediate and long-term levels. Such disturbances disrupted trade. The Boxer Uprising would have done so on a large scale had it not been for the protective policy towards foreigners, adopted by high Chinese officials in the central and southern provinces where British interests were most deeply entrenched. There was, however, a more far-reaching repercussion of the missionary question. In pressing for compensation after anti-missionary incidents generally instigated by anti-dynastic elements, Britain was undermining the prestige of the Manchus who had in the first place conceded her privileged claims in China.

The British government's reaction to this dilemma was ambivalent: while it refused the Manchu request to curb missionary activities for fear of influential opposition from the churches, on the other hand it did discourage further missionary work in China. Most British missionaries saw their government's ambiguous attitude as an important cause of the growth of Chinese anti-Christian hostility.[2]

The problems mentioned so far were essentially situations arising in China. One has also to consider international rivalry, which challenged Britain's privileges and threatened her chance of expansion in China. Foreign encroachment and competition increased towards the end of the nineteenth century with the growing weakness of Ch'ing China. The climax came in 1897–1898 with the so-called 'scramble for concessions', when Germany controlled Shantung province, with exclusive mining and railway rights; France dominated south and southwest China around Kwangchow Bay; Russia was in the northeast, centering on Dairen and Port Arthur; and Japan in Fukien. Britain's response to these territorial claims followed her traditional China policy. To safeguard her interests in central China, she demanded from the Chinese government the non-alienation of the Yangtze region. To avoid over-committment herself, however, Britain did not go so far as to seek conversion of the Yangtze area into her specific sphere of influence.[3]

With the dawning of the new century, Britain's position in China was still plagued by the same problems—a feeble Manchu government, Chinese anti-foreignism, and international rivalry—but with greater intensity and new forms of expression.

The previous century had witnessed many serious anti-Manchu uprisings, but on the whole they lacked continuity. This was no longer true in the twentieth century. The *Tung-meng hui,* founded in 1905, organized a series of rebellions, culminating with the 1911 Revolution which ended the Ch'ing dynasty. No less detrimental to Manchu interests, and occuring almost simultaneously, was the constitutional movement. Ironically, this movement was initiated by the Manchus, who had been forced by their dismal defeat in the Boxer Uprising to admit that reforms were necessary to save the dynasty and the country. The country, however, became dissatisfied with the government's meagre innovations and clamoured for a more extended division of power which of course gradually diluted the absolute rule of the Manchus.

The anti-foreign sentiment of early twentieth century Chinese was no longer motivated by xenophobia which resulted in the blind killing of foreigners. The seeds of modern Chinese nationalism were sown, and took the form of boycotts and demonstrations against the powers' imperialist ambition in China, and rebellions against the Manchu government for failing to protect China's rights.

Among concessions from China, railway rights were the most sought after by Britain. Contrary to the belief of many British traders that China would be a great market for their manufactured goods, China's import trade until the end of the nineteenth century had remained discouragingly small. However, British merchants discovered that investments in mining, shipping, banking, and especially railway construction, were extremely lucrative.

In 1898 the Hongkong and Shanghai Banking Corporation associated with Jardine, Matheson and Company to form the British and Chinese Corporation for railway building in China.[4] With the support of the Foreign Office, the new corporation and other British firms obtained a fair number of railway rights from the Chinese during the scramble for concessions in 1898. It is not an exaggeration to say that railways formed an integral part of Sino-British relations from the end of the nineteenth century onwards, replacing missionaries as a cause of conflict between the two countries. In fact, the so-called 'rights recovery movement' in China reached such intensity at the turn of the century that it made a deep impression on Sir Ernest Satow, the British minister at Peking. Shortly before he left his post early in the summer of 1906, he submitted a memorandum advising the Foreign Office to abandon the old policy of extorting railway rights from China and, if possible, refrain from implementing those agreements already obtained. Sir Edward Grey, secretary for foreign affairs since the end of 1905, seemed well-disposed towards Satow's advice and was prepared 'to adopt a more conciliatory attitude, meeting the Chinese half-way, as long as they showed a disposition to do the same'.[5]

International rivalry for assets in China continued in the twentieth century. The previous pattern of scrambling among the powers was replaced by co-operation to exert joint pressure on China for investment opportunities. An international consortium for obtaining railway rights was founded in 1910, which consisted of American, British, French, and German financial interests. The consortium quickly expanded, diversifying into other forms of investment, and in 1912 it included Russian and Japanese participation, though not without unwillingness from some of the original members.

During 1912–1914 China shared the uneasy calm before the storm of World War I. The war in Europe also upset the balance of power in East Asia. As one by one the powers became involved with the war, Japan was left with a free hand to achieve her long-cherished ambition in China. Before the war, Britain had been the most influential power in

East Asia, though, as I. H. Nish suggests, the Anglo-Japanese Alliance of 1902 already indicated that Britain could no longer shoulder 'the burden of maintaining the Pax Britannica'[6] alone in the area. Between 1911 and the outbreak of war there was already 'growing disharmony' between Britain and Japan, arising from Britain's concern to maintain her position and Japan's growing ambitions in East Asia.[7] Serious conflict between the two allies did not occur until after August 1914. Japan was then able to exploit the power vacuum in the East while the war in Europe steadily debilitated Britain. Britain's rapid decline as a power effected Japan's growing dominance in East Asia.

Britain's representative in China during this transitional and difficult period was Sir John Newell Jordan.[8] Jordan was born on 5 September 1852 at Balloo, Ireland. His friends attributed his deep sense of justice and conscientiousness to his Irish origin and strict Presbyterian upbringing. His involvement with China began in 1876, when as a student interpreter he joined the China consular service. Between 1881 and 1886 he occupied various consular posts in South China. In 1886 he was transferred to Peking where he at first discharged the duties of accountant to the legation. In 1889 he was promoted to the position of assistant Chinese secretary, and in 1891 he became full Chinese secretary, winning the approval and confidence of the British minister at Peking, N. R. O'Conor.[9] By 1896 Jordan had enhanced his position as Chinese secretary in two other ways. He had gained an adequate knowledge of the Chinese language, a unique qualification amongst the British ministers to China, as well as acquiring first-hand experience of Chinese politics and Sino-foreign diplomacy at the highest level.[10]

In 1896 Jordan was appointed consul-general at Seoul, capital of Korea and at that time the pivot of Russo-Japanese rivalry. In 1898 he became chargé d'affaires and in 1901 minister resident in Korea, while retaining the position of consul-general at Seoul. Jordan left Korea late in November 1905. Not long after, Britain withdrew her diplomatic mission, anticipating Japan's hold on Korean foreign policy, which was exercised in February 1906. While Jordan might well have been 'only a distant observer of events in China' when he was in Seoul,[11] his Korean experience had a profound effect on his later service in China. Frequent references to Korea in Jordan's correspondence during World War I—when China's sovereignty was severely threatened by Japan—show that his mind was haunted by the spectre of Korea's humiliating occupation by Japan.[12]

After a reshuffle of British diplomatic and consular personnel in East

Asia in late 1905 and early 1906 Jordan succeeded Sir Ernest Satow as minister to China. Early in April 1905 Lord Lansdowne, secretary for foreign affairs, decreed that, barring special circumstances, every *chef de mission* should automatically vacate his post after a five years' tenure.[13] On receipt of the new regulation, Satow telegraphed Sir Eric Barrington, private secretary to Lansdowne, to ascertain his status in Peking after October, when he would have served out his five years in China.[14] Barrington, acting on his own initiative, replied in August that Lansdowne hoped that Satow would remain at his post 'for at least another year from September'.[15]

Satow received the answer with mixed feelings. He had for some time complained about the hot summer and the 'continuous dull monotonous unpleasant work' in Peking. In addition, his conscience was troubled by the way China had been 'most unjustly treated' by the powers, and he felt that he should 'have no more share' in the matter. In fact, even before Barrington's reply, Satow had expressed his hope to F. V. Dickens, his long standing correspondent outside the Foreign Office, that his Peking tenure would not be extended.[16]

On the other hand, Satow was both hurt and disappointed by Barrington's reply, interpreting the phrase 'at least another year from September' to mean that 'more than that w[ou]ld not be expected' of him. In a telegraph to Barrington, Satow expressed willingness to remain at his post for another year, after which, for reasons of health, he would rather leave Peking before the hot season began and 'not to return to China'.[17] The Foreign Office took Satow's response at face value and considered he had earned 'a rest after all the hard work and anxiety'.[18] In his diary, however, Satow confessed that though he would not himself ask for an extension, he would have agreed to remain in Peking had Lansdowne offered him another five years' tenure, or if later Sir Edward Grey had asked him to stay.[19]

Meanwhile, Japan's ally status by virtue of the Anglo-Japanese Alliance caused for the expansion of the British legation at Tokyo. The Foreign Office was confronted with the task of appointing the first British ambassador to Japan. The British minister in Japan then was Sir Claude MacDonald who was considered unsuitable for the ambassadorial post by the British government. Dr George Ernest Morrison, the *Times* correspondent at Peking since 1897, who had great influence on the British East Asian policy, regarded MacDonald as 'garrulous, inaccurate, long-winded'. Sir Charles Hardinge, permanent foreign under-secretary, considered MacDonald ignorant and incapable.[20]

Furthermore, the prime minister, Arthur James Balfour, was convinced by long experience that it was 'very difficult to get a point into [MacDonald's] head'.[21]

Lansdowne shared these views about MacDonald and agreed that 'it would be better to appoint someone else to the new Embassy', providing that 'it could be arranged that [MacDonald] should be withdrawn under conditions which he could not complain'. Lansdowne's rationale was that while MacDonald had not performed his duties with 'conspicuous ability', at the same time he had not made any 'serious mistakes' during a period of great stress.[22] Apparently the 'conditions' for the removal of MacDonald as prescribed by Lansdowne did not arise, and MacDonald had to be promoted as ambassador. At first the appointment was offered only on a temporary basis which greatly upset MacDonald who felt that the Foreign Office had done him grave injustice.[23]

At this stage of MacDonald's fortunes—when his promotion was confirmed—Satow, the British minister in Peking, became involved. Some of Satow's friends were indignant that he was not given the Tokyo post for which they thought he was most qualified.[24] In fact, Satow had been the minister to Japan before MacDonald, who first took up the position late in 1900. Later, back in London, Sir Edward Grey himself told Satow that had it been at all possible he would have been offered the ambassadorship. Well-intentioned as they were, these words only intensified the pangs of unfulfilled hopes.[25]

As Satow's departure from Peking drew near, the Foreign Office had to decide on appointing his successor. Also keenly interested in the matter was Morrison of *The Times,* who was thoroughly disgusted with Satow's weakness and was firmly convinced that Jordan, rather than 'a European diplomat ignorant of the very rudiments of the China question', would be the most suitable choice. This idea had been with him at least as early as late 1903. On returning to London in the autumn of 1905, one of Morrison's objectives was to secure Jordan's appointment to Peking. He wrote to Jordan in Korea of his intention and was heartily thanked. By the time he set out for China again, Morrison strongly believed that he had convinced Lansdowne, William G. Tyrrell, assistant head in the Far Eastern Department, and Louis Mallet, then précis-writer to Lansdowne, of Jordan's 'incomparable qualities' for the ministerial post.[26] However, Lansdowne left the Foreign Office before the year ended and Jordan's appointment was made by Grey early in 1906. It is quite possible that either Lansdowne or Mallet, who succeeded

Barrington as private secretary to the foreign secretary, suggested Jordan to Grey on the strength of Morrison's recommendation.

Meanwhile, the situation in Korea favoured Jordan's appointment to China. On 14 September 1905 Jordan telegraphed the Foreign Office for permission to take leave of absence from Korea in about the middle of November and the request was readily granted. It was well known that Jordan's leave was long overdue, pending the peace settlement between Japan and Russia. The Foreign Office's concern was to find someone to act in his place because the last chargé d'affaires had been a failure.[27] Jordan was asked his opinion, and suggested Henry Cockburn, Chinese secretary to the British legation at Peking then on leave in England.[28] Cockburn was to regret his acceptance of the acting appointment shortly after he had assumed duties when Britain made an agreement with Japan to withdraw her legation from Seoul, leaving behind a consulate-general.[29] This also meant that Jordan was suddenly without a post. The Far Eastern Department did not wish him to be reduced from minister and consul-general to only consul-general at Seoul.[30]

With the return of spring, the Foreign Office could no longer postpone their decision about the Peking post, especially as at that time China was a considerable cause of anxiety. The boycott of American goods was followed by the murders of missionaries at Nanchang. Other disturbing events occurred: continuous Chinese agitation for the return of railway and mining rights; virulent anti-foreign utterances in the Chinese press; and inflammatory speeches against foreigners at public meetings.

On 3 March 1906 Grey telegraphed Satow that if his decision to retire that year was final, arrangements had to be made 'under present anxious circumstances in China' for someone to succeed him as soon as he left. Grey told Satow that Jordan had been considered as the 'eventual successor', but nothing as yet had been mentioned to him.[31] Grey's suggestion that the new minister should take charge immediately after Satow's departure was rather unprecedented. Satow's tenure as minister would only terminate in October, until when he would receive the minister's pay except one quarter of it which would be paid to the chargé d'affaires who was normally the next senior man in the legation. Thus the British government would incur much greater expenses if the new minister assumed duty before Satow's term officially expired.

Apart from confirming his intention to leave Peking that year, Satow in his reply raised some of his personal views with Grey. He believed that the China situation was 'difficult' rather than 'anxious' and considered that Lancelot D. Carnegie, legation secretary, and Charles W.

Campbell, acting Chinese secretary, could be trusted to handle the work of the legation until the arrival of the new minister. As to the question of his successor, he did not 'know Sir J. Jordan personally', but would himself recommend either Reginald Tower or Walter Townley, as each had served under him with great distinction as legation secretary.[32] Satow's views went unheeded. Two days after Satow's intention to retire was confirmed, Sir Charles Hardinge wrote to the King: 'Sir E. Grey has seen Sir J. Jordan, and the latter is to go out shortly to China as Chargé d'Affaires with the rank of Minister until October, when Sir E. Satow retires, and he will then be definitely appointed Minister at Peking'.[33] The Foreign Office justified such 'extravagance' to the Treasury on the ground that 'the unsatisfactory state of affairs in China' made it 'essential to place H.M. Legation at Peking in the hands of an officer of special ability and experience'.[34]

According to some Chinese, the Foreign Office chose Jordan for another, more important reason; that is, his close friendship with Yüan Shih-k'ai who by this time had become a key political personage in China. An enthusiastic exponent of this view was Yeh Kung-cho, not only a well-known figure in recent Chinese economic and railway history, but also a close associate of Liang Shih-i, who was intimately connected with Yüan Shih-k'ai for many years. According to Yeh, Jordan had once saved Yüan's life in Korea, shortly before the outbreak of the Sino-Japanese War in 1894. The Japanese had plotted to assassinate Yüan, believing his influence was grossly detrimental to their position in Korea. Yüan narrowly escaped by boarding a man-of-war—put at his disposal by Jordan who was then consul in Korea—and eventually returned to Tientsin. Yeh claims that the British government intended to use the Jordan/Yüan relationship to achieve Britain's ends in China, and hence took the unusual step of appointing a man in the Consular Service to a conventionally diplomatic post.[35]

This view poses the question as to when this significant friendship began. The common assumption is that it began when Jordan and Yüan were both serving in Korea. This idea was accepted by people who had had close ties with Yüan Shih-k'ai, including his son, K'e-wen, who was more interested in literature than politics, and also T'ang Shao-i, and Yeh Kung-cho.[36] It is not surprising, therefore, that this view has been accepted by many historians and writers.[37]

However, the validity of this view is clearly open to doubt. In the first place, it is chronologically impossible. Jordan's term of service in Korea did not overlap at any period with that of Yüan Shih-k'ai. Yüan first went to Korea in 1882 and left in August 1894, shortly after hostilities had broken out between China and Japan.[38] He was back in China for less than two months before he left for Manchuria, where he was responsible for the supply of reinforcements to the Chinese forces fighting in Korea.[39] Yüan did not finally return to China until the beginning of 1905.

Jordan, on the other hand, did not take up his first posting in Korea until late 1896. Early in July that year Sir Walter Hillier, consul-general at Seoul, applied for early retirement because of a serious eye disease which threatened him with blindness. Sir Claude MacDonald, then British minister in China (1896–1900) who was also responsible for overseeing British interests in Korea, recommended Jordan for the vacancy.[40] The Foreign Office approved of the recommendation in September.[41] By the time Jordan officially assumed duties at Seoul on 26 October,[42] Yüan Shih-k'ai had been away from Korea for two years and two months.

Moreover, neither Jordan nor Yüan confirmed the Korean origin of their friendship. Jordan did not once mention the point in all his voluminous writings. The most natural and likely place for him to have done so was in his letter to Sir Walter Langley, assistant under-secretary overseeing the Far Eastern Department, written shortly after Yüan's death in 1916. In it Jordan says that during Yüan's 'early life in Korea he, Yüan, formed friendships with a number of Englishmen—Baker [sic. E. C. Baber?], [Walter] Hillier, [John] McLeavy Brown and others'.[43] Jordan himself does not appear on the list. Also Jordan does not mention the Korean episode in 'Some Chinese I have known', an article he wrote after he had retired from China.

Another answer must be sought. Jordan might have first met Yüan in the two years' interval between Yüan's return to China from Korea, and his own departure from China to Korea during the period when he was Chinese secretary to the legation. Yüan was either in the Peking-Tientsin area between his return from Korea and departure for Manchuria, or training China's first modern army in Hsiao-chan, a place between Peking and Tientsin. Alternatively, the initial encounter might have taken place after Jordan's return to China in 1906. Neither premise, however, is supported by positive documentary evidence. However, Jordan's account of his first visit as British minister to Yüan, who was then viceroy of Chihli at Tientsin, certainly does not read like a meeting between two strangers, but there are no references to previous encounters.[44]

CHAPTER II

JORDAN, YÜAN AND CHINESE POLITICS
1906–1911

WHEN Jordan returned to Peking in 1906 he found that society had changed 'wonderfully'. Many of the social changes signified that 'a new China' was emerging. Chinese ladies were seen on the street riding or driving in carriages; and princes and other high dignitaries increasingly abandoned their traditional seclusion from dinner parties and other social occasions. More and more Chinese sought to eliminate opium-smoking and foot-binding of women, regarding these traditions as positive vices.[1]

The political scene, however, was less encouraging. Between 1906 and the outbreak of the revolution in October 1911 Jordan observed, in a somewhat over-simplified way, three basic trends in Chinese politics: increasing weakness of the Manchu government; the growing strength of the anti-Manchu elements; and Yüan Shih-k'ai, representing the middle course between the corrupt but conservative government and the radical anti-government forces.

The Manchu government had been overtly incompetent since the middle of the nineteenth century, and barely survived the Boxer Uprising. Jordan's view of the situation was more pessimistic after the death of the august empress dowager, Tz'u-hsi, on 15 November 1908. The emperor Kuang-hsü died the day before, but the event was relatively insignificant. The empress dowager had been the effective ruler of the country, and most people believed that it was her efforts which prevented China's immediate collapse after the Boxer catastrophe.

The empress dowager's death had been dreaded for some time in official circles, and it was feared that her disappearance would cause an upsurge of anti-Chinese sentiment from the Manchus and disorder generally.[2] Many interested foreigners shared the same feeling. Yüan Shih-k'ai at this time was both president of the Ministry of Foreign Affairs *(Wai-wu pu)* and a member of the Grand Council *(Chün-chi ch'u)*. Jordan had had the additional worry that with the demise of the Empress, the emperor would wreak vengeance on Yüan for his betrayal of the Hundred Days Reform in 1898 which, if successful, would have installed the emperor as the effective ruler. The 'simultaneous deaths of both monarchs' were therefore to Jordan 'a fortunate solution of the difficulty'.[3]

Jordan's optimism was short-lived. Early in 1909 Yüan Shih-k'ai was summarily dismissed from the government by the regent, Prince Ch'un, who was the father of the infant emperor, Hsüan-t'ung, and a brother of the late emperor, Kuang-hsü. Furthermore, the Ch'ing government lost other indispensable officials: the veteran Chang Chih-tung died early in October, shortly followed by the dismissal on trivial grounds of Tuan-fang, whom Jordan regarded as the most able Manchu official at the time.[4]

As expected by some Chinese officials before the imperial deaths, considerable tension in the government arose from the regent's obvious preference for Manchus than for Chinese. This resulted in marked Manchu ascendency in many departments. In order to strengthen the Manchus militarily, Prince Ch'un in January 1909 organized under his command a new army of hand-picked Manchu Imperial Guards *(Chin-wei chün)*. He ordered it to be trained by his younger brother, Tsai-t'ao, and his kinsmen, Yü-liang and T'ieh-liang. In May Prince Su (Shan-chi), Tsai-tse, the regent's cousin, T'ieh-liang, and Sa-chen-ping were instructed to make preparations for a navy. In June the regent declared himself commander-in-chief of both the army and the navy, and an office of military supplies was established under Yü-liang's direction. In August Tsai-hsün, another brother of the regent, and Sa-chen-ping were ordered to inspect the military defenses of all the provinces along the coast and those bordering the Yangtze. Shortly afterwards they were sent to study the navies of various European countries. At the end of 1910 Tsai-hsün was appointed minister of the navy, and in May 1911 a General Staff Council *(Chün-tzu fu)* was set up under Tsai-t'ao.

Jordan obviously did not favour these developments because they would widen the rift between the Manchus and the Chinese. Furthermore, he had little faith in the Manchu leaders; apart from distrusting T'ieh-liang for being an avowed enemy of Yüan Shih-k'ai, he did not credit the two brothers of the regent with much ability.[5]

Jordan, though concerned at the steady decline of the Ch'ing government, was more disturbed by the growing autonomy of the provinces. He was convinced that the weakness of the central government *vis-à-vis* the provinces could gravely affect foreign interests in China.

In 1898 the British and Chinese Corporation obtained in the lower Yangtze two concessions, namely the rights to build the Shanghai-

Nanking Railway and the Soochow-Hangchow-Ningpo Railway. The final Shanghai-Nanking Railway Loan Agreement of 9 July 1903 was condemned by the Chinese as greedy and extortionate. The objectionable points of the agreement were a heavy commission; the purchase of the Shanghai-Woosung Railway (which had been built by the Chinese themselves), as a branch line of the Shanghai-Nanking Railway; the great power enjoyed by the British chief engineer; and the predominant control of the British over the construction and management of the line.[6] These harsh terms not only aroused Chinese resentment, but stimulated greater Chinese effort in railroad development, especially in Kiangsu and Chekiang provinces.

The preliminary agreement of the Soochow-Hangchow-Ningpo Railway was more or less identical with that of the Shanghai-Nanking Railway. As the British dealt with the two concessions at the same time, one can safely assume that the final agreements of the two railways would have been fairly similar. However, between 1898 and 1903 the Soochow-Hangchow-Ningpo line seemed to have attracted little attention from the British and Chinese Corporation.

On 24 May 1903 Sheng Hsüan-huai, director-general of the Railway Administration *(T'ieh-lu tsung kung-ssu)*, which was founded by the Ch'ing government early in 1897 in Shanghai, notified the corporation that if surveys and estimates of the Soochow-Hangchow-Ningpo line were not made within six months, the preliminary agreement of 1898 would lapse.[7] No answer was received and Sheng encouraged the Chekiang gentry to proceed with their railway plans. In 1905 the Chekiang Provincial Railway Company *(Che-chiang ch'üan sheng t'ieh-lu kung ssu)* was established with imperial sanction. The company then proposed a provincial railway scheme to centre on Hangchow, which clashed directly with the British Soochow-Hangchow-Ningpo concession.

At the end of the year Sheng informed the British and Chinese Corporation that he had received imperial instruction to cancel the preliminary agreement of 1898.[8] The corporation objected and a deadlock ensued for eight months (until Jordan's arrival in Peking in September 1906). During this period the behaviour of the Chinese was most inconsistent. The Chekiang gentry had actually begun surveys for construction by the end of February,[9] yet the Ministry of Foreign Affairs, represented in this matter by Prince Ch'ing and T''ang Shao-i, was willing to carry on negotiations with the British on the basis of the preliminary agreement. The inconsistency reflected disagreement between the province and the part of the government dealing with foreign relations. The government, unable to quell the opposition of the province, was sandwiched between the hostile provincials and the indignant British.[10] In the middle of the year Prince Ch'ing suggested that the whole question be shelved until the negotiations over the Canton-Kowloon Railway, another concession obtained by the British and Chinese Corporation, were settled.[11] To this proposal the British agreed.

However, on 10 September, the very day of Jordan's arrival in Peking, Carnegie, who had been acting as chargé d'affaires, sent a disheartening report to the Foreign Office. An imperial rescript issued in late August had authorized two new provincial railway companies to build a line from Soochow to Hangchow to Ningpo—exactly the right given to the British![12] Impatient though he was, Jordan could do little to improve the British situation while the Canton-Kowloon Railway Loan Agreement remained unratified by the Chinese. Meanwhile, he received constant reports on the progress made by the Chekiang gentry in railway construction. The Chekiang Provincial Railway Company at its first shareholders' meeting on 26 October declared that the company had about 6,000 shareholders, and the amount already paid up was between 4,210,000 and 4,219,000 dollars.[13] In the middle of November the formal opening of work was attended by important provincial authorities.[14] By the end of 1907 the ambition of the provincial gentry had increased considerably; the Kiangsu and Chekiang railway representatives announced their intention to build the Soochow-Kashing and Kashing-Hangchow sections respectively.[15]

During this time Jordan's inability to act forced him to draw two conclusions: capital investment made by provincial gentry posed a real threat to British interests; and provincial enterprises, however promising they might first appear, would fail in the end. Jordan believed that as yet it was a wasteful and time-wasting procedure for the Chinese to build their own railways. To support this theory he reported early in February that corruption existed in the Chekiang Provincial Railway Company, which squeezed contributions from the population who were anxious for the railway to be built.[16]

At the end of May the Chinese government renewed contact with the corporation. Negotiations were to be opened within two months, on the arrival in Peking of Wang Ta-hsieh, a member of the Chekiang gentry who had been Chinese minister to Britain. Wang, however, suggested that the matter again be postponed until the conclusion of the Anglo-German Tientsin-Pukow Railway Agreement. Jordan refused to accept this proposal. He did not agree that the Soochow-Hangchow-Ningpo line, a British interest, should be secondary to the Tientsin-Pukow line which was only half a British interest.

Negotiations finally resumed early in August. At the second meeting the Chinese gave Guy Hillier, the representative of the corporation, three choices. The first two basically nullified the preliminary agreement; the third provided that 'the corporation should furnish a loan for the construction of the whole line by China herself, the loan being secured by Chinese Government revenues other than those of the railway, but repayable out of the surplus earnings of the line'.[17] In short, the Chinese offered a compromise in which the corporation could provide the loan but have no part in building and operating the railway.

Jordan, taking into account the hostile attitude of the provinces, reluctantly advised Hillier to accept the Chinese offer.[18] However, the British minister refused the Chinese request that the British loan be used for another project, arguing that the provinces had accumulated sufficient capital for building the railway.[19] This resulted in the issue of an imperial edict: the governors of Kiangsu and Chekiang were to persuade the gentry to accept the compromise which had been reached between the government and the corporation.

However, the provinces would not comply with this. Towards the end of the year they decided to defy both the central government and the British. The gentry bombarded the local and central authorities with angry telegrams. Tuan-fang, then viceroy at Nanking, received a belligerent letter from the provincial railway companies. Mass meetings were held in the provinces; the British loan was denounced as an alienation of the people's rights and anti-British boycotts were discussed. The Chinese press, especially in Shanghai, threatened anti-dynastic risings and assassinations. Wang Ta-hsieh was said to have been warned by his fellow provincials that if he allowed the agreement to be signed, his ancestral tomb would be desecrated.[20] The central government dared not conclude the settlement with the corporation. Sheng Hsüan-huai was called to Peking to act as an intermediary between the government and the provinces. The government even invited provincial representatives to Peking for consultation. These representatives, however, were determined to block any compromise agreement.[21]

While Jordan was fully aware that the Peking government was under great pressure from the provinces, he nevertheless adopted a most intransigent attitude which he deemed vital under the circumstances: 'The Central Government is now between the Devil and the deep sea. . . . The provincials are bombarding the Wai Wu Pu with furious telegrams threatening open rebellion if they yield, while we go down once a week and tell them that they have no claim to be considered a government if they cannot bring the provincials into line. There has never before been such a distinct test case between Peking and the provinces, and the result, whatever way it goes, must have far-reaching effects'.[22]

Despite what he felt, Jordan was forced to compromise regarding the precedence of the Soochow-Hangchow-Ningpo line over the Tientsin-Pukow line. The Chinese government argued that the publication of the lenient terms of the latter would expedite further negotiations, especially when it was made known that the two agreements were to be identical.[23]

Provincial vehemence began to subside early in 1908, partly due to the laxity of the Tientsin-Pukow Railway Agreement. More important however, was the central government's concession that the Soochow-Hangchow-Ningpo loan would be borne not by the provinces but by the Ministry of Posts and Communications *(Yu ch'uan pu)*.

The final agreement was signed on 6 March 1908. Compared with the Shanghai-Nanking Railway Loan Agreement, the Shanghai (instead of Soochow)-Ningpo Railway Loan Agreement[24] represented considerable loss of British rights. In the case of default the Shanghai-Ningpo line, unlike the Shanghai-Nanking Railway, could not be mortgaged or taken over by British creditors. The loan was secured not on the surplus earnings of the railway itself, but on those of the Imperial Railway of North China. There would be no British auditor as stipulated in the preliminary agreement. The British chief engineer was to be selected by the Ministry of Posts and Communications and was to function under Chinese authorities.[25] In short, the railway was to be a 100 per cent Chinese property.[26] Jordan considered such reduced privileges 'the best' the British could obtain under the circumstances.[27]

Not long afterwards negotiations began for the building of the Hukwang railway from Hankow (Hupei) to Canton (Kwangtung). Initially the American Chinese Development Company obtained in April 1898 the right to build a railway from Hankow to Canton. On 6 September 1905 the Chinese government redeemed the right from the Americans for US$6,750,000,[28] to which sum the British government in Hong Kong contributed £1,100,000 in the form of a loan. In return for their assistance the British were assured by Chang Chih-tung, then viceroy of Hupei and Hunan provinces, of priority in railway development in the two Hu provinces.[29]

During the following three years, however, Hupei, Hunan, and Kwangtung undertook to build the Canton-Hankow line themselves. In this Kwangtung made the most headway, although its achievement was negligible. By now Chang Chih-tung had realized that a foreign loan was necessary if the railway was to be completed at all, and to become a viable source of revenue. At the end of 1907 Chang was relieved of his provincial duties and was called to the capital to assume the position of a grand councillor. In July 1908 he was given the additional responsibility of directing the construction of the Canton-Hankow line and at this point he recalled his promise to the British in 1905. In October through contact with Everard Fraser, British consul-general at Hankow, he requested British financial aid for building the Hupei section of the railway.[30]

Jordan was pleasantly surprised by Chang's overture and, for a while enjoyed the progress of the negotiations between the Chinese and the British and Chinese Corporation.[31] Deadlock came in February 1909 when the representative of the corporation, J. O. P. Bland, insisted on adhering to the terms of the Canton-Kowloon Railway Loan Agreement. These he regarded as the irreducible minimum for the protection of the lending party. Chang Chih-tung would not concede anything more than the Tientsin-Pukow terms, which of course were more advantageous to the borrowing party.

Jordan at first agreed with Bland, but changed his mind when the Germans offered a loan to Chang on the basis of the Tientsin-Pukow agreement.[32] Three months later in May, the situation became more complicated. On 14 May 1909 the Hongkong and Shanghai Bank, which had replaced the British and Chinese Corporation, made an agreement with the Banque de l'Indo-Chine and the Deutsch-Asiatische Bank. They would make equal loans to Chine to build not only the Canton-Hankow line but also a railway from Hankow to Szechwan which together would comprise the Hukwang railway system. Jordan objected strongly but the British Foreign Office agreed to the arrangement, being anxious not to strain further the already tense Anglo-German relations. Jordan was mildly happier when the British group was alloted complete engineering right over the whole Canton-Hankow line.[33]

The British minister was still embittered about the internationalization of the Hukwang loan. Nevertheless, he now reasoned that 'it matter[ed] not so much who buil[t] the railways as that they should be built quickly in the interests of trade'.[34] But the railways were not to be built quickly:

delay was caused by Chinese provincial opposition, and the claim by the United States' government to the right to share in the loan.

Much to the annoyance of the British government and financiers, the American intrusion delayed matters until 23 May 1910 when a quadruple agreement was signed, accepting American participation and raising the total sum of the loan to £6,000,000.[35] Jordan however, was spared much frustration because early in 1910 he became seriously ill and left China shortly afterwards.

Turning to the question of provincial hostility, opposition came first from Kwangtung. Discussion of borrowing foreign money to build the Canton-Hankow line was first broached in 1908. The president of the Kwangtung Canton-Hankow Railway Company *(Kuang-tung yüeh-han t'ieh-lu kung-ssu)* assured the British acting consul-general at Canton, Harry H. Fox, that the company had sufficient funds to complete the Kwangtung section of the railway.[36] Later that year when Chang Chih-tung, who had become well known to be in favour of a foreign loan, was responsible for overseeing the construction of the Canton-Hankow line, Jordan noticed increased agitation in Kwangtung. Chang himself was conscious of the danger of the situation, and assured the provinces that the government would bear their interest in mind.[37] Compared with Kwangtung, Hupei and Hunan were then much less militant in attitude. They had made much less progress in building their sections of the railway; and Chang Chih-tung, despite his transfer to the capital, maintained his influence in the two provinces.[38]

Not long after Chang Chih-tung's death in October 1909, Hupei and Hunan became unruly. Matters relating to the Hukwang lines were now placed in the charge of the Ministry of Posts and Communications. It was brought to Jordan's attention that the Hupei Railway United Association *(Hu-pei t'ieh-lu tsung chü)* had forced contributions from the farming and business classes in the province. The press in both Hupei and Hunan quoted freely from British newspapers, notably *The Times* which attached political significance to the loan negotiations, to show the powers had ulterior motives in competing to build the railways. Moreover, the two provinces clearly acted with the knowledge, if not support, of the local authorities.[39]

Consular reports reached Jordan that in Szechwan there was zeal to build the railway to Hankow with provincial resources.[40] The whole situation had become explosive, and an imperial edict was issued not long before Jordan left China early in 1910. The Hupei gentry were granted the right to issue stocks for building the Hupei sections of both

Canton-Hankow and Szechwan-Hankow lines. Jordan and his French and German colleagues protested strongly against the Chinese edict.[41]

During Jordan's absence there were anti-foreign outbursts in the provinces connected with the Hukwang loan. When he returned to China at the end of 1910 the provinces remained hostile and the loan agreement was still unsigned. This situation continued for the next 'strenuous six months', during which time Jordan gave 'no peace' to the Chinese Ministry of Foreign Affairs.[42]

A ray of hope glimmered through the intricate and fruitless negotiations in the middle of January 1911, when Sheng Hsüan-huai was appointed president of the Ministry of Posts and Communications. Sheng had by then formulated the policy of nationalization of trunk railway lines and commercialization of branch ones.[43] Between February and May Sheng negotiated actively with the four banks. His object was to secure the Hukwang loan and have the railways built for inclusion in his nationalization scheme.

Sheng's plans, however, were seriously hampered by continued provincial agitation. The Chinese government, though afraid of the provinces, used them as a lever to extract better terms from the foreign banks. By the beginning of spring both Jordan and the banks with their respective governments had exhausted their patience. All were anxious to conclude the loan, particularly after they had heard rumours of the formation of a rival international consortium.[44] In March the foreign banks agreed, as a conciliatory gesture to the Chinese, to exclude the Ching-men-chou-Hanyang branch of the Szechwan-Hankow line from the agreement.[45]

In the middle of April another problem occurred, which mainly affected the British group, and Jordan secured its removal. At the meeting with the foreign bankers on 12 April Sheng Hsüan-huai announced that in face of increasing provincial hostility the groups would have to make further concessions. Sheng now requested that on the eventual signing of the loan agreement half of the loan would be deposited with the Ta-Ch'ing Government Bank and the Chiao-t'ung Bank, so that China might receive better interest than the 3 per cent which was all the foreign banks would give her.

Hillier, the Hongkong and Shanghai Bank's representative in the negotiations, urged the bank to agree to the Chinese demand. Jordan, on his part, telegraphed the Foreign Office, advising immediate sanction.[46] The Hongkong and Shanghai Bank, being the chief issuing bank, feared that the new arrangement would severely undermine foreign control over the loan. Charles Addis, manager of the bank in London, finally relented after Jordan's strong recommendation which was supported by the French, German, and American ministers and all the bank representatives in Peking.[47] Jordan explained to the Foregin Office that although the 'arrangement [was] not an ideal one . . . such a favourable opportunity for a settlement [was] very unlikely to recur'.[48]

However, the matter did not end here. On being informed by Sheng Hsüan-huai of the growing instability in the provinces connected with the Hukwang loan, Hillier thought he should advise his bank to rescind its consent to Sheng's latest request. It would be disastrous to the British bank if the situation in China became untenable after large sums of money had passed into Chinese hands. Hillier, moreover, told Jordan that the Hong Kong and Shanghai offices of the bank had the additional worry that large transfers to the Chinese banks might cause disorganization of the money market. This in turn, would gravely affect the British bank which was the chief issuing bank and the chief exchange bank in the consortium. Jordan managed to dissuade Hillier, emphasizing that it was 'no time for mincing matters or considering the interests of any particular institution when the larger interests of British trade in China and of a British colony [were] at stake'.[49]

Thereafter, negotiations between the consortium and the Chinese government continued, but provincial repudiation of the loan remained violent. To facilitate the signing of the final loan agreement, at Sheng's insistence an imperial edict was issued on 9 May, transferring all trunk railway lines to the control of the Ministry of Posts and Communications. Jordan warmly approved of the edict as representing a significant victory of the government over the provinces.[50] On 20 May 1911 the Hukwang Railways Loan Agreement was at long last concluded. Jordan could hardly wait for the time when Peking would be directly connected with the British colony of Hong Kong by rail.[51]

Thus between 1906 and the outbreak of the revolution in 1911 Jordan was much preoccupied with negotiations over railways. To Jordan the Shanghai-Ningpo Railway Loan Agreement and the Hukwang Railways Loan Agreement were important not only as British interests, but critical in the power struggle between the central government and the provinces, the outcome of which would have a far-reaching effect on Britain's position in China. Between the government and the provinces, Jordan's choice was obvious. The provinces worked persistently against foreign interests while the government, represented in this period by officials such as Prince Ch'ing, Yüan Shih-k'ai, Chang Chih-tung, Liang

Tun-yen, T'ang Shao-i, and Wang Ta-hsieh, at least acknowledged its foreign obligations. Even Sheng Hsüan-huai who in Jordan's opinion was anti-British and an enemy of Yüan Shih-k'ai,[52] was reconciled to foreign concessionaries at the final stage of the Hukwang loan negotiations.

While the central government was to be preferred and upheld, it was clearly fighting a losing battle with the provinces. Jordan's optimistic view of the government quickly evaporated after the Hukwang Railways Loan Agreement was signed. For five months there was unremitting agitation in the provinces against the government's nationalization scheme. In late August serious revolts occurred in Szechwan. Later, Jordan always regarded these uprisings as the precursors of the October revolution which terminated the Ch'ing dynasty.[53] Jordan had won only a pyrrhic victory in pushing the railway agreements because in the long run the position of the government *vis-à-vis* the provinces was seriously compromised.

To Jordan the second distinct feature of Chinese politics between 1906 and 1911 was the growth of anti-Manchu forces, which comprised both the revolutionary movement and the constitutional movement. As far as the revolutionary movement was concerned, Jordan no doubt regarded it a growing threat to the Manchus, but he never quite believed that it would eventually overthrow the Ch'ing dynasty. In December 1906 anti-dynastic risings, which represented the first attempts of the *T'ung-meng hui*, broke out in P'ing-hsiang, Li-ling, and Liu-yang prefectures on the border of Hunan and Kiangsi. Jordan reported their quick suppression and expressed no anxiety whatever.[54] However, the revolts greatly shocked the authorities in the Wuhan area. In the following weeks a purge was carried out in the New Army in Nanking, which was suspected of being highly infiltrated by revolutionaries. There was also an intensive search for secret societies in the central Yangtze region. The consul-general at Shanghai sent Jordan reports on these activities, together with a translation of the views of Chang Chih-tung, then viceroy of Hupei and Hunan, on the revolutionary organizations in the Yangtze provinces. Jordan considered that Chang had exaggerated the case and that his fears were 'improbable'. Jordan did not intend to convey Chang's views to the Foreign Office until he heard 'similar rumours' from Sir Robert Hart, the British inspector-general of the Imperial Chinese Maritime Customs Service. Sir Robert added that Yüan Shih-k'ai had alerted his troops to go to the Yangtze at a moment's notice.[55]

Thus for some time the Yangtze area was closed to the activities of the *T'ung-meng hui*. Moreover, the Ch'ing government later discovered that the *T'ung-meng hui* headquarters and its leaders were in fact in Tokyo. Japan therefore was requested by the Chinese government to extradite Sun Yat-sen, Hu Han-min, Wang Ching-wei and other revolutionaries, who afterwards set up a new headquarters at Hanoi in Annam. Consequently, most of the uprisings organized by the *T'ung-meng hui* during the following years occurred in south and southeast China.

At the end of May and beginning of June 1907 the *T'ung-meng hui* directed revolts in Swatow and Waichow in Kwangtung. Again, Jordan attached little significance to the disturbances which were easily suppressed by the Manchus. Furthermore, the consuls at Swatow and Amoy, who were the British officials nearest to the scene, had not taken the trouble to report them. On being asked by Jordan, both consuls assured the legation that newspaper accounts of the incidents were grossly exaggerated.[56]

On 6 July 1907 the Manchu governor of Anhui province, En-ming, was assassinated by a revolutionary, Hsü Hsi-lin. The assassination was followed by an abortive uprising in Anking, the provincial capital, in which the well-known woman revolutionary, Chiu Chin, was involved. Hsü, Chiu, and several other revolutionaries were caught, severely tortured,and then executed.[57] While the assassination caused great tension among the grand councillors in Peking and high ranking officials in the provinces, Jordan thought that such a state of nerves was unwarranted.[58] Jordan paid scant attention to the series of unsuccessful revolutionary attempts in the following three and a half years.[59]

The uprising at Canton in April 1911[60] has been regarded as the most large-scale revolt the *T'ung-meng hui* had organized before the revolution broke out later in October that year. On 10 April Jordan received news of the assassination two days before of the tartar-general at Canton by a revolutionary. The consul-general at Canton, James W. Jamieson, viewed the incident as 'merely the act of an isolated individual'.[61] Two and a half weeks later, the revolt erupted. No consular reports were sent to the legation until Jordan, on being asked by Sir Edward Grey for information to answer parliamentary questions, enquired into the matter. On 3 May, nearly a week later, Jordan informed the Foreign Office that Canton had already been brought under control and that accounts of the disturbance had been grossly exaggerated.[62]

Compared with this revolutionary movement, Jordan considered the constitutional movement a much more potent anti-Manchu force. The constitutional reform movement was launched by the Manchu government shortly after the Boxer Uprising. The tragic outcome of the Boxer Uprising forced the empress dowager at last to realize that, if the Manchus were to remain rulers in China, she would have to make certain political concessions, in form if not in reality. Thus constitutional reforms, with a constitutional government as the ultimate goal, which had been anathema to the Manchus in 1898, were now granted by the Ch'ing government.

The constitutional movement embodied administrative reforms as well as political and institutional ones. At the end of 1906 Jordan noted with pleasure that most of the decrees which had been issued dealt with such matters as the reorganization of the metropolitan and provincial administration, promotion of education, suppression of opium, and control of railway, telegraph, and postal administration.[63] In the middle of 1907 another series of decrees provided for administrative and judicial reform at the provincial level.[64] Jordan was even more delighted in late 1907 when the Manchus decided to disband their garrisons and treat the Chinese on an equal footing with them. At the same time codification of the laws and improvement of the fiscal system was also decreed.[65]

Jordan reacted quite differently to the political aspect of the constitutional movement. In September 1906 the throne announced the gradual implementation of a constitutional government on the recommendation of the mission which had just returned from a study of various constitutions abroad. By August 1907 the Commission to Investigate Modern Governments *(K'ao-cha cheng-chih kuan)* had been reorganized into the Constitutional Government Commission *(Hsien-cheng p'ien-ch'a kuan)*, a more powerful and permanent agency charged with supervising the necessary reforms. In September a national assembly *(Tzu-cheng yüan)*, meant to be the precursor of the parliament, and in October provincial assemblies *(Tzu-i chü)* and various local assemblies were promised.

The legislation for a constitutional government culminated in August 1908 when the court promulgated a programme indicating that constitutional reforms would be completed in nine years, that is in 1917, by which time the parliament proper would have replaced the national assembly.[66] Jordan was sceptical about the feasibility of the nine years' plan. He realized that China was modelling her reforms on Japan but he believed that China, with less political experience and fewer leaders, would need more than nine preparatory years.[67]

However, it was not so much the people's political immaturity as what

Y. C. Wang calls 'the wide discrepancy developed between [the Manchu] intention and practice'[68] which eventually caused the movement to threaten the very existence of the Manchu regime. This 'discrepancy' occurred with the emergence of two parties with irreconcilable aims. The Manchus naturally wanted to control the reforms in order to regain their prestige and reassert their influence. Conversely, the so-called constitutionalists were eager to promote constitutionalism for reasons which sharply contradicted the Manchu purpose.

The constitutionalists fell broadly into two categories. One group consisted of reformists under the banner of K'ang Yu-wei and Liang Ch'i-ch'ao, who were still living in exile abroad after their abortive *coup d'état* in 1898 to bring about a constitutional government. Jordan, however, attached more significance to the second group of constitutionalists—moneyed provincial gentry determined to use the constitutional reforms to acquire power and benefit nominally for the provinces, but in practice for themselves.[69]

Jordan foresaw the conflict between the Manchus and the constitutionalists from the start. His experience of the provincial gentry during the railway negotiations led him to predict that the Manchus would raise 'a Frankenstein by their propagation of constitutional theories'.[70] In saying this Jordan meant that the balance of power between the local government officials and the gentry would be upset; the latter would dominate the provincial assemblies which would certainly not stop at being merely deliberative in function.[71] In the capital, with the calling of the national assembly, the government would have to face opposition from the 'rabid members from Canton and the South'.[72]

Jordan felt no gratification in having his prophecy fulfilled. The gentry in the provinces acted immediately after the court had made known in September 1906 the intention of granting a constitutional government. In the same year the Association to Prepare for the Establishment of Constitutional Government *(Yü-pei li-hsien kung hui)* was founded in Shanghai by leading gentry members in Chekiang, Kiangsu, and Fukien provinces, represented by T'ang Shou-ch'ien, Chang Chien, and Cheng Hsiao-hsü respectively. Similar organizations were founded in Hupei, Hunan, and Kwangtung.

Early in 1908 the Association to Prepare for the Establishment of Constitutional Government took the lead in petitioning the court for a parliament. The association first contacted the Constitutional Government Association *(Hsien-cheng kung hui)* in Hunan, the Constitutional Government Preparation Association *(Hsien-cheng ch'ou-pei hui)* in

Hupei, the Self-government Association *(Yüeh-shang tzu-chih hui)* in Kwangtung, and the constitutionalists in Honan, Anhui, Chihli, Shantung, Shansi, Szechwan, and Kweichow. Together in July they sent representatives to Peking. At the capital the provincial representatives had gained the support of a number of officials before they made the petition in August. At the end of the month the government was forced to announce the nine years' plan to prepare for the parliament.[73]

Among the various provincial constitutionalist organizations, Jordan no doubt found the Self-government Association in Kwangtung most objectionable. Early in 1908 it played a leading role in organizing the anti-Japanese boycott to protest against the *Tatsu Maru* incident.[74] On 29 November a Chinese passenger died on his way from Hong Kong to Canton on board the Butterfield & Swire river-streamer *Fatshan*. The Self-government Association, supported by the local Chinese press, insisted that the man had died after having been ill-treated by a Portuguese ticket collector, named Noronha. The British acting consul-general at Canton, Harry Fox, duly conducted an enquiry, but the verdict was death from natural causes. As a result, the Self-government Association worked to stir up anti-British feelings among the populace. The promise of a second enquiry temporarily calmed the people down. However, when the same verdict was returned at the beginning of 1909, the association instigated a boycott against the *Fatshan*.[75] According to the acting consul-general the association derived its strength from two sources: control of the local press, and large contributions from influential people in Canton as well as Cantonese residing in the British colonies in Southeast Asia.[76]

The assemblies in most provinces met for the first time in the middle of 1909, when consular officials were instructed to provide the legation with detailed reports. Jordan was wary of the attitude of the assemblies in Hunan, Hupei, and Kwangtung, the provinces who had fought hard against the Hukwang loan. A gloomy overall picture emerged from the consular reports: local officials were either not strong enough to overcome gentry opposition, or were openly sympathetic with the assemblies in rejecting the central government's policies.[77]

Shortly afterwards Chang Chien, president of the Kiangsu provincial assembly, founded the Association of Provincial Assemblies *(Ko sheng tzu-i chü lien-ho hui)*—representing sixteen provinces—to press the government to set up a parliament without further delay. In spring 1910 the Association of Comrades to Petition for a Parliament *(Kuo-hui ch'ing-yüan t'ung-chih hui)* was formed first in Peking and later in the provinces. Despite his illness and subsequent absence from China that year, Jordan was well aware that the two associations had petitioned the throne to institute a parliament in one year, instead of in 1917 as had been decreed in 1908.[78]

The situation steadily deteriorated. The second sittings of the provincial assemblies at the end of 1910 were largely marked by serious clashes between the assemblies and the government. Jordan heard that the Kwangsi provincial assembly had resigned *en masse* after disagreement with the local authorities over the policy of opium suppression in the province. The Chekiang assembly left when the governor refused to take up with the throne problems relating to the Chekiang Provincial Railway Company, the interest of which was a great concern to many assembly members. The assemblies in Hunan and Shensi pledged support for the Chekiang assembly. In Kwantung the assembly insisted on taking part in governing the province and demanded that the provincial budget should be submitted for its approval.[79]

Troubles over the provincial assemblies had hardly subsided before the national assembly met for the first time on 3 October 1910. The new establishment initially appeared to Jordan as much less of a threat to the Ch'ing government. Only half of the assembly's total membership (196 or 200) was elected by the provincial assemblies from their own membership; the other members were selected by the emperor mainly from the Manchu, Mongolian, and Tibetan nobilities, and top literary circles. Bearing this in mind, Jordan might have hoped that the national assembly would exercise a moderating influence on the provincial bodies. Moreover, the national assembly was to function under the direction of a president selected from princes, dukes, or state officials 'of recognised merit', and a vice-president who had to be an official above the third rank. Among its various functions the national assembly was to intervene in disputes among the provincial assemblies and mediate between the assemblies and provincial authorities if such a need arose.[80]

The national assembly was an immediate disappointment. On the day of its inauguration the Association of Comrades to Petition for a Parliament presented the throne with its petition to institute a parliament within one year, requesting that the national assembly should discuss it. Towards the end of the month the assembly decided unanimously to support the petitioners, declaring that it would resign if their request was rejected.[81] On 4 November the regent finally agreed to the compromise whereby parliament would be convoked in 1913 instead of 1917.

Not surprisingly, the news upset Jordan a great deal when it reached him in London.[82] On returning to China he attended some of the meetings of the national assembly and soon discovered the reason for its 'independent attitude': 'provincial members . . . are carrying all before them, and, so far, there has practically been no opposition on the part of the representatives of the Government'.[83] Jordan ceded that many members attended to assembly matters with great seriousness.[84] What he could not tolerate however, was their condoning the provincial assemblies to defy authority and make attacks on the government.

The summit of defiance against the central government came in November when the national assembly denounced the Grand Council as 'an irresponsible body' which should be subordinated to their control. The Grand Council retaliated by resigning *en masse*—a wholly unprecedented event in its history. Although the regent did not accept the council's resignation and confirmed its power over the national assembly, an imperial decree issued on 25 December instructed the Constitutional Government Commission that a responsible cabinet would replace the Grand Council and all other advisory bodies. Jordan sympathized with the grand councillors whom he thought had suffered unjustly from 'the extravagant pretentions of these inexperienced representatives of the people'.[85]

In the midst of these depressing Chinese political scenes, Jordan regarded Yüan Shih k'ai as the one redeeming element. When Jordan arrived in Peking in 1906 Yüan Shih-k'ai was viceroy of Chihli province where he devoted himself to implementing the constitutional reforms announced by the throne. Under Yüan's guidance several means had been devised to popularize the idea of constitutionalism in the province, and study centres had been set up where the gentry were trained in the art of self government. For several years Chihli was rated by the Constitutional Government Commission as the best prepared province for the constitution.[86]

Though suspicious of the constitutional movement, Jordan had peace of mind when it was in the hands of Yüan Shih-k'ai. Moreover, Jordan was outspoken in his admiration for Yüan's achievement in putting a stop to the growing and smoking of opium, promoting technical education, and improving and modernizing Tientsin, the provincial capital. In short, Chihli was the 'model on which the reform of the country should be based'.[87]

It was therefore natural that Jordan rejoiced early in September 190; at Yüan's appointment as a president of the Ministry of Foreign Affairs. The British minister anticipated that Yüan's new position woul(

improve Sino-British relations apart from being an asset to the ministry concerned. Two months after Yüan had assumed duties, the British Foreign Office presented the Chinese minister in London with a memorandum, listing the outstanding grievances Britain held against China. The most serious complaint was the Chinese obstruction in the negotiations over the Soochow-Hangchow-Ningpo railway line. In Jordan's opinion the conclusion of the railway loan agreement early in 1908 was due largely to Yüan Shih-k'ai, who had asked the British legation for a strongly-worded letter of protest, with which he could advise his government to settle the matter quickly.[88] Britain was also dissatisfied with China's delay in implementing the currency reform which she had promised in the Commercial Treaty of 1902. This Yüan attempted to remedy late in 1908. One of his trusted henchmen, T'ang Shao-i, was about to leave China on a mission to thank the United States for using her share of the Boxer indemnity as scholarships for promising Chinese students to study in America. Yüan instructed him to discuss the question of currency reform with the British Foreign Office on his way home.[89]

During the one and a half years when Yüan was in charge of foreign affairs, Jordan was impressed by his ability to bring the provinces in line with the government in fulfilling foreign obligations. At the end of 1908 the Far Eastern Department in the Foreign Office summarized the impact of Yüan's appointment on Sino-foreign relations: 'We are able to record a sensible improvement in the conduct of foreign affairs in China. The improvement may be said to date from the appointment of Viceroy Yüan Shih-k'ai to a seat at Wai Wu Pu and from the promotion of Liang [Tun-yen], a graduate of Yale, to a Vice-Presidency of the Ministry. The Viceroy brought to the Wai Wu Pu the requisite strength of character, prestige and influence among his contemporaries, while Liang has supported the Viceroy with a knowledge rarely equalled among his countrymen of Chinese and English. Complaints are now rarely heard of unanswered dispatches, of exasperating evasion and trickery'.[90]

Thus Yüan's sudden dismissal on 2 January 1909 was a heavy blow to Jordan, especially as he had believed that the simultaneous deaths of the empress dowager and the emperor Kuang-hsü meant safety for Yüan. Moreover, there had been two overt signs of the regent's favour: Yüan was charged with arranging the imperial funerals, and also appointed as a senior guardian of the infant emperor.

The news of the dismissal caused a commotion in the foreign legations, especially the British one.[91] That very afternoon Jordan and his American and German colleagues agreed that the foreign ministers should warn the regent jointly that 'China's foreign relations would suffer severely by the dismissal of a statesman who was universally considered the guarantee of his country's political stability'.[92] This opinion was endorsed by the foreign diplomats at an informal meeting the following day, after which the French minister was asked to draft a joint statement to be presented to the Chinese, pending the approval of the home governments. Jordan urged the Foreign Office for immediate authorization, which it gave not without a twinge of conscience for interfering in China's internal affairs.[93]

On 9 January, however, Jordan reported the failure of the diplomatic body in exerting pressure jointly on the Chinese. Since the meeting on 3 January opinions differed as to the form the representation should adopt and the manner in which it should be made. Jordan largely blamed Japan for the situation. He was greatly displeased by the 'marked indifference' of the Japanese minister, Ijuin Hikokichi, and Japan's argument that, since Yüan's personal safety had been guaranteed, there was no further ground for interference.[94]

Jordan shared the belief of many Chinese officials and foreigners in China that Japan was elated by Yüan's downfall.[95] Since April 1907, Yüen's trusted advisers Hsü Shih-ch'ang had been viceroy of Manchuria and T'ang Shao-i governor of Fengtien (a province in Manchuria). It was well known that for some time Yüan, Hsü and T'ang had been trying hard to curb Japan's fast expanding influence in South Manchuria. Japanese activities in South Manchuria had not only offended the Chinese, but had somewhat soured British opinion towards the Anglo-Japanese Alliance after 1906. British merchants were enraged by Japanese commercial immorality in particular the piracy of British trade marks.[96]

Despite the attitude of Japan and some other powers, Jordan continued protesting to the Chinese. He agreed with the American minister, William W. Rockhill, that they should ask permission from their governments to approach the Chinese government, on the basis of the French draft which had resulted from the ministers' meeting on 3 January. Although 'originally doubtful', Sir Edward Grey gave his consent to the move because of his 'confidence in Sir J. Jordan's knowledge of the Chinese and his judgement as to its probable effect'.[97] As a result of Britain's decision, the United States government, though reluctant to take the lead in any action, authorized Rockhill to associate with Jordan in protest against Yüan's removal.[98]

Jordan and Rockhill made their representations at an interview with

Prince Ch'ing, the most senior minister in the Ministry of Foreign Affairs, on 15 January. Jordan stressed that any violent change of the Chinese government was of great concern to Britain who possessed such vast interests in China. Prince Ch'ing answered that the regent's decision concerning Yüan was final, but it did not denote a change of policy either in internal reforms or foreign relations.[99]

Significantly, Jordan never regarded the dismissal early in 1909 as Yüan's final exit from the arena of Chinese politics. He was concerned that there might be a wholesale removal from the government of Yüan's protégés,[100] but Yüan's son, K'e-ting, his henchmen such as Feng Kuo-chang, Yang Shih-ch'i, Hsü Shih-ch'ang, and Chao Ping-chün continued to occupy important positons in the Army, the Ministry of Posts and Communications, and other government departments. Moreover, there were repeated talks of Yüan's reappointment between early 1909 and the outbreak of the 1911 Revolution, when Yüan was urgently recalled by the Manchus to control the situation.

Rumours of Yüan's return to government were rife from late 1910 onwards. Daily conferences concerning his reinstatement were said to have been held in September 1910 among government officials. It was alleged that these meetings were inconclusive because of the opposition of the empress dowager, the consort of the late emperor Kuang-hsü. Expectation again rose high on the eve of the 1911 Revolution when Prince Ch'ing resigned from the premiership and recommended Yüan as his successor. However, the prince's resignation was rejected by the throne.[101]

Chinese politics between 1906 and 1911 convinced Jordan that only Yüan could solve the problems created by the growing disunity of the country. On the whole Jordan believed that the Manchu government genuinely intended to fulfill its foreign obligations. However, when the government was unable to control the forces obstructing foreign interests sincerity alone was meaningless. By contrast, Yüan Shih-k'ai's ability to restrain the separatist tendency of the provinces was proven while he was serving in the foreign ministry. Moreover, sympathetic as Jordan was with the Manchu government, he realized that only reforms could ensure its survival. However, he was concerned that changes must not be so drastic as to bring about the collapse of the *status quo* on which British interests depended. Here Jordan had in mind the constitutional movement, which he believed must be in the hands of 'a leader capable of controlling it and guiding it along the path of moderation and safety'.[102] Such leadership Jordan had seen displayed by Yüan Shih-k'ai when he was viceroy of Chihli.

CHAPTER III

THE 1911 REVOLUTION

To Jordan the outbreak of the 1911 Revolution had at least one good outcome: the recall of Yüan Shih-k'ai by the panic-stricken Manchu government. Jordan's immediate reaction was that Yüan would be perfectly able to cope with the situation.[1] Jordan realized before long that he had underestimated the extent of the revolution, which spread first along the Yangtze and then across the whole country. He could no longer maintain his hitherto unsympathetic attitude towards the revolutionaries and he devised a policy of neutrality, by which his country sought to safeguard British life and property during the upheaval.[2]

The policy of neutrality was imperative to cope with the situation, but it did not tally with Jordan's concept of the ideal situation for Britain's long term interests in China. Behind the official neutral stand Jordan's sympathies were with Yüan Shih-k'ai and the Manchu government which had recalled Yüan.

Contrary to his initial expectations, Jordan soon realized that Yüan's position was much weaker than he had originally thought. Firstly, Yüan's arrival in Peking early in November did not cause the powers to retract their refusal to lend money to the Manchu government. About a week after Yüan's reappointment the Ministry of Posts and Communications and the Ministry of Finance *(Hu pu)* had each approached the international consortium for loans which together amounted to twelve million taels. The representatives of the foreign banks and the American, French, and German ministers in Peking, whose faith in the Manchu government had been boosted by Yüan's recall, were anxious to comply with the Chinese requests. Jordan's immediate reaction, however, was defensive: he feared vengeance from the revolutionaries, and financial loss if the debtors were to emerge a loser in the revolution. Almost the next moment Jordan thought he was being over cautious, and ambiguously advised the Foreign Office that while it was 'no doubt desirable to render every assistance to the Chinese government in its present difficulties', it was 'equally certain that requests for money must in the end entail some form of international control'.

By 23 October Jordan's preference for the retention of the Manchu dynasty overcame his cautiousness; as a complete *volte face,* he now recommended financial assistance to the Manchus. However, he insisted on certain terms to safeguard the expenditure and the repayment of the loan, as well as several conditions to be complied with by the Chinese before they received the money. The first and foremost of these was a reformed government in Peking with Yüan Shih-k'ai as leader. At his time Yüan was still bargaining with the Manchu government over the terms of his recall in his native province, Honan. In the end the Manchu requests for money were not granted because the consortium powers, except Germany, were unwilling to renounce their professedly neutral attitude.

On 1 November M. W. Townsend, acting manager of the Hongkong and Shanghai Bank in London, suggested to the Foreign Office that the Chinese government might be reminded of its claim to half of the Hukwang Railways loan funds (£3 million) to be deposited in the Chinese banks. In this way the situation could be stabilized for the general benefit of commerce without angering the revolutionaries, since such an advance could not be regarded as a new loan. However, the Foreign Office quickly turned down the proposal.

The following day Townsend again urged the British government to comply with a new Chinese request for five million taels to stabilize the money market in Shanghai. Townsend made special mention of the expected arrival in Peking of Yüan Shih-k'ai, who had already left Honan and was then commanding the government troops in the Wuhan region, the area where the revolution first broke out. Shortly afterwards Townsend dispatched to the Foreign Office similar requests from the American, French, and German bank representatives in Peking. Their main concern, besides steadying the Shanghai money market, was that Yüan should have money at his disposal in Peking for reorganization purposes. Britain still firmly refused to lend, and on 8 November the same attitude was officially adopted by the consortium at an inter-bank conference. Even Yüan Shih-k'ai's personal appeals for funds after his arrival in Peking on 13 November did not change the situation.[3]

Jordan no doubt was somewhat relieved to learn that Yüan was given access to the palace treasure hoarded by the late empress dowager, Tz'u-hsi. Yüan was said to have been given about £400 thousand of the palace hoard to defray the current expenses of the government, buy ammunition for the war ministry, and pay for the movements of troops.[4] The question was how long this palace treasure would last. The month of November saw the rapid spread of revolutionary success. One province after another declared independence from the Manchu government.

Taxes would certainly not be forthcoming from these independent provinces; and neither from the 'loyal' ones which all claimed that they needed the money, and much more from the government, to maintain stability.

Jordan had hoped that Yüan's reappointment would 'ensure loyalty of the northern troops [*Pei-yang chün*] which was doubtful',[5] but he was disappointed. On 29 October the 20th Division of the Northern Army stationed at Luanchow, which was under the command of Chang Shao-tseng, mutinied and refused to entrain for the Wuhan area. Chang and several of his colleagues then presented the Manchu court with a petition of twelve articles. If these petitions were accepted, there would be a national parliament before the end of the year, a constitution to be drawn up by the parliament, and exclusion of members of the imperial household from all offices of state. In short, a constitutional monarchy was demanded.[6]

The Manchus were terrified by this turn of events. Luanchow was a strategic point on the Peking-Mukden Railway on which they depended for reinforcements and as a possible way of retreat to their homeland in Manchuria. Jordan, too, was upset although Yüan K'e-ting, Yüan Shih-k'ai's son, assured him that the Luanchow troops had acted on his father's order.[7] Jordan accepted the assurance in good faith, but was concerned lest Yüan's loss of administrative control over the Northern Army between 1907 and 1911 might weaken his personal loyalty from the troops, despite his close links with top-ranking officers during the period.[8]

If the Luanchow incident could not prove the disloyalty of the Northern Army, there was no doubt about the ensuing mutiny of the 6th Division, one of the original divisions of the army, at Shih-chia-chuang. The commander in this case was the revolutionary Wu Lu-chen who had only secured his position in the winter of 1910 through the influence of a Manchu noble, Liang-pi. There were close connections between the two mutinies. Shortly after his success Wu attempted to contact Chang Shao-tseng and Lan T'ien-wei, the assistant commander of the 20th Division to start a revolution in the north. Both these men were Wu's old friends of his student days in Japan. Thoroughly alarmed at the news of the plot, the Manchu government appointed Wu as the new governor of Shansi, the capital of which had just been captured by the revolutionaries, with the intention of making it impossible for Wu, Chang, and Lan to join forces. Wu resolved to play along with the Manchus and accepted the appointment. He met the Shansi revolutionaries at Niang-tzu-kuan where they co-operated in feigning a surrender to allay the government's suspicion of Wu. Afterwards Wu stationed his troops at Shih-chia-chuang, awaiting an opportunity to meet with the 20th Division and then march on to Peking. While at Shih-chia-chuang Wu did his best to disrupt the transport of munitions to the imperial troops fighting in the Wuhan region.[9]

These happenings seriously disturbed the Manchus. Now not only the Peking-Mukden Railway, but also the Peking-Hankow Railway were being endangered. Moreover, Luanchow, Niang-tzu-kuan, and Shih-chia-chuang were all within striking distance of Peking. Fortunately for the Manchus, the Shih-chia-chuang crisis was soon resolved with the assassination of Wu Lu-chen.[10] Nevertheless, the incident cast grave doubts in Jordan's mind as to Yüan's ability to control the Northern Army.

Thus the recall of Yüan succeeded in solving neither the financial nor the military difficulties of the Ch'ing government as the Manchus and their sympathizers had hoped. There was yet another hope to be frustrated—this concerned Yüan's alleged influence over the national assembly. On 22 October the national assembly began its second session in the midst of turmoil. After five days it made the following demands: the abolition of the existing 'imperial cabinet' (so called because most of its members were from the imperial family), an amnesty for political offenders; popular participation in making the constitution; and the immediate convocation of parliament. Two days later the Luanchow generals presented their demands. Jordan was struck by the similarity between the two sets of demands and suspected collaboration.[11] His suspicion was confirmed on 2 November when Yüan K'e-ting told him that the Luanchow demands had been instigated by Yüan Shih-k'ai who had also conferred with the assembly.[12]

The frightened court quickly succumbed to the Luanchow demands. On 2 November the national assembly drew up the constitution which was produced on the following day, and accepted by the regent. He promised to promulgate it at the end of the month in the imperial ancestral temple. As a further proof of submission to constitutional limitations, the court announced the appointment of Yüan Shih-k'ai as the new premier. The national assembly, on being requested by the court, endorsed the appointment on 7 November.[13]

The day after the release of the Luanchow demands Jordan sent a telegraph to the Foreign Office. He hoped that the national assembly could persuade the provinces, through its influence on the provincial assemblies, to accept under adequate guarantee the concessions made by the court.[14] In fact, immediately after the court's acceptance of the constitution, the assembly dispatched delegates to the provinces to gain support for a Manchu constitutional monarchy. The atmosphere of the assembly was said to be 'languid', because the most active and eloquent members had been sent to the provinces.[15] On 6 November Jordan told the Foreign Office that the Manchus' hope for survival depended on 'Yüan and the National Assembly being able to convince the country that it [was] better to keep the Manchu dynasty in position, shorn of all powers, than to the prospect of probable confusion and disorder'.[16]

However, any optimism was shortlived. About the middle of the month Jordan reported to his government that the delegates had not received 'a very cordial reception' at Hankow, Shanghai, and other revolutionary strongholds.[17] By the end of the month, despite the regent's constitutional oath on 26 November in the imperial ancestral temple, Jordan believed that the national assembly and Yüan Shih-k'ai behind it had lost their cause.

Jordan's assessment of the relative strength of the revolutionaries, and the Manchu government led by Yüan Shih-k'ai is essential for appraising his mediation between the two parties at the end of November and beginning of December. Jordan was not the first person to suggest mediation. On 26 October Townsend of the Hongkong and Shanghai Bank and Hillier, the bank's Peking representative who was then in London, called on the Foreign Office with a letter from the bank's office in Hong Kong, suggesting that the powers might mediate for the Chinese. Hillier in particular was keen on the idea and tried to convince Sir Francis Campbell that mediation was highly acceptable to the Chinese mentality.[18] The Foreign Office was sceptical and conferred with the Peking legation. Jordan strongly opposed the bank's proposal, expressing anxiety that Britain must not be involved and the Manchu cause not prematurely compromised.[19]

Meanwhile, fighting continued in the Wuhan area. On 25 November Herbert Goffe, acting consul-general at Hankow, telegraphed Jordan that stray shells fired by the government troops, who were operating to retake Hanyang, were falling on the British concession in Hankow. On the following day Jordan told Yüan Shih-k'ai of his grave concern about the safety of the British community at Hankow. Yüan replied that the government forces were only acting on the defensive and he was prepared to agree to an armistice on mutually beneficial terms. Yüan then requested Jordan to make his wish known to Li Yüan-hung who was at the top of the Hankow revolutionary government. Jordan acted immediately on Yüan's request for mediation. He instructed Goffe to convey to Li Yüan-hung a verbal and unofficial message, stressing that the object of mediation was to 'avert useless bloodshed and to prevent prolongation of dangerous situation in which the British community [had] now been placed for some six weeks'.[20] The next day the revolutionaries lost Hanyang to the imperial forces. There was now greater scope for mediation. Goffe reported that many revolutionaries, demoralized by the defeat, fled to Wuchang where the situation became quickly untenable. Li Yüan-hung was said to have been forced by circumstances to agree to a constitutional monarchy,[21] and later that day he accepted an armistice.

On 1 December Yüan Shih-k'ai presented his terms for a ceasefire which Jordan telegraphed to Goffe to offer the revolutionaries. Yüan's terms provided for continued possession on both sides of territories already occupied, and an initial three-day truce to be followed by cessation of reinforcement by both parties. To ensure that his terms would be honoured by the revolutionaries, Yüan's last condition was that Goffe would have to sign the armistice as a 'witness'. Jordan felt he 'had no time' to consult Sir Edward Grey, and authorized Goffe's signature entirely on his own initiative.[22] He was anxious that the ceasefire should be a *fait accompli* before either side regretted it.

Jordan's independent decision caused considerable turbulence in the Foreign Office. It was feared that Britain might be constantly embarrassed if the terms of the truce were not adhered to. This worry was later justified. The British consulate-general at Hankow was inundated by complaints of infringement of the armistice agreement, especially from the revolutionaries.[23] Sir Arthur Nicolson, permanent undersecretary, was more concerned about the reaction of the other powers. Japan, in particular, had just approached Britain to intervene in favour of the Manchus.[24] Campbell, however, warmly supported Jordan's action for two reasons. As witness, Goffe was not obliged to guarantee the smooth operation of the armistice; his main service was to exercise a deterrent influence on the two opposing parties.[25] The debate ended when Sir Edward Grey decisively ruled that 'Sir J. Jordan [had] acted quite rightly'.[26]

Meanwhile, the imperial troops at Nanking were defeated on 2 December by the revolutionaries who then occupied the city. Jordan sent an immediate message to Yüan Shih-k'ai, urging him not to retake

Nanking by force and 'irretrievably compromise the cause of a peaceful settlement'.[27] On 3 December a truce of three days was at last arranged. When it ended a second truce of three days was agreed upon, followed by an armistice of fifteen days. The armistice was prolonged indefinitely, although the threat of a renewal of hostilities was present for a long time.

It is pertinent at this point to query Jordan's quick response to Yüan's request for mediation, whereas a month before he had strongly opposed a similar suggestion from Townsend and Hillier. Jordan claimed that his action was intended to bring to an end the 'dangerous situation' in which British life and property had been placed since the revolution began. This was the ostensible explanation, but represented only part of the truth.

Jordan had rejected the earlier mediation proposal for fear that Britain's role might be resented by both the Manchus and the revolutionaries—a situation which would certainly have an undesirable effect on Britain's interests. By the end of November, however, Jordan realized that prolonged fighting would also exert an adverse effect on Britain's position in China, taking into account the general disruption of trade and the unenviable state of the British concession at Hankow. He was genuinely concerned that continued fighting with shortage of pay might result in the degeneration of both the revolutionary soldiers and government troops into bandits. Moreover, there was the possibility that bandits originally in the provinces might take advantage of the chaotic situation to pillage on a grand scale. If such events were to materalize, British subjects, especially those in the interior, would suffer greatly.

The British minister was so worried at the end of November that he requested Admiral Alfred L. Winsloe, commander-in-chief of the British China Squadron, to defer his annual visit to Hong Kong and stay north during the winter. Jordan was anticipating general lawlessness, misery and distress, especially in the central provinces.[28] Thus Yüan Shih-k'ai's request for the British to bring about a truce came at the time when Jordan's misgivings were most intense. Had Hillier's earlier suggestion been followed, Britain would have interfered on her own initiative, but now Jordan was acting on the invitation of Yüan Shih-k'ai, with the tacit agreement of Li Yüan-hung.

Was Jordan aware of his argument a month before that mediation might unjustly compromise the Manchu cause? Although he did not refer to this question again at the end of November, it was obvious that he now considered the Manchu cause fully tried. It is interesting that Jordan was not surprised by Yüan's suggestion of a ceasefire. Was he here projecting on Yüan his own assessment of the situation? The peaceful means of salvaging the Manchu dynasty, as attempted by the national assembly, had clearly failed; yet chances of a military victory for the Manchus were remote.

Jordan's unfavourable opinion of the Manchus' military strength did not change even after the government victory at Hanyang. This victory has been most frequently quoted to argue that it was not beyond Yüan Shih-kai's ability to crush the revolution had he really intended to do so.[29] For some time after the revolution Jordan himself was the focus of criticisms from pro-Manchu quarters. They regarded his mediation as forestalling an eventual success of the government in the Wuhan area, which might have brought about the collapse of the entire revolutionary movement. The severest attack came perhaps from the Peking correspondent of the *New York Herald*, J. K. Ohl, who had a personal grudge against Jordan, and was generally anti-British in his attitude. However, Jordan retorted with confidence that had he not mediated, 'at best a long and bloody war would have ensued'.[30]

Moreover, it seems probable that at the end of November Jordan rather believed that intervention, instead of compromising the Manchu cause, might prevent the fast deterioration of the Manchu power. As it was, when the truce and armistice eventually came into effect, the Manchus' position was still not completely untenable. The retention of the dynasty might still be possible in view of Li Yüan-hung's agreement to a constitutional monarchy after the revolutionary defeat at Hanyang. It is likely that in mediating between the Manchus and the revolutionaries, Jordan strove for two results—an end to hostilities, and a last chance for Yüan Shih-k'ai to save the Ch'ing dynasty.

Once the fighting stopped, peace talks were to take place. It had been agreed during negotiations for the truce that a peace conference would be held at Wuchang. On 9 December T'ang Shao-i, Yang Shih-ch'i, T'ang's aide, and nine other delegates of the Manchu government left Peking for the conference. However, when the government retinue reached Hankow two days later, the revolutionaries there insisted on holding the conference at Shanghai instead. This change in locality and Li Yüan-hung's subsequent refusal to go to Shanghai, were to influence Jordan's reaction towards the revolutionaries' demand for a republic at the peace conference.

Great tension marked the first meeting of the conference, held on 18 December in the International Settlement. Both sides accused each other of breaking the armistice. On 19 December Everard Fraser, British consul-general at Shanghai, received a visit from T'ang Shao-i. The latter had been informed that at the second meeting of the conference scheduled for the following day, the revolutionaries would demand acceptance of a republic in return for further negotiations. T'ang asked Fraser to reason with Wu T'ing-fang, the commissioner representing the revolutionaries at the conference. Fraser did as requested but found Wu extremely truculent.[31]

At the meeting on 20 December the revolutionaries declared that a republic would be the future form of government in China, and 'no compromise whatever could be discussed'. When the session was over T'ang Shao-i again approached Fraser, this time to convey a message to Yüan, through Jordan, that a 'republic became the only solution'. T'ang himself sent a personal telegram to Yüan to the same effect.[32]

Until now Jordan had hoped that the Manchu dynasty might be retained, and his actions had been influenced within limits by this desire. However, the revolutionaries' categorical demand on 20 December and Yüan's subsequent behaviour finally convinced Jordan that a republic was inevitable. Here it is appropriate to discuss the significance of holding the peace conference at Shanghai instead of at Wuchang. Shanghai was under the influence of such revolutionary leaders as Wu T'ing-fang, Wen Tsung-yao, and Wang Ch'ing-wei who, though not left-wing revolutionaries like Sun Yat-sen, Huang Hsing, and Ch'en Ch'i-mei, were ardent believers in republicanism. These leaders differed from Li Yüan-hung who was neither a revolutionary nor a republican, and had earlier on even agreed to a constitutional monarchy after the revolutionary defeat at Hanyang.

More important still, Shanghai was the base from which the majority of British firms and businessmen operated. The British mercantile community in the city was extremely anxious to remain on good terms with the revolutionaries, and this sentiment naturally had considerable influence on Jordan.[33] Moreover, G. E. Morrison's stay in Shanghai just at this juncture was no doubt to the advantage of the revolutionaries. Morrison had been openly sympathetic towards the revolution from the beginning, and it was known that he had persuaded Yüan Shih-k'ai to abandon the Manchu cause.[34] Jordan could hardly slight the studied opinion of someone who had recommended his current appointment, and who was instrumental in moulding British public opinion on Chinese affairs.

It was, however, what appeared to be Yüan Shih-k'ai's acceptance of a republic after 20 December that convinced Jordan of the exhausted mandate of the Manchus. Chinese historians widely regard Yüan as playing off one party against another since the start of the revolution for his own benefit, and believe that he had never been sincere about the Manchu cause. Jordan had until now for the most part believed in Yüan's professed loyalty to the Manchus.

As early as the beginning of November, Jordan was aware that Yüan Shih-k'ai was in communication with the revolutionaries. The British minister believed that Yüan was trying to induce the revolutionaries to put down their arms and accept a limited monarchy, just as he was attempting to achieve the same with the Manchus through the Luanchow demands and the national assembly.[35] The day after Yüan Shih-k'ai's arrival in the capital, Yüan K'e-ting paid a visit to the British legation 'on his father's behalf'. He brought the message that Li Yüan-hung had offered the presidency to Yüan on the condition that he would defect from the government and accept a republic, emphasizing that 'the republic would only be a transitional stage'. The news was clearly distasteful to Jordan, who expressed his opinion that the best solution was to maintain the Manchu dynasty, but with the constitutional concessions made by the court to the national assembly a fortnight before.

At the interview with Yüan Shih-k'ai himself the following day, Jordan found that Yüan's attitude was not the same as his son had implied. Yüan declared his firm adherence to the dynasty despite the revolutionaries' insistence on a republic. Jordan was most pleased and dismissed Yüan K'e-ting's visit merely as 'a feeler'.[36]

Yüan was repeatedly offered the position of president by the revolutionaries, and as far as Jordan was aware the last offer was made at the beginning of December.[37] Yüan's behaviour was ambiguous enough to prompt Jordan to notify Sir Francis Campbell at the end of November. Referring to Yüan's threat to resign because of the regent's refusal to abdicate, Jordan maintained that Yüan had no real intention of effacing himself, and that he would probably keep to the winning side if he did not 'fall between the stools' in the meantime.[38] At the same time, however, the revolutionaries' overtures were not positive evidence of Yüan's betrayal of the Manchus, because he was not known to have accepted any of the offers.

Perhaps the most convincing argument which demonstrates Yüan's disloyalty to his Manchu masters was the government's loss of Nanking to the revolutionaries on 2 December. Yüan has been accused of planning the event, and thus greatly boosting the revolutionaries' morale which had been much dampened by their earlier defeat at Hanyang.

Jordan himself informed the Foreign Office that the revolutionaries' victory at Nanking was effected by some arrangement between the generals of both sides, and that Tuan Ch'i-jui, a trusted general of Yüan who was in charge of the campaign, had received orders from Peking to abandon the city.[39] Jordan, however, fully expected this turn of events for he had specifically advised Yüan against a forcible recapture of Nanking so as not to jeopardize the chance of bringing about a truce.

One can conclude that up to the time of the Shanghai peace conference Jordan had generally regarded Yüan as a faithful servant of the Manchu throne. After 20 December, this belief in Yüan rapidly waned. In the first place, it was strange, to say the least, that Yüan's representative at the conference should be none other than T'ang Shao-i who yielded readily to the revolutionaries' demand for a republic. Jordan had to admit that T'ang's behaviour at Shanghai was 'a bit of a mystery to everybody and why Yüan ever sent him there if he knew T'ang's sentiments [was] only explicable on the theory that Yüan, in spite of all his protestations, would in the end accept the presidency of a republic'.[40]

What happened afterwards further confirmed his theory. Since Japan's role was becoming increasingly dominant, it is worth noting her response to the revolution since it began in October. Firstly, one has to distinguish between the attitude of the Japanese government and that of the pan-Asiatic Japanese nationalists, or *shishi,* among whom the most well-known was perhaps Miyazaki Torazo who had for some time been closely associated with Sun Yat-sen.[41]

The policy of the Saionji cabinet, unlike that of the nationalists who were overtly sympathetic with the Chinese revolutionaries, was formulated by officials who were totally unprepared for the Chinese revolution, and whose opinions on the subject differed widely. For example, the newly appointed foreign minister, Uchida Yasuya, was uninformed about Chinese affairs after his long term as ambassador to the United States. For a week or so the Japanese government, apparently influenced by the army, was more inclined towards the Manchu cause. On 16 October Uchida decided to supply the Manchu government with arms and ammunition through private merchants. This was in compliance with a Manchu request made three days earlier through the Japanese legation in Peking.[42]

The general staff, however, were in favour of aiding the revolutionaries, whom they considered as the weaker party and more deserving of Japan's help. This idea was rejected by Saionji Kimmochi and Uchida, but Hara Kei, the home minister, was uncertain. He urged the cabinet to watch the situation vigilantly instead of being content with the resolution of helping the Manchus because of the expanding influence of the revolutionaries. As a result of the split in opinion the cabinet, at its meeting on 24 October, laid down a dubious policy. While exploiting the revolution to consolidate Japanese influence in China and Manchuria, Japan should at the same time associate herself with the other powers, especially Britain and Russia whose response to the China situation had been cautious. The second part of the policy was designed to be acceptable to both the Manchus and the revolutionaries while the situation remained unclear.[43]

Official Japanese policy was more committed when Yüan Shih-k'ai returned to the capital in the middle of November. The change was largely brought about by the Japanese minister at Peking, Ijuin, upon whose judgement Uchida relied to deal with the China exigency. Ever since his days as consul at Tientsin, Ijuin had respected and felt well disposed towards Yüan Shih-k'ai. Having observed the Manchus' total dependence on Yüan, the Japanese minister was further convinced that his country should invest her support in him. Ijuin had in fact established secret ties with one of Yüan's confidants, Chao Ping-chün, even before Yüan's arrival in Peking.[44]

On 16 November the Japanese Ministry of Foreign Affairs *(Gaimusho)* instructed Ijuin to ascertain Yüan Shih-k'ai's intentions, but without committing Japan to a definite course of action. Uchida later added that if Yüan indicated reliance on Japan to save the situation, Ijuin should promise some help.[45] The Japanese minister came out of his interview with Yüan Shih-k'ai with the strong belief that Yüan's intention was to preserve the Manchu dynasty. Ijuin subsequently urged his government to intervene in favour of a constitutional monarchy in China.[46] The influential Elder Statesmen *(Genro)* also put pressure on the cabinet to adopt a similar policy.[47]

The outcome was that on 28 November Uchida instructed Yamaza Enjiro, Japanese chargé d'affaires in London, to present two memoranda to Sir Edward Grey. The first document described the current situation in China which the Japanese government considered dangerous if allowed to continue. It also analyzed the relative strength of the Manchus and their opponents, concluding that the powers interested in China 'should not maintain any longer an attitude of mere onlookers', but 'to take proper measures as soon as possible with a view to safeguarding their interests'. However, Japan would not approach the other powers before she had reached an agreement with Britain.

The second memorandum expressed the 'proper measures' which Japan thought should be adopted by the powers to protect their interests. In short, the Japanese government regarded a republic as the most unsuitable form of government for China. Since the Manchus by themselves were incapable of regaining control, Japan suggested that Britain and the other powers should actively intervene to secure a constitutional monarchy with nominal Manchu sovereignty.[48]

Japan's desire was thwarted by Britain's coincidental decision to mediate between the Manchus and the revolutionaries. Anxious to make the situation less galling for Japan, Sir Edward Grey instructed Jordan at the beginning of December to invite the Japanese minister to co-operate in prolonging the armistice and in putting pressure on the regent to abdicate. This was a step which Jordan, under Yüan Shih-k'ai's influence, believed as 'an essential preliminary to a settlement'.[49]

Since Ijuin was responsible for the Japanese memoranda of 28 November, he felt particularly embittered by Jordan's mediation. Suspecting Yüan of duplicity, the Japanese foreign ministry was willing to abandon the idea of active intervention. Yüan had simultaneously approached Japan for aid to preserve the Manchu dynasty, and Jordan to mediate between the Ch'ing government and the revolutionaries. Ijuin, however, attributed this state of affairs almost entirely to Jordan.

Jordan, on his parts, was fully aware of Ijuin's suspicion and hostility but he wasted his time explaining to his Japanese colleague the impracticability of Japan's proposal and his reasons for mediation. In order to avoid further misunderstanding, Jordan suggested that Japan should be invited to participate at the peace conference which was to be held at Shanghai, although he himself would remain as sole intermediary.[50] Both the British Foreign Office and the British ambassador in Tokyo warmly welcomed the idea, which was also acceptable to the Japanese government.[51]

This marked the beginning of a close relationship between Jordan and Ijuin during the Chinese revolution, whereas before Jordan had been more inclined towards discussing the situation with the American minister.[52] On 11 December Jordan suggested to Ijuin that he should communicate directly with Yüan Shih-k'ai to improve the chance of successful peace negotiations. It seems that since his return to Peking Jordan was completely unaware of the transactions which had been taking place between Ijuin and Yüan. Having made the suggestion, Jordan was not surprised to learn from Yüan later the same day that he had just been reminded of the existence of the Anglo-Japanese Alliance by Ijuin. The latter had also requested that in future he should be informed of all the discussions between Yüan and the British minister.[53]

Jordan apparently knew nothing about the interview between Yüan and Ijuin the following day when, according to Ijuin's report to the Japanese foreign ministry, Yüan again denounced the idea of a Chinese republic. Ijuin was now tempted to revive his proposal of active intervention to retain the Manchu dynasty.[54] The Japanese foreign ministry, determined not to be fooled a second time, instructed Ijuin that Japan must act in co-ordination with her ally.[55]

Ijuin saw Yüan again on 17 December, the day before the peace conference began. Jordan was later told by Yüan that at the interview he had reiterated his preference for a limited Manchu monarchy by retaining the child emperor and instituting a council of regency. Ijuin had inquired what Yüan's policy would be if the Shanghai conference did not achieve the desired result. Yüan claimed that he would solicit the good offices of 'friendly powers'. At this point Ijuin insisted that in the event of Yüan asking for foreign help, only Britain and Japan should be approached. Yüan replied that 'he would of course have to inform Great Britain and he was willing to inform Japan also, if the two governments wished that he should do so'. When Ijuin pressed the point again Yüan said 'emphatically that if Great Britain and Japan were agreed on the point, he would be quite prepared to approach British and Japanese governments alone and to follow advice and decision of the two powers'.[56] Yüan was clearly anxious to stress Britain's lead in the Anglo-Japanese relationship.

Jordan immediately felt that Ijuin had committed him beyond his instructions which 'only covered negotiation at Shanghai'.[57] Sir Claude MacDonald in Tokyo also warned against any independent action such as that proposed by Ijuin.[58] On 20 December, when the revolutionaries at the Shanghai conference insisted on a Chinese republic, Jordan told Ijuin that Britain considered his suggestion impracticable.[59]

Troubles did not cease here, and the next few days were utter confusion for Jordan. On 20 December the Japanese consul-general was told by G. E. Morrison, in no uncertain terms, that the only solution for China was a republic with Yüan Shih-k'ai as president.[60] Ijuin telegraphed Uchida the following day, after an interview with Jordan, that the Japanese government should object to Morrison's opinion which the British minister seemed to endorse.[61]

On 24 December Sir Edward Grey received a visit from the Japanese ambassador who wanted to confirm if 'the opinion expressed by Sir J.

Jordan . . . [was] shared by the British government'.[62] Grey could not give an answer until he had first ascertained Jordan's opinion, which was most emphatic; 'I am not in favour and never have been in favour of supporting Yüan Shih-k'ai as president of Republic'.[63] Indeed, if Jordan had never been in favour of a republic, how could he have favoured Yüan as president?

However, Ijuin had not made a mistake, as Uchida later explained, because of his deficiency in English.[64] Jordan did tell Ijuin that Britain, with vital interests in central and south China, could not ignore the revolutionaries' demand. Moreover, Morrison had already spoken on the suitability of a republic for China. Jordan had begun to realize the inevitability of a Chinese republic, but it was Yüan's behaviour which forced him to deny in public his preference for the retention of the Manchu dynasty.

On 22 December Yüan Shih-k'ai asked to see Jordan and Ijuin separately, and in that order, to discuss the telegrams which Yüan had received from T'ang Shao-i since 20 December. The most pressing one had suggested a representative national assembly to decide on the future form of government. Yüan stressed his desire for a constitutional monarchy and asked Jordan if 'he could look to foreign intervention for support'. Jordan answered that it would mean coercing half of the country and that Britain only 'wanted a strong and united China, under whatever form of government the Chinese people wished'. This was certainly the first time since the outbreak of the revolution that Jordan, in Yüan's presence, made no reference to his support of a Manchu constitutional monarchy. Yüan then argued that the Shanghai republican revolutionaries did not indicate the view of the masses, who were conservative and monarchical. Jordan counter-argued that if what Yüan had said was true, T'ang Shao-i's suggestion of a representative assembly would be even more appropriate. It was obvious now that Jordan would not oppose a republic.[65]

That afternoon Yüan repeated to Ijuin his earlier comments to Jordan. Ijuin, unlike the latter immediately assured Yüan that the Japanese government favoured a constitutional monarchy in China, and telegraphed Yüan's appeal for aid to Tokyo.[66]

The following day these lines appeared in *The Times*:

'The present issue is complicated by the openly expressed fears of Yüan Shih-k'ai that England and Japan, acting in union, are determined to maintain a monarchical government in China, if necessary by force. Absurd though the story is, it is believed by Yüan Shih-k'ai and is having a baneful effect that the British Foreign Office might wisely dispel'.[67]

The news created an uproar in the Foreign Office, the British legation in Peking, and in Shanghai. Jordan was warned by T''ang Shao-i from Shanghai that any intervention by the powers would unite all classes and parties against the foreigners.[68] Jordan was also instructed by Grey to deprecate Yüan Shih-k'ai's statement which was 'mischievous' and 'quite untrue'.[69] Jordan accordingly told Yüan, in Morrison's words, that Britain 'had done her best to bring the contending factions together, but cared not a damn whether there was a republic or a monarchy'.[70] Meanwhile, the British legation instructed the consul-general at Shanghai to refute statements in the local press which repeated the views reported in *The Times*.[71]

Later, Morrison revealed the source of the message published in *The Times*—T''ang Shao-i who, in his turn, had received it from Yüan Shih-k'ai by telegraph. Morrison explained the confusing situation to Willard Straight, the American bank representative:

'Sir John Jordan, the British Minister, and Ijuin, the Japanese Minister, acted under explicit instruction from their chiefs to cooperate. They both separately so informed Yüan. Ijuin, however, without telling Jordan, advised Yüan that Japan would never recognise a republic and would interfere with force, if necessary, to prevent its establishment. In view of what both Jordan and Ijuin had said about cooperation Yüan took this as meaning that Great Britain agreed to this attitude'.[72]

This might have been Morrison's own view, and was certainly what Yüan wanted Morrison and others to believe, but it was not the truth. If Yüan had truly thought that Jordan and Ijuin were in close co-operation, why had he taken such great pains on 22 December to see the two ministers separately?

The incident could have only one explanation: Yüan Shih-k'ai had agreed to a republic. Historical investigation reveals that if Jordan had known of the secret transactions between Yüan and the revolutionaries, he would have avoided much confusion and embarrassment. Simultaneously with the formal conference, negotiations were held in the Wen-ming Bookstore in Kansu Road, Shanghai, between Liao Yü-ch'un, representing Tuan Ch'i-jui who in turn represented Yüan Shih-k'ai, and Ku Chung-shen, representing the well-known revolutionary, Huang Hsing. On 20 December, when the revolutionaries at the peace conference demanded a republic, a fivefold agreement was also reached in the bookstore: '(1) A republican government will be established as the only government of China; (2) the imperial house will be treated with generosity and courtesy; (3) the man responsible for overthrowing the Manchu regime shall be made president of the republic; (4) the soldiers of the north and south, including both Hans and Manchus, will be treated with due consideration and will not be held responsible for destruction during the revolutionary war; and (5) temporary administrative councils will be created in the provinces to maintain peace and order'.[73]

There was another perplexing factor. Wang Ching-wei, an important revolutionary delegate at the Shanghai conference, had also been appointed by Yüan Shih-k'ai as a member of the government delegation to the conference. It seems that shortly before the conference Yüan Shih-k'ai had become very worried about his own position at the news of Sun Yat-sen's impending return to China. Yüan therefore asked Wang Ching-wei to do his best to negotiate on his behalf especially with Wang's old friend Huang Hsing, who had been staying in Shanghai since his retreat from Hanyang at the end of November.[74]

There are two possible explanations of Yüan's dishonesty during his talks with Jordan and Ijuin on 22 December. They involve the two strongest opponents to a Chinese republic: the Manchu court and the Japanese government. Ever since his recall to office, Yüan had repeatedly professed in public that he would not betray the Manchus whom he and his ancestors had served, and go down in history as an usurper. Here one has little reason to doubt Yüan's sincerity, for although he cannot be looked upon as a scholar, his upbringing was certainly traditional and Confucian in character. It is unlikely that a person of such convictions would lightheartedly play the role of traitor and burden himself with considerable guilt.

G. E. Morrison seemed to have understood the problem. Writing to a friend on 29 December, he had the ingenious idea that the best solution was to arrange for the Manchus themselves to support Yüan's appointment as the president of the republic. This would be a face-saving device for both Yüan and the Manchus. On 31 December Morrison proposed his scheme to Yüan Shih-k'ai through Tsai T'ing-kan, a trusted subordinate of Yüan. Morrison's biographer, Cecil Pearl, suggests that this was the 'germ of the idea that was to produce the most remarkable event in China's long history: the creation of a republic by the edict of an Empress'.[75] However, in retrospect the whole idea seems to have been conceived earlier by Yüan himself, as suggested by his interview with Jordan on 22 December, and Jordan's forced denial in public of Britain's support for the retention of the Manchu dynasty. Yüan hoped to convince the Manchus of the hopelessness of their cause and the inevitability of a republic.

The British minister's statement also served to influence Japan's attitude towards a Chinese republic. Yüan could now tell Ijuin that, since Britain would not support the Manchus, continuation of the Ch'ing dynasty was most unlikely. Indeed, in the presence of Prince Ch'ing on 24 December, Yüan separately showed Jordan and Ijuin a telegram he was about to send to T'ang Shao-i at Shanghai, approving T'ang's proposal of a national assembly to decide on the future form of government. Jordan considered the proposal a 'fair one' which, if rejected, would make the revolutionaries morally responsible for continuing the civil war.[76] Ijuin, however, asked Yüan not to dispatch the telegram until an answer was received from Tokyo about Yüan's request for help made on 22 December.[77]

Just at this time the Japanese cabinet decided to make a last attempt to salvage the Manchu dynasty.[78] This action was due largely to the insistence of the Elder Statesmen who shunned the idea of a republic so close to imperial Japan. However, with confirmation of Britain's stance, Yüan Shih-k'ai could now openly defy Japan's wishes. He telgreaphed his approval of a national assembly to T'ang Shao-i on 26 December, without waiting for a reply from the Japanese government as Ijuin had suggested.[79] The court signed what J. O. P. Bland calls 'the death warrant of the dynasty'[80] on 28 December 1911 when it issued an edict accepting the national assembly.

While Sir Edward Grey resented Yüan Shih-k'ai's intrigue, Jordan quickly recovered from his initial displeasure. He was now reconciled to the idea of a republic and was anxious for the return of peace and normalization of trade. For Jordan, events had already begun to develop satisfactorily. On 29 December the Shanghai peace conference decided to extend the armistice to 5 January, by which time questions concerning the election and composition of the assembly would have been discussed.[81] The meetings on 30–31 December were devoted to preparing for the assembly, and the first sitting was scheduled to be held on 8 January 1912.[82]

Quite unexpectedly, Jordan wrote on 1 January that Yüan Shih-k'ai had become 'unwell and very depressed'. Yüan was embroiled in an impossible situation and threatened to resign. Two problems caused the crisis. In the north he had become most unpopular because of his concession to the revolutionaries in agreeing to the national assembly.

Secondly, the peace conference had broken down because of the revolutionaries' insistence that the assembly must convene at Shanghai where the sentiment was exclusively republican. Jordan was rightly puzzled by Yüan's attitude. If Yüan had initially agreed to the assembly, the outcome of which was a foregone conclusion, its location should not pose such a difficult problem. Jordan therefore 'could not resist' asking Yüan if 'any outside influence' was at work.[83]

There certainly was. On 25 December the charismatic revolutionary figure, Sun Yat-sen, arrived in Shanghai. Four days later the revolutionaries, who had established a united provisional republican government at Nanking, elected Sun as their president. Sun was duly inaugurated on 1 January. Yüan Shih-k'ai was furious and felt that he had been cheated by the revolutionaries who had repeatedly offered him the presidency. Both the day before his inauguration and in his inauguration speech Sun promised that he would immediately vacate the post of president on the abdication of the Manchus.[84] But Yüan was not to be easily pacified. In accusing T'ang Shao-i of having exceeded his power at the meetings on 30–31 December, and in accepting T'ang's resignation the following day, Yüan disrupted the peace conference at Shanghai.

To Jordan's relief, the differences between Yüan and the revolutionaries were reconciled more quickly than expected. Further assurances given by Sun Yat-sen on 2 January and by Wu T'ing-fang three days later allayed much of Yüan's suspicion. Moreover, ambiguious personalities such as T'ang Shao-i, Wang Ch'ing-wei, Liang Shih-i, and Yang Shih-ch'i were busy as intermediaries between the two parties. By now negotiations were between the revolutionaries and Yüan himself, instead of Yüan representing the Manchu government. The exit of the Manchus was inevitable, and Yüan and the revolutionaries, while distrusting each other, each wished to secure the best possible terms in the impending change.

The underground transactions at this stage between Yüan and the revolutionaries were known to Jordan. He was therefore not surprised on 11 January when Liang Shih-i informed him that 'all parties had come to the conclusion that the abdication of the emperor and the retirement of the Court formed an indispensable preliminary to any settlement'. Liang stated as his personal view that the court would either abdicate in favour of Yüan or authorize him to establish a provisional government. He then asked Jordan if in either case Yüan would be recognized by Britain.

If such events materialized, they would contradict the agreement

which had supposedly been reached between Yüan and the revolutionaries. Instead of receiving power from the revolutionary provisional
government at Nanking, Yüan asked Jordan and Britain to recognize a
provisional government to be set up in the north under his exclusive
control. Jordan assumed an 'attitude of reserve', but he did assure Liang
Shih-i that the powers had confidence in Yüan.[85] Three days later Ts'ai
T'ing-kan informed Jordan that the empress dowager, Lung-yü, would
soon issue an abdication edict, which would put Yüan in temporary
charge of the government, pending the election of a president.[86] It is
significant that Yüan did not send Liang and Ts'ai to see Ijuin.[87]

Events did not develop as smoothly as Jordan had been led to expect.
Yüan Shih-k'ai soon found himself sandwiched between the Manchu
fanatics and the revolutionary die-hards. This situation, which for Yüan
was the most critical period since the revolution began, lasted for about
a fortnight. Jordan naturally shared Yüan's tension and uncertainty.

At the final stage of the secret negotiations between Yüan Shih-k'ai
and the revolutionaries concerning the Manchu abdication, Yüan Shih-
k'ai asked Prince Ch'ing, his great admirer, to raise the matter at court.
At a meeting in the palace on 12 January Prince Ch'ing presented the
case for abdication, but it was rejected by the majority of the imperial
kinsmen present. This occasion led to the founding of the Imperial Clan
Party *(Tsung-she tang)*, which consisted of imperial kinsmen and
Manchu nobles who were determined to save the dynasty, such as
Prince Kung, Prince Su, the ex-regent, Duke Tsai-tse, Liang-pi,
T'ieh-liang, and Yü-liang. Some of the group, notably Prince Kung,
sold their antiques and valuable paintings to raise funds for a final
showdown with the revolutionaries.[88]

On 16 January Yüan Shih-k'ai narrowly escaped an attempt on his
life when he was on his way home from an audience with the empress
dowager on the question of abdication.[89] The abortive assassination was
carried out by an underground revolutionary organization in Peking.
Its leaders, Chang Hsien-p'ei and Yang Yü-ch'ang, decided to eliminate
Yüan, regarding him as the sole obstacle to a revolutionary victory. This
was chiefly because, however, being in the north they were unaware that
negotiations were still going on between Yüan Shih-k'ai and the
revolutionaries in the south. Since this incident Yüan never went to the
palace again, although he continued to press the court to abdicate
through his followers Wu Wei-te, then minister for foreign affairs, Chao
Ping-chün, minister of the interior, and Liang Shih-i.[90]

At the imperial conference held the day after the attempt on Yüan's life, no conclusion was reached. Prince Ch'ing and P'u-lun were in favour of voluntary abdication; Prince Kung and a Mongolian prince strongly denounced the idea; and all the others were silent. The diversity of opinion became even more pronounced at the meeting on 18 January, after which the Imperial Clan Party decided to take action. The following morning they published a strong statement of their views and vowed to adopt stringent measures to retain the dynasty.[91]

A new situation emerged at the imperial conference on 19 January: Chao Ping-chün and Liang Shih-i suggested that the question of abdication should be decided by the cabinet, the premier of which was Yüan Shih-k'ai. They also proposed that the governments in Peking and Nanking should be simultaneously dissolved, and replaced by a new integrated government at Tientsin.

That same day Yüan assured Jordan that 'arrangements had been completed with the southern leaders'. The arrangements which had in fact been agreed upon did not, of course, relate to the proposed integrated Tientsin government. Jordan was asked to recommend the British Foreign Office to recognize the Tientsin government and Yüan's position in it. This Jordan gladly did, emphasizing that 'recognition of Yüan Shih-k'ai afford[ed] only hope of securing anything like a stable Government in China'.[92] Sir Edward Grey agreed to support Yüan's proposal if it had indeed been made 'in arrangement with southern leaders'.[93]

Meanwhile, the imperial princes and Manchu nobles continued their deliberation. The empress dowager, whose faith in Yüan Shih-k'ai's sincerity had greatly increased since the attempted assassination, was prepared to abdicate. The Imperial Clan Party strongly objected, and the embarrassed empress was particularly ruffled by the uncompromising attitude of Prince Kung. The morale of the noblemen was greatly boosted by general Feng Kuo-chang who told Duke Tsai-tse, obviously without Yüan's knowledge, that if he could be furnished with three months' expenses he would be able to suppress the revolution. While most of the members of the imperial party were unwilling to part with their personal wealth, they nevertheless maintained a militant stand.[94]

On 23 January Ts'ai T'ing-kan told Jordan that Yüan was going to resign because of the difficulty posed by the Imperial Clan Party. Jordan was extremely perturbed by the news. He immediately approached Ijuin with the argument that unless suitable measures were adopted, Yüan's resignation would cause havoc in the north. Ijuin had clearly had enough of Yüan and was 'disinclined to take any action'.[95] The Foreign Office wondered what action Jordan could have in mind and guessed that it might be 'a joint warning from the Powers to the Manchu Princes'.[96] The British government, however, was determined to adhere to its policy of non-intervention, feeling that it knew too little about the ever-changing situation in China to be certain of its ground.[97]

Relations between Yüan Shih-k'ai and the 'reactionary party', Jordan's name for the Imperial Clan Party, were fast deteriorating. Jordan even feared a resumption of fighting, as the princes had persuaded the empress dowager to postpone abdication. Yüan Shih-k'ai was now forced to revert to the earlier decision that a national assembly should decide on the form of government.[98] A decree to the above effect was in fact issued on 25 January. The Imperial Clan Party was not upset by Yüan's threat to resign, and arranged to set up a new cabinet after the resignation with T'ieh-liang as the commander of the Manchu troops.

The Imperial Clan Party, however, was only half of Yüan's trouble. He was under severe pressure from the revolutionaries who were both surprised and infuriated by his Tientsin scheme. As a result, William Wilkinson, the British consul at Nanking reported that Sun Yat-sen immediately withdrew his offer of the presidency and instructed Wu T'ing-fang to telegraph his conditions to Yüan: The emperor was to abdicate, and abstain from the organization of a provisional amalgamated government; Nanking was to be the seat of the new provisional government; Sun Yat-sen would resign when, and only when, the provisional government was recognized by the powers; and finally, Yüan was not to concern himself with the provisional government until after Sun's resignation.[99]

Two days later Sun Yat-sen telegraphed another five points to Yüan through Wu: Yüan's official announcement of the emperor's abdication to the foreign ministers; a public declaration by Yüan of his support of republicanism; the resignation of Sun Yat-sen when informed of the abdication by either the Diplomatic Corps at Peking or the Consular Corps at Shanghai; and an oath by Yüan after his election as president to be faithful to the constitution promulgated by the Nanking senate.[100] These terms were also released to the press.

Sun's concern to detach Yüan from the Manchu government and to put him under the control of Nanking was understandable. Even Wilkinson wrote to Jordan that the 'conditions laid down by Dr. Sun . . . [were] by no means impossible ones for Yüan Shih-k'ai to accept, especially if, as was no doubt, intended, pressure was brought upon him to do so by the foreigners at Peking'.[101]

The British minister felt otherwise, and was extremely annoyed by

Sun Yat-sen's actions. He lamented to the Foreign Office that there would be 'great difficulties in forming an amalgamated Government of the north and south'.[102] Here Jordan was clearly biased; the revolutionaries did not oppose an amalgamated government, but opposed one which would be exclusively under Yüan's influence and in no way responsible to them.

To the great relief of both Yüan Shih-k'ai and Jordan, the Manchu clique succumbed after two incidents on 26 January. On that day the leader of the Imperial Clan Party, Liang-pi, was assassinated by a revolutionary Peng Chia-chen. The party suffered a serious setback from Liang-pi's death, and soon dispersed: Prince Su fled to Port Arthur, Prince Kung to Tsingtao, and some others to Tientsin.

On the same day over forty generals of the Northern Army, led by Tuan Ch'i-jui, petitioned for an abdication. It was obvious to Jordan that they 'had acted under the inspiration of Yüan Shih-k'ai'. Instead of accusing Yüan of disloyalty, as many historians have done, Jordan regarded him as 'the astute politician, whose masterly brain [had] been directing all the moves in this long drawn-out game of Chinese statecraft'.[103]

With the disappearance of the Manchu extremists, the empress dowager finally decided on 30 January to abdicate. Two days later Wu Wei-te informed Jordan that the court had authorized Yüan to negotiate terms with the revolutionaries.[104] On 12 February three imperial edicts were announced. By the first one, the Manchu dynasty would be replaced by a republic, with Yüan Shih-k'ai empowered to organize a provisional republic in co-operation with the southern republican party. The second edict dealt with the treatment of the imperial family upon abdication, and the third urged the people and officials to serve the new government.

Thus between 26 January and 12 February Yüan Shih-k'ai had only to worry about the revolutionaries. Jordan learned from Wilkinson of the existence of a strong militant group in the Nanking government. These extremists wished to continue fighting, not against the Manchus, but against Yüan Shih-k'ai who was suspected of trying to out-manoeuvre the revolutionaries to attain imperial honour for himself.[105] Indeed, the clamouring among the southern revolutionary leaders for a northern expedition was increasingly fierce and vociferous.

The spirit of militancy was evident in the *Provisional Government Gazette (Lin-shih cheng-fu kung-pao)*, published by the revolutionary provisional government at Nanking. The Wuchang Military Government *(Wu-chang chün cheng-fu)*, for example, telegraphed the Nanking government on 26 January that it would resume fighting if abdication had not taken place three days later when the armistice expired.[106] Other revolutionaries sought to convince the Nanking government that only a northern expedition could forestall the cunning devices of Yüan Shih-k'ai, and lead to a general settlement of the situation.[107]

Jordan was aware that about 3,500 revolutionaries had already been dispatched to Shantung where they were to join troops from the north before marching on to Peking. On 27 January, two days before the armistice expired, fighting resumed on the Tientsin-Pukow Railway. Moreover, the revolutionaries widely distributed their pamphlets which advocated that the national problem could only be solved by force.[108] Though anxious about the situation, Jordan nevertheless believed that Yüan Shih-k'ai could somehow reach an agreement with the revolutionaries, whose northern expedition was greatly hampered by financial difficulties.[109]

On 30 January the empress dowager, as mentioned before, authorized Yüan to negotiate with the revolutionaries for conditions of the Manchu abdication. Before that date all negotiations between Yüan and the revolutionaries were, legally speaking, unauthorized. Jordan observed Yüan Shih-k'ai's two aims between 1 and 12 February as being the finalization of terms on which the Manchu court would retire, and the establishment of a coalition government as quickly as possible after the abdication. To achieve the second objective, Yüan desired to crowd into one day the announcement of the abdication, Sun Yat-sen's resignation, his own election as president, and the formation of an amalgamated cabinet.[110]

Jordan appreciated the wisdom of Yüan's intention to bring about a *fait accompli* by a series of quick actions. Sun Yat-sen also understood the point and demanded that Yüan himself should be at Nanking when he was elected president. For Sun, Yüan's election as president by the Nanking senate was recognition that the republic was created by the revolution.

The abdication edict of 12 February was, therefore, a severe blow to Sun and his close associates, such as Hu Han-min, Ch'en Ch'i-mei, and Ma Chün-wu who represented the left-wing revolutionaries. The edict provided for an amalgamated government which was almost a replica of the Tientsin provisional government scheme which Yüan Shih-k'ai had proposed about a month before. Although not at Tientsin, the new government was to be led by Yüan who would derive his status from the last Manchu imperial edict and not the revolutionaries. Much to Jordan's relief, Sun Yat-sen resigned shortly after the abdication, and Yüan shih-k'ai was elected on 15 February as the new provisional president by the Nanking senate.

When the revolution was over, G. E. Morrison wrote: 'I have kept poor old Sir John straight throughout this crisis. . . . But for me I believe that long before this he would have had a nervous breakdown'.[111] It is highly doubtful that Jordan shared Morrison's view of his good service to him. Many a time during that critical period Jordan must have been annoyed by Morrison's statements, to say nothing of the latter publishing some of his telegrams in *The Times*.

It is, however, true that Jordan had been under a great strain during the revolution, even though the final outcome was a compensation. Since late December 1911 Jordan had come to terms with the facts: 'China is not suited and will not for many years to come be suited, either for constitutional government or a republic, and that it matters little what form of government is adopted, provided she can obtain some capable men to govern the country'.[112] Who could have been more capable, both with regard to Britain's interests and China's own well-being, than Yüan Shih-k'ai? It would have been disastrous if the Chinese republic had fallen into the hands either of Sun Yat-sen who was an 'armchair politician', 'a wild visionary' ignorant about his own country, and 'a coward', or of the other revolutionary leaders, none of whom was a 'man of any capacity or marked ability above his fellows'.[113]

CHAPTER IV

YÜAN'S PRESIDENCY, 1912–1915

A PROMINENT feature of Yüan's presidency was his personal control over the government. These few years mark Yüan's growing autocracy, and culminate in his attempt in 1915–16 to revive a monarchy and assume the throne himself. This chapter deals with Yüan's struggle for power, of which the critical point was the 'Second Revolution' in the summer of 1913.

Yüan Shih-k'ai's consolidation of his power up to 1913 was achieved by three progressive steps: the reorganization loan made by the international consortium; T"ang Shao-i's resignation from the premiership; and Sung Chiao-jen's assassination. Both Jordan and Yüan were actively involved in the question of the reorganization loan, but Jordan was purely an observer in the dramas of T'ang's departure and Sung's death.

Yüan was inaugurated as president amidst loud and desperate appeals for money from all quarters. He himself urgently needed funds, not only to set up a coalition government, and to meet current administrative expenses, but also to wind up the Nanking government. The latter was incessantly requesting money for the disbandment of soldiers, whose demands for pay in arrears were particularly intense in Shanghai and Nanking. If not quickly satisfied these men could easily deteriorate into bandits. About 500 thousand irregular soldiers, mostly recruited by the revolutionaries, were waiting to be disbanded. Yüan, however, wanted money to build a personal army in the north. The Manchu court also clamoured for its stipulated pension. At the same time the powers were demanding that China should liquidate her outstanding foreign debts and pay the arrears of the Boxer indemnity incurred during the 1911 Revolution.

It was no simple task early in 1912 for China to solve her financial problems. The government was not sufficiently restored to be able to collect taxes regularly from the provinces. Moreover, the Customs had been completely under foreign control since the outbreak of the revolution; the Likin Excise and Salt Gabelle were chaotic, corrupt, and governed by monopolies. Finally Yüan was forced to turn to foreign money-lenders after his dismal failure in floating an internal loan in January.[1]

On 28 February the Hongkong and Shanghai Bank paid, on behalf of the consortium, 2 million taels to Yüan. This money was to be used by the Nanking government to disband troops and liquidate its outstanding liabilities. The following day T'ang Shao-i, who had become the first premier of the Chinese republic, asked the consortium for 3 million taels for March for the Peking government, and 64 million taels each month for April, May, and June—half for Peking and half for Nanking. T'ang assured the foreign bankers that all these advances would be covered by a comprehensive loan of £60 million, which China would conclude with the consortium in June. This loan was to cover all matured provincial loans and arrears of indemnity; as well as to reorganize the country, with special regard to productive enterprises, the army, navy, and education. The loan was to be secured as a second charge on a reorganized Salt Gabelle.

On 2 March Yüan Shih-k'ai made an urgent request for 1,015,000 taels so as to meet the exigencies caused by mutinies at Peking, Paoting, and Tientsin. On 9 March the consortium handed over another 1,100,000 taels to Peking, but demanded in return a firm option on the monthly provisions for March, April, May, June, and possibly July and August of the reorganization loan. Yüan Shih-k'ai agreed to these terms in his letter to the bank representatives on the same day. On 12 March the banks agreed to furnish Yüan Shih-k'ai with monthly provisions until August, inclusive, and to grant his most recent request, made the day before, for 2 million taels to pay the troops at Wuchang and to support the Hupei provincial currency. The banks laid down regulations governing the monthly payments; namely, immediate reorganization of the Salt Gabelle through the help of foreign experts, and prudent expenditure of the loan proceeds.

However, the bankers were not optimistic for long. On 14 March the Peking bank representatives learned that T'ang Shao-i had made an independent agreement with a Belgian syndicate for a loan of £1 million at 5 per cent interest. The security was the net income and property of the Peking-Kalgan Railway and the general revenue of the country. China then agreed to conclude with the syndicate a £10 million reorganization loan, on terms equally as advantageous as those offered by other parties. The consortium banks and governments took immediate action by suspending all money advances to China, and Yüan Shih-k'ai was forced within a short time to make repeated appeals to the consortium to resume lending. Before China was to receive money again, T'ang Shao-i had to suffer the humiliation of apologizing in person to each consortium legation, and China had to acknowledge at the end of the month that the Anglo-Belgian loan was 'a breach of faith' on her part. The Belgian loan was cancelled on 2 May 1912, and Jordan reflected on the outcome as 'a blessing in disguise'. It had made China more conscious of her obligations as 'a suitor for foreign financial assistance'. Secondly, he realized that a monopoly by the consortium in lending to China, as opposed to free competition among the foreign countries, was imperative for strict supervision of the expenditure of loan funds— crucial for the benefit of both China and her lenders. Jordan's second rationale was not without foundation. A large part of the Belgian loan, which amounted to £1,250,000 by a subsequent issue of £250 thousand was mostly 'frittered away' in political buying and selling, and T'ang Shao-i was unable to produce a full statement of expenditure although he had repeatedly been asked to do so.

As soon as the negotiations resumed the consortium received numerous appeals for money from China. Jordan believed that such requests should be met only upon conditions of control, laid down by the bank representatives after consultation with the ministers. Consequently, with guidance from the British legation, Hillier and the representative of the British and Chinese Corporation, S. F. Mayers, drafted a scheme to control Chinese expenditure of the provisional advances.

This proposal, later revised and endorsed by the other representatives, was most rigorous. It provided for the consortium to select an experienced auditor whose function was to sign all requisitions on the monthly advances. It also controlled expenditure for payment and disbandment of troops, and payment of civil officials' salaries and administrative expenses. For the effective disbandment of troops, a commission, made up of the military attachés from the legations of the consortium powers was to be formed. For the second purpose, the co-operation of consular officials would be enlisted. The Chinese government, however, refused to accept the proposal unless the powers replaced the military attachés with foreign commissioners of Customs who, though foreign, were nevertheless employees of the Chinese government.

Meanwhile, the consortium was preoccupied with the conditions for the reorganization loan, and the inclusion of Russia (the Russo-Asiatic Bank) and Japan (the Yokohama Specie Bank) in the consortium community. By 20 June the foreign bankers had drawn up the reorganization loan terms. Conditions included the effective control of loan expenditure through foreign personnel to be employed by the Chinese government; the reorganization, under foreign direction, of the Salt

Gabelle which was the security of the loan; the prohibition of borrowing by China from other sources until the entire reorganization loan of £60 million had been issued; and the consortium's appointment of financial agents for five years to assist in the reorganization of China. These terms were categorically rejected on 24 June by the Chinese who were averse to the principles of supervision of expenditure and control of security. Five days later the Chinese government reduced its request from £60 million to £10 million in the hope that the consortium might relax its conditions. The Chinese were to be disappointed. On 9 July the six foreign ministers jointly declared in Peking that their governments would not allow the consortium to make further advances to China, unless the conditions laid down at the end of June were respected.

Jordan, though participating in the joint declaration, doubted whether the powers were acting correctly. He had expected the Chinese government to turn down the consortium terms, in view of recent agitation against foreign control of the expenditure of the provisional advances. Opposition was further aggravated by the so-called National Subscription Drive *(Kuo-min chüan)*, which was especially popular in the south.

Jordan was clearly uneasy about the situation, in which he saw 'a sinister resemblance to the similar movement against the Hukwang Railway Loan, which proved the precursor of the revolution'. Worst still, the consortium scheme to supervise the expenditure of the preliminary advances had failed, largely because the Chinese central government was unable to control the provinces. For the time being, however, Jordan decided to back up the other five ministers, and his own government, who insisted on strict control and supervision.

In August came a serious challenge to the policy of the British government, regarding its exclusive support to the Hongkong and Shanghai Bank in lending to China. On 23 August Mr Birch Crisp informed the British Foreign Office in person about another loan which his syndicate had been negotiating with China since 30 May. The Foreign Office was in a difficult position. It was certain that Crisp would not give up the loan, supported by such influential banking houses as Lloyd's Bank, the London Country and West Bank, and the Capital and Counties Bank (all determined to break the monopoly of the Hongkong and Shanghai Bank), and by Morrison who had just resigned from *The Times* and was then in London in his new capacity as political adviser to president Yüan Shih-k'ai. Yet the Foreign Office had pledged exclusive support to the Hongkong and Shanghai Bank until a reorganization loan with China was concluded.

As a way out of the difficulty, Sir Edward Grey suggested Britain's possible withdrawal from the consortium. Still mindful of the Anglo-Belgian loan, Jordan advised against the idea; firstly, China had not definitely rejected the consortium, and secondly, if the consortium broke up, ruthless competition among the powers would cause even greater financial chaos in China. Influenced by Jordan's advice, the more flexible attitude of the Chinese, and the pressure from the Hongkong and Shanghai Bank, the British government agreed, for the time being to remain in the consortium.

Later, the parties concerned arrived at a compromise which was telegraphed to the British legation in Peking on 16 September. A speedy conclusion of the reorganization loan was sought through relaxation of the terms regarding foreign administration of the Salt Gabelle, but not those concerning expenditure of loan funds. The British group had accepted the arrangement and was going to exert pressure on the other consortium groups to follow suit immediately.

Simultaneously, Jordan reached the same conclusion that the consortium terms must be relaxed. Though fully aware of the difficulty in which the home government found itself, Jordan was essentially influenced by developments in China. On 13 September Jordan was assured by Yüan that, if the consortium agreed to more lenient terms, the Chinese government would cancel the Crisp loan. On the following day Yüan even threatened to resign if he was not given money. Jordan's telegram to the Foreign Office of 15 September, stating that the 'only feasible solution' was to relax the consortium conditions, crossed with an almost identical message from the Foreign Office. Jordan, however, also urged the relaxation of the terms governing both the control of the security and of the expenditure of loan funds.

Britain's new policy was not to come into effect immediately. On 23 September the bank representatives rejected a set of counter-proposals for the resumption of negotiations which the Chinese minister of finance had presented two days before. The next day the Crisp Syndicate paid over £5 million to China. Yüan informed Jordan that he had been forced to accept the advance because of the uncompromising attitude of the banks.

Jordan was greatly upset. Both he and Sir Edward Grey had considered the Chinese counter-proposals a reasonable basis for resuming negotiations. In addition, the approach of the presidential election in

China prevented Yüan Shih-k'ai from accepting the consortium's original demands, which were especially disagreeable to the southern provinces. To exacerbate matters, the consortium could not decide on the terms on which they would reopen negotiations with China. At the end of September a Belgian firm, taking advantage of the deadlock between the consortium and China, contracted a loan agreement of 250 million francs to build a railway from Lanchow to Haichow.

Jordan now pressed the Foreign Office to grant bank representatives in Peking greater freedom in negotiating with the Chinese, instead of having the consortium principals draw up hard and fast terms in Europe. Half a month later the consortium still faced a stalemate, and resolved that the six bank representatives were to confer with the six ministers in an effort to conclude the reorganization loan.

Jordan seized this opportunity to convince the other ministers that leniency was the only way to resolve the situation. On 5 November negotiations formally resumed between the consortium and the Chinese government on the basis of the Chinese counter-proposals of 21 September. There is, however, another circumstance, apart from Jordan's initiative, to be taken into account. Earlier on the Chinese government had learned that the Crisp Syndicate might be unable to pay over the second half of its loan, and was therefore more willing to comply with the consortium. The Crisp loan was eventually cancelled on 23 December after China had agreed to make a considerable compensation payment.

By the end of 1912 a general agreement had been reached between the consortium and China. The loan was to be £25 million, pledged on the Salt Gabelle. Supervision of expenditure and security would be achieved by the establishment of a central salt administration, a national debts department (for China's foreign loans generally), a loan department (for the reorganization loan exclusively), and an audit bureau. Compared with the consortium terms presented at the end of June there was one significant concession in the agreement. Instead of insisting that the top personnel of the salt administration would be exclusively foreign, the foreign banks now accepted the appointment of a Chinese co-inspector-general on a par with the foreign inspector-general.

The agreement would have been signed at the beginning of 1913 if it had not been for the eruption of internal dissension among the signatory powers. Early in January China indicated that she would appoint three foreign advisers—one each for the Salt administration, the public debts department, and the audit department. The French minister, with the support of his Russian colleague, insisted on the appointment of six advisers, one from each of the consortium nationalities. The other foreign ministers disagreed with the French point of view. Jordan in particular denounced it for entailing a foreign commission of control which would never be acceptable to the Chinese. There were further complications about a month later when Sir Edward Grey became determined that Germany should on no account obtain the post of inspector-general of the salt administration.

China threatened to break off negotiations because of the long delay caused by the powers' rivalry among themselves. Sir Edward Grey, discouraged by the stalemate, was once more tempted to abandon the consortium, but Jordan warned against the idea. Instead, he suggested, there should be one British inspector-general of the Salt Gabelle at Peking, one German deputy inspector-general at Shanghai, one French and one Russian adviser to the audit department, and one German director of the national loan bureau. Such an arrangement would be acceptable to the powers, while confining the presence of foreign advisers to three departments as the Chinese had originally intended. By mid-March Jordan's proposal brought accord among the foreign governments.

Britain wanted the matter to be settled quickly but unfortunately this was not the case. The American group withdrew from the consortium shortly afterwards, under pressure from President Woodrow Wilson's new administration which denounced the loan as 'touching very nearly the administrative independence of China'. An uproar immediately arose: the other bank groups feared that China might now be encouraged to turn away from the consortium, and in Britain the sudden prominence of the Chinese loan question heralded severe criticism of the government's consortium policy.

The American move came as the final blow to Grey who had been suffering from considerable tension since the question of the Crisp loan arose. Now he was more determined than ever to withdraw the British group from the consortium. It was only after Jordan had assured Grey that the American withdrawal would not weaken the consortium that Grey agreed to let Britain stay in the consortium.

From this point onwards the situation in China developed in favour of the five-party consortium. Two days after the American withdrawal Sung Chiao-jen was assassinated. Yüan Shih-k'ai's involvement in the plot forced him to accept financial assistance from the foreign banks on almost any terms. Sung was the founder and actual leader of the Kuomintang, which Yüan regarded as hampering his path to autocracy. On 10 April the bank representatives in China were notified that, if the consortium reduced the interest from $5\frac{1}{2}$ per cent to 5 per cent, the Chinese government would sign the agreement 'at once and without reference to New Parliament'.

The reduced interest rate was quite acceptable, but the consortium doubted whether it was wise to ignore the parliament which had a Kuomintang majority. Grey too was uncertain and asked for Jordan's opinion. Jordan replied that as far as the consortium was concerned it was irrelevant whether the Chinese parliament had been consulted; a loan agreement communicated to the legations by the Chinese foreign ministry would alone be binding for the Chinese government and its successors. Jordan explained to Grey that it was important to have the loan concluded immediately. This would enable Britain to recover her freedom for economic enterprises, and at the same time encourage Yüan Shih-k'ai on the eve of his dispute with the Kuomintang. The Reorganization Loan Agreement was finally signed, without the approval of the Chinese parliament, on 26 April 1913, the day after Sun Yat-sen had denounced it at Shanghai.

Before the agreement was concluded Britain had been the first consortium power to suggest the relaxation of loan terms. Jordan played a significant role in this international project which involved many British interests. He appeared to be the first foreigner who queried the stringency of the terms which the consortium originally intended for the loan. In September 1912 both Jordan and the Foreign Office concluded independently that the consortium must relax its demands if the loan was to be speedily effected.

However, Jordan proved to be more steadfast and consistent in adhering to this view. Grey at first would only relax control over the security, while Jordan was in favour of relaxing control over the expenditure of the loan funds as well. Grey was tempted to abandon the consortium every time he was criticized for it or there was deadlock in the negotiations, whereas Jordan insisted on its maintenance until the reorganization loan was contracted. One could justifiably argue that since Britain had been so involved in the matter, Grey would only have given up the loan if the situation had become untenable, but Jordan's strong convictions and his efforts to speed up matters in China must have convinced Grey to support the consortium.

Although the Foreign Office and Jordan were both in favour of alleviating the consortium terms, their reasons were quite different. Grey wished to remove the stigma attached to the Foreign Office on account of this business, so that Britain could compete freely with other nations again in the industrial development of China. Jordan was concerned about these problems, but he was also fully aware of the Chinese political situation. Compared with the other foreign ministers, he was unique in being closely associated with Yüan Shih-k'ai throughout the loan negotiations. This point is reflected in his letter to Langley, written about a month before the Crisp loan: 'Yüan works . . . upon me as a sort of renegade. At our last interview he pictured the six ministers as trying hard to strangle him but said he knew I kept the knot from being tied too tightly'.

Jordan was instrumental in urging the British government, and through it the other consortium powers, to sanction the reorganization loan without the approval of the Chinese parliament. He has been condemned by Chinese Communists and Nationalists alike, as one party inciting the Second Revolution, of which a major cause was the Kuomintang's opposition to the signature of the loan agreement without parliamentary consent.

It was vital that Yüan received money, as he did, from the powers immediately prior to his struggle with the Kuomintang. The material aspect of the reorganization loan was no doubt important in the spring and summer of 1913. However, one could argue that Yüan would have somehow obtained money if the consortium had eventually failed him. Significantly, Jordan pointed out that in making the loan the powers were 'virtually backing [Yüan] against the rest of the field'. In short, the reorganization loan was a token of the powers' approval and support of Yüan's growing autocracy in republican China.

The reorganization loan did not by itself cause the Second Revolution. Shortly after the reorganization loan negotiations had begun, T'ang Shao-i resigned from the premiership—an action widely accepted as the first overt expression of Yüan Shih-k'ai's autocratic aims.

Yüan's investiture as provisional president took place on 10 March 1912. To establish an amalgamated government it was now imperative to form a cabinet. On 13 March Yüan appointed T'ang Shao-i as the first premier of the Chinese republic, a choice which had previously been approved by the parliament at Nanking. By the end of the month T'ang had assembled a cabinet.

Jordan always regarded the relationship between Yüan and T'ang as one of master and subordinate. The two men first met in Korea where Yüan was the Chinese commissioner for military affairs and T'ang a Customs official. Yüan quickly recognized T'ang's ability and, during the following decade T'ang was the acting commissioner for military affairs whenever Yüan was absent from Korea. T'ang continued to serve Yüan, in the capacity of secretary, after the latter had left Korea and was training soldiers at Hsiao-chan. As governor of Shantung, Yüan entrusted T'ang with the handling of diplomatic and commercial affairs. On becoming the viceroy of Chihli, Yüan commissioned T'ang to the Tientsin Customs to help collect provincial revenues with which to pay off Chihli's share of the Boxer indemnity. After the Russo-Japanese War the viceroy of Chihli was, for the first time, made responsible for the defence of Manchuria. Yüan's influence secured T'ang's appointment in the spring of 1907 as the governor of Fengtien, one of the three Manchurian provinces. Late in 1911, as referred to earlier, Yüan sent T'ang to negotiate with the revolutionaries at Shanghai.[2]

Like Yüan Shih-k'ai, Jordan recognized T'ang as a man of ability,[3] but he also believed that without Yüan Shih-k'ai's support, T'ang by himself accounted for little. Jordan's assessment of T'ang was perhaps based on T'ang's mission to Britain early in 1909. At the end of the previous year the Chinese foreign ministry had sent T'ang Shao-i to thank the United States for giving over part of her Boxer indemnity to educate Chinese youth. Yüan Shih-k'ai, who was then a president of the foreign ministry, informally entrusted T'ang with the additional task of seeking expert assistance from Britain for a number of schemes concerning the Chinese navy. Jordan was delighted and attached great importance to T'ang's visit to his country. The Foreign Office was asked beforehand to 'secure a good reception for T'ang'.[4]

However, in January 1909 came Yüan's dismissal from the government. Jordan told Sir Francis Campbell despondently that T'ang's visit to Britain was no longer of 'any practical importance' because it 'depended entirely on Yüan's presence' in the government.[5] Again, at the beginning of 1911, Jordan thought that T'ang was wise to resign from the acting post of minister in the Ministry of Posts and Communications; with Yüan Shih-k'ai out of office, T'ang 'would have no power'.[6]

In appointing T'ang Shao-i as premier Yüan had assumed that the new president—premier relationship would again be one of master and protégé. Yüan was quickly disillusioned. Once he became premier, T'ang insisted on strict adherence to the provisional constitution promulgated by the senate at Nanking. The document loosely defined the powers of the president, the ministry, and the constitution itself and would 'probably be a source of frequent dispute in the future'.[7]

T'ang was determined from the start that the cabinet, and not president Yüan, should wield executive power in the government. During his term of office T'ang did not allow the president's office to issue any statement without his prior approval and co-signature. He even edited Yüan's inaugural speech before it could be published. Yüan Shih-k'ai in turn exhausted every means to handicap the cabinet. For instance, Chao Ping-chün, Yüan's faithful supporter and minister of the interior, never once attended cabinet meetings. In the president's office T'ang Shao-i was the target of ridicule and hate.[8]

The relationship between Yüan and T'ang was finally severed by two events: the Belgian loan of March 1912 and the appointment of the governor-general of Chihli. It has been seen that the loan was denounced by the consortium and the powers as a breach of faith by China. There have so far been two views concerning the involvement of Yüan and T'ang in the matter. One theory asserts Yüan's genuine intention to keep his promise to the consortium and that the Belgian loan was T'ang's independent action. Yüan was subesquently most displeased with T'ang when the consortium suspended all advances to China on account of the new loan.[9]

The other view is that Yüan was extremely unhappy about the terms demanded by the consortium bankers, which if accepted, would be highly detrimental to his political future. He was therefore not an unwilling party to T'ang's attempt to push through the Belgian loan. Even if the loan was eventually aborted, it could at least be used to extract better terms from the consortium. Opposition from the groups was unexpectedly strong, and Yüan resorted to feigning complete ignorance of the matter. T'ang Shao-i, the scapegoat, was made to apologize to each of the consortium legations so that China could receive money again.[10]

Of the two views, Jordan chose to follow the first. During the impasse caused by the Belgian loan, he wrote to Walter Langley, who had become head of the Far Eastern Department on Campbell's death at the end of 1911, that T'ang had been 'at his old tricks again and [had] got the President and his party into a mess'.[11] It is of course open to interpretation as to whether Jordan really believed in Yüan's innocence or, knowing his financial difficulty, tried to remove the deadlock by using T'ang Shao-i as a scapegoat.

Contrary to Jordan's opinion, it was not the Belgian loan which cost T'ang his premiership, but the appointment of the governor-general of Chihli. In the middle of March the provisional government at Nanking decreed that governor-generals and governors of the provinces would be called *tu-tu* and elected by the provincial parliaments. Wang Chih-hsiang, a military officer whose sympathies had been with the revolution-aries, was accordingly, elected *tu-tu* by the Chihli parliament. The revolutionary members of the Chihli assembly intended Wang to keep a close watch on Yüan Shih-k'ai.

At the time of Wang's election, T'ang Shao-i was organizing his cabinet at Nanking. The revolutionaries there pressed him to promise that the government would endorse the election. On his return to Peking, T'ang succeeded in obtaining Yüan's approval of Wang, who was then asked to go to the capital to be officially appointed. Wang's arrival coincided with the government's receipt of a telegram from five military leaders in Chihli, objecting to the appointment. On the basis of this telegram Yüan decided to send Wang to Nanking where he was to help disband the troops. T'ang, anxious to respect both his promise to Nanking and the integrity of the government, refused to co-sign Wang's new commission which was nevertheless released on 15 June. The next day T'ang left for Tientsin, leaving behind a letter of resignation.[12]

Jordan felt sorry about T'ang's 'bolt to Tientsin' because he regarded both Yüan and T'ang as his 'old friends'. However, unlike Yüan's dismissal in 1909, Jordan was not the least disturbed by T'ang's resigna-tion, except that it might provoke the 'Southern men'.[13] In a way he even believed that Tang's departure might be for the good of the Chinese government because of his 'emotional nature and general unsteadiness of purpose'.[14]

T'ang Shao-i's resignation did not cause an immediate crisis; in fact the political scene in China was calm and peaceful for more than a year. T'ang was first succeeded as premier by Lu Cheng-hsiang, a well-meaning diplomat who could be easily influenced.[15] When Lu was replaced by Chao Ping-chün in September the same year, the cabinet became a pliant tool in the hands of president Yüan. Yet relations between Yüan and the ex-revolutionaries appeared to be harmonious. For instance, Yüan's assassination of Chang Chen-wu and Fang Wei, generals who had belonged to the revolutionary camp, was allowed to pass almost unnoticed.[16] Moreover, Sun Yat-sen and Huang Hsing visited Yüan in August and September respectively. Even Jordan had been rather relaxed in following Chinese internal political affairs, although during the same period he was preoccupied with the reoragnization loan negotiations.

The assassination of Sung Chiao-jen late in March 1913 abruptly upset the tenor of events, and once again focused Jordan's attention on

Chinese politics. Sung Chiao-jen had founded the Kuomintang in August 1912, using the T'ung-meng hui members as the nucleus. Sung's two principal political beliefs were a responsible party cabinet and local self-government, both heresies to Yüan Shih-k'ai.[17] In touring around the country Sung not only zealously preached his political ideals; he also denounced Yüan's government.[18]

Jordan was Yüan Shih-k'ai's staunch ally in opposing Sung Chiao-jen and the Kuomintang. Quite apart from the Kuomintang's threat to Yüan's power, Sung's propagation of local self-government unpleasantly reminded Jordan of the feud between the Ch'ing government and the provinces before the 1911 Revolution. Might he, therefore, have been biased in asserting that the Kuomintang had achieved its success in the elections for the provincial assemblies in January 1913, by 'a gross display of corruption and intimidation'?[19]

By March 1913 returns in the election for the national parliament had clearly indicated a Kuomintang majority. Sung Chiao-jen, as party leader, was expected to be the next premier. On 20 March he was shot in the back at the North Station in Shanghai, just before boarding a train for Peking where he was to consult Yüan Shih-k'ai about the opening of parliament early in April. Two days later Sung died from his wounds.

Sung's assassination immediately provoked a serious political crisis because president Yüan Shih-k'ai was suspected of being implicated. The assassin, Wu Shih-ying, and the alleged instigator of the crime, Ying Kuei-hsing, were arrested shortly after the murder and held in custody by the authorities of the French and International Settlements respectively. Before long Jordan received the report from the consul-general at Shanghai that the Municipal Police of the International Settlement had documentary evidence that Ying had instigated the murder under orders from Hung Shu-tsu, private secretary to premier Chao Ping-chün.

Jordan was further informed that the Kuomintang knew of such evidence and that Ying had already telegraphed to Peking, urging that he and the French minister be asked to intervene in the matter. Fraser, aware of Jordan's feelings towards Yüan Shih-k'ai, warned: 'I do not see any advantage in trying to have evidence withheld or holding sitting *in camera* and I think men and papers must be handed over if there is reasonable evidence of guilt'.[20]

Jordan agreed. Evidence of Yüan's implication seemed too obvious to be overlooked. The British minister became further convinced of Yüan's involvement on learning that the French consul-general at

Shanghai had been asked by the Chinese commissioner of foreign affairs at Tientsin to delay the trial of the assassin until he had seen all the evidence compromising the government. At the same time, C. D. Bruce, superintendent of the Municipal Police of the International Settlement, was asked to detain Ying Kuei-hsing for as long as possible.[21]

Apart from the likelihood of Yüan's complicity, Jordan had other reasons for not interfering in the matter. He had for some time been optimistic about a compromise: 'the present struggle between the north and south, like any street brawl, will probably terminate in both sides eventually adjusting their differences in deference to the counsels of peace makers'. After all, the national parliament did open 'smoothly' as scheduled. Even if a compromise failed to take place, Jordan was confident of Yüan emerging victoriously out of an armed struggle; his troops, numbering about 100 thousand, were 'immeasurably superior to any forces which the south [could] command'.[22] Meanwhile, Jordan devoted his energies to securing the timely conclusion of the reorganization loan.

Immediately after Sung Chiao-jen's death, Sun Yat-sen, hurried back to Shanghai from Japan on 25 March. Sun as nominal chairman of the Kuomintang, consulted the other Kuomintang leaders as to the steps to be taken against Yüan Shih-k'ai. Huang Hsing and Huang Fu opposed Sun and Ch'en Chi-mei who advocated the immediate use of force to expel Yüan from office: it was still possible to impeach Yüan through legal and constitutional means; and secondly, the Kuomintang was simply not prepared for an armed clash with Yüan. Even Hunan, Kwangsi, Anhui, and Kwangtung—provinces where the Kuomintang had the strongest influence—could scarcely cope with problems of internal order and military discipline.

The argument of Huang Hsing and Huang Fu was approved by the majority of the Kuomintang leaders then in Shanghai. Instead of making military preparations, the party set about organizing a special court to ensure a fair trial of the Sung case. The Kuomintang continued its policy of constitutional opposition, even after the conclusion of the reorganization loan and Yüan's refusal to allow Chao Ping-chün to appear as witness in the Sung trial, as decided by the Shanghai court and demanded by the Kuomintang members.[23] A compromise seemed to be on the way.

Yüan Shih-k'ai, however, was unwilling to compromise. He rejected the Kuomintang's suggestion of a special court, insisting that the case should be tried in a regular court by the *tu-tu* and the civil commissioner of Kiangsu. Moreover, Yüan used the reorganization loan money to his own advantage. He bought over many Kuomintang members, and provided Liang Ch'i-ch'ao with ample funds to organize the Progressive Party (*Chin-pu tang*), which soon became a tool of the government and an opponent to the Kuomintang in the new parliament.[24] On 29 April Yüan Shih-k'ai sought a confidential interview with Sir John Jordan. At the meeting Yüan praised Britain's role in the reorganization loan and commented generally on the Sung case. He then told Jordan that Sun Yat-sen and Huang Hsing intended to reduce him to a mere figure-head, and that the two Kwang provinces were contemplating an independent movement. Jordan was then asked if the powers were happy to see Sun and Huang in power; if not, would they condone Yüan using force against the recalcitrant provinces? While deprecating the idea of a civil war, Jordan assured Yüan of the unanimous support of the foreign ministers in Peking, and that he would personally regard Yüan's retirement 'a great misfortune'. Jordan also allayed Yüan's fear that Japan might help the Kuomintang, by emphasizing that the Japanese minister shared the general foreigners' attitude.[25] Sir Edward Grey, however, was not so forthright in giving support to Yüan.[26]

At the end of the interview Jordan realized that China was on the brink of further civil strife. The 'root cause'[27] of the struggle was the Kuomintang's insistence on limiting Yüan Shih-k'ai by constitutional regulations. Unless the Kuomintang was prepared to compromise, their efforts to bring about a peaceful settlement during May would be futile.

Early in May, Sun Yat-sen explicitly told colonel Bruce of the Municipal Police, who had been on close terms with the Shanghai Kuomintang leaders, that force would not be used against Yüan.[28] Shortly afterwards the Shanghai party members, disturbed by the movement of government troops into Hupei, made a similar statement.[29] In the middle of the month the Kuomintang approached Timothy Richard, a highly respected veteran missionary, to ask Jordan if he would mediate between the party and Yüan Shih-k'ai. The Kuomintang would no longer object to Yüan as president on certain conditions: that he would delegate offices equally among the parties; establish an audit of public expenditure; give the Sung case a fair trial; and abide by constitutional laws.[30] On 20 May Jordan learned that E.S. Little of the well-established Brunner Mond—a company with Kuomintang leanings —was about to leave for Peking to present Yüan Shih-k'ai with the Kuomintang's proposals for mediation. Jordan answered decisively that 'no foreigners could hope to do any good by interfering in such a question'.[31]

The Kuomintang at long last realized that their peace offers were unacceptable to Yüan Shih-k'ai. By the end of May both sides were preparing for an armed confrontation. At a dinner given in honour of Baron Kato Komei, Sun Yat-sen pointedly asked the Japanese guest if the Kuomintang could rely on Japan's help in its imminent struggle against the government. The reply was negative.[32] By this time Huang Hsing had already been stripped of his military rank and publicly denounced by the government. While large bodies of government troops were moving into the Yangtze area, Yüan Shih-k'ai rejected an offer of mediation from Ts'en Ch'un-hsüan, a well known ex-Ch'ing official. Yüan believed that the crisis hinged not on the difference between north and south, but the submission of the provinces to the central authority.[33] No one could agree with Yüan more than Jordan on this point.

At the last interview with Yüan before going on leave, Jordan was assured that the Kuomintang provinces could easily be dealt with. The government needed only to remove the *tu-tu* of Kiangsi, Li Lieh-chün, before it could have the Yangtze area under full control. Actions would then have to be taken against Canton. In short, Yüan was 'determined at all costs to secure the unification of the provinces under the central government'.

Apart from the situation in the provinces, Yüan's main concern was his position as president. He was confident of being elected first president of the Chinese republic in the forthcoming election; even the Kuomintang could not suggest an alternative to him. However, he refused to become a figure-head, with powers limited by party cabinets and other regulations.

Jordan's response to the points raised by Yüan was most gratifying. He endorsed the view that a strong centralized government was imperative for China. Instead of discouraging civil war as at the interview on 29 April, Jordan now hoped that no more force than necessary would be used to subdue the provinces. Moreover, Jordan expressed appreciation on behalf of the Diplomatic Corps of Yüan's success in maintaining peace and order in face of overwhelming difficulties since the 1911 Revolution. The British minister, though unable to attend the presidential inauguration, assured Yüan that Britain would recognize the republic as soon as the president was elected.

Once the principles were agreed upon, Yüan discussed the details of mplementation. He sought Jordan's help in preventing the import of arms to Canton from Hong Kong, the sanction of loans to the provinces, and the use of the Shanghai International Settlement as a screen by political agitators. Again, Jordan's response was most satisfactory. He and the Chinese foreign ministry had previously agreed to the two conditions on which the Hong Kong government could issue an export permit of arms: another permit issued by the Chinese war ministry, and notification of British legation in Peking. By this arrangement one large consignment of arms for Canton had already been held up. Nevertheless, Jordan undertook to remind the governor of Hong Kong on this point. On the question of provincial loans, there would be no sanction without the approval of the Chinese government. The problem of the Shanghai settlement was more complicated because of the other powers' involvement. However, the Diplomatic Corps had always objected to the settlement being used as a refuge by political agitators, and would certainly continue to do so.[34]

Three days after Jordan's departure from China, on 9 June, Yüan Shih-k'ai stripped Li Lieh-chün, *tu-tu* of Kiangsi, of his title. The Kuomintang *tu-tus* of Kwangtung, Hu Han-min, and Anhui, Po Wen-wei, were dismissed on 14 and 30 June respectively. The Second Revolution broke out on 12 July when the government troops clashed with Li Lieh-chün's soldiers: Li then moved to Hu-k'ou, where he declared himself independent of the government. Huang Hsing took up military command against Yüan at Nanking on 14 July, and two days later Ch'en Ch'i-mei did the same at Shanghai. Following this, declarations of independence were made closely one after another by Kuomintang leaders in Anhui, Kwangtung, Fukien, Hunan, and Szechwan. However, by the end of August the Second Revolution had ended with the defeat of the Kuomintang.

Despite his absence from China during the upheaval, Jordan played a significant part, in the Second Revolution. It was he who effected the reorganization loan for timely use by Yüan. The £25 million loan was twelve times over-subscribed on the day of issue.[35] China, however, could only have access to £21 million because the loan was paid over at the issue price of 84 per cent.[36] Of this amount, £10 million was assigned to payment of matured or maturing liabilities of the Chinese government; £3 million to disbandment of troops; £5.5 million to 'current expense of administration'; and £2 million to reorganization of the Salt Gabelle.[37]

Specific amounts of the loan were earmarked for specific purposes, and there seemed to be scant opportunity for abusing the loan especially with regard to liquidating foreign liabilities and the reform of the salt administration.[38] However, the other two headings of expenditure, current administrative expenses and disbandment of troops, were defined so loosely that it was difficult to exercise stringent control over them, and foreign banks and governments chose not to follow matters closely. There are clear references to the misappropriation of the funds, which had been intended for the disbandment of troops, being used to finance the Second Revolution. In protest against such activities, Chou Hsüeh-hsi, the minister of finance who had signed the Reorganization Loan Agreement, is said to have resigned and gone to Tsingtao.[39]

Although the British legation in Peking could not say how much of the loan money had been used for the rebellion, it estimated that during the summer and autumn of 1913 Yüan's government had received about £8 million.[40] Thus before the revolution broke out, Yüan was able to bribe Kuomintang members in the Peking parliament and form opposing political parties. After the outbreak of hostilities, Yüan had the means to buy the loyalty of some of the Kuomintang generals,[41] while retaining that of the government troops.

A vivid example of the last point was an incident involving the Chinese navy which is described in detail in the book *Pulling strings in China*.[42] The author, William Ferdinand Tyler, a self-proclaimed 'strong partisan of Yüan' who had served in the Chinese navy during the Sino-Japanese War, was later appointed adviser to the Chinese naval commander-in-chief on neutrality affairs.[43] At the time of the revolution in 1913, Tyler was employed in the Customs at Shanghai.

Puzzled by the fact that the Chinese fleet was still anchored opposite the Kiangnan Arsenal which the Kuomintang was about to attack, Tyler paid a visit on 17 July to admiral Li Ting-sing (Tyler's transliteration for Li Ting-hsin). On arrival, Tyler was informed by the admiral that at a captains' meeting the day before, two of them had threatened to carry the fleet over to the side of the Kuomintang. This would mean a joint attack on the arsenal by the Kuomintang and the mutinied fleet. The only solution, according to Li, was to obtain immediately one million taels to pay the men who had not been paid for two months, and who had been promised pay by the Kuomintang if they would rebel against the government.

Tyler immediately called on A. G. Stephen, manager of the Hongkong and Shanghai Bank at Shanghai, and enquired about using the considerable reserve of Chinese government money which the consortium bankers held against Chinese liabilities. Stephen did not give an answer then.

The next day Tyler was introduced to admiral Tseng Ju-cheng, a faithful follower of Yüan who had been commissioned to reinforce the fleet at Shanghai. The admiral claimed that if money could not be obtained by the following noon, the arsenal would most probably be attacked the same night.

Meanwhile, the newly-appointed commander-in-chief of the British China Squadron, admiral T. M. Jerram, had just arrived in Shanghai on the *Newcastle*. Tyler immediately secured an interview with the British admiral as well as the acting consul-general, H. E. Fulford. While Jerram favoured Tyler's efforts to save the Shanghai fleet for Yüan Shih-k'ai's government, Fulford's cautious attitude was understandable. Even Tyler himself admitted that his intervention was improper, but he argued that it was the lesser evil compared with Yüan Shih-k'ai's downfall.

On 19 July Tyler received a cheque for a quarter of a million taels, with the guarantee of further advances on the condition that he himself administered the funds. At the same time he received a telegram from the chief secretary of the Customs service, C. A. V. Bowra, allowing him freedom of action at his discretion. No longer uneasy about implicating the Customs, Tyler immediately rented a flat to serve as a naval office where he carried out the duties of a treasurer. In return for being furnished with funds admirals Tseng and Li had to submit a summary of expenditure for each vessel, including those on the upper Yangtze. Thus, during the Kuomintang attack on the arsenal on 23 July, the government troops who defended it were assisted in their operation by Chinese men-of-war.

Tyler's account is well reinforced by the British Foreign Office archives, which explain the rationale of the Hongkong and Shanghai Bank, the British consulate-general at Shanghai, the British legation in Peking and the consortium. After the interview with Tyler, Fulford had another visitor—Stephen of the Hongkong and Shanghai Bank, who wanted to know if a British naval man could correctly act as the pay master-general to guarantee the loyalty of the Chinese fleet. Fulford was against the idea but suggested that Stephen should telegraph Hillier in Peking to find out whether funds could be used from the reorganization loan, with a member of the bank implementing payment to the Chinese on a private basis.[44] On receiving an urgent telegram from Stephen,[45] Hillier consulted Beilby Alston, acting British minister in Jordan's absence, who in his turn, consulted the other four ministers of the consortium. The five ministers decided to sanction the immediate advance of funds to the Chinese admirals through the banks in Shanghai.[46]

The reorganization loan money was also used to retain the loyalty of the government troops defending the Kiangnan Arsenal, and the allegiance of general Chang Hsün. It is alleged that the latter had previously encouraged the *tu-tu* of Mukden to become independent of the government in return for a bribe from Japan who was on the side of the revolutionaries.[47] No one was more aware of the material significance of the loan than Alston, who wrote:

It must, in the first place be conceded that the principal weapon used by the Central Government and its supporters has been bribery. No decisive success in the field was gained by the northern generals nor anything in the nature of a 'lesson' inflicted on the rebel forces. Desultory fighting . . . was followed, in almost every case, by protracted negotiations, resulting in the fixing of a definite price at which the leaders were prepared to be 'bought off' and the men to disperse after laying down their arms and receiving a bonus in cash.[48]

When Jordan resumed duties late in November, Yüan Shih-k'ai had been elected president, and the Chinese republic was officially recognized by the powers. Moreover, to prevent the Kuomintang-inspired Draft Constitution of the Altar of Heaven *(T'ien-t'an hsien-fa ts'ao-an)* from taking effect, on 4 November, Yüan Shih-k'ai had rid the parliament of a quorum by expelling all the Kuomintang members.

Shortly after Jordan's return, the prime minister, Hsiung Hsi-ling, organized an advisory body, the Administrative Council *(Cheng-chih hui-i)* to replace the disabled parliament. Jordan was amused to observe that the Administrative Council was 'a much more pliant instrument of [Yüan's] will than the ordinary legislative Council [was] in the hands of a British Colonial Governor'.[49] On 10 January 1914 Yüan Shih-k'ai dissolved the parliament altogether, and less than two months later ordered the dissolution of all provincial assemblies and self-governing bodies throughout the country.

Having removed the obstacles to power, Yüan now set about strengthening his autocratic position. A special committee was appointed to amend the Nanking Provisional Constitution. On 1 May 1914 the Constitutional Compact of the Chinese Republic *(Chung-hua min-kuo yo-fa)* was promulgated. The compact was perhaps misnamed, in view of unlimited power it accorded the president. Yüan was to appoint all officials and cabinet ministers; to conduct foreign affairs independently and to declare war if necessary; to draft, together with the newly established Council of State *(Ts'an-cheng yüan)*, and promulgate the constitution; and to issue financial measures and emergency bills as circumstances required. The Council of State, replacing the Administrative Council and composed of highly conservative members, was set up late in June. By the end of December the new council had finalized the regulations governing the presidential election: the president was to be in office for ten years and eligible for re-election. Moreover, he was to nominate three candidates, not necessarily excluding himself, from whom the new president was to be elected.

Besides these measures, Yüan Shih-k'ai controlled the provinces by appointing only his close associates to authoritarian posts.[50] Jordan of course was most satisfied with these developments. After all his years in China, the political situation in early 1914 was nearest to his ideal for the country. Even finances were no longer a major problem; the central coffer was receiving an ever-increasing amount of revenue from the provinces.[51] This Jordan attributed to Yüan Shih-k'ai's outstanding achievement in centralizing the administration of the country. Moreover, the reorganization of the salt administration had begun to show effect, and the monthly yield of salt revenue increased greatly.[52] Jordan was now confident that on the strength of the Customs service and the salt administration, China would be able to repay her foreign liabilities. He reacted favourably to the talks of a fresh reorganization loan to China in the spring of 1914.[53]

Jordan's optimism continued even after the outbreak of World War I. Despite the shadow cast by Japan's activities in Shantung, he wrote three months after the war had begun: 'China is going along quietly, keeping her head above water and just managing to pay her way financially. Unless there are some unexpected complications, I see no reason to be apprehensive about the immediate future'.[54]

CHAPTER V

THE MONARCHICAL MOVEMENT

THE monarchical movement of Yüan Shih-k'ai, which started in August 1915, was the climax of his ambition. Undoubtedly it was the most far-reaching political event in China between the 1913 'Second Revolution' and Yüan's death in June 1916. The movement emerged slowly, and was not unexpected when it was formally inaugurated in the summer of 1915.

It is commonly asserted that Yüan had aspired to imperialism for some time before the movement. This view has several foundations: his increasing disregard of parliamentary rule since the 1913 Revolution; his worship, in late 1913 and early 1914, of Heaven and Confucius which had been the prerogative of the emperor in imperial China; and his tacit approval of those in favour of imperialist restoration under the previous Ch'ing dynasty, such as Sung Yu-jen, Lao Nai-hsüan, and Liu T''ing-shen.[1] Liang Ch'i-ch'ao is said to have rejected a bribe to support Yüan's monarchy early in 1915.[2] Moreover, there have been allegations that later in the year Yüan Shih-k'ai bowed to most of Japan's twenty-one demands in return for her connivance in the monarchical plan.[3]

By the early summer of 1915 rumours were rife in Peking that a Yüan dynasty was imminent. Such hearsay prompted Feng Kuo-chang, then *tu-tu* of Kiangsu province, to visit the president in person and ascertain the truth. Yüan emphatically denied his desire for the dragon throne, knowing that Feng was not in favour of such a change.[4] Shortly afterwards, however, the *tu-tus* of Shantung, Kiangsi, Shansi, Mukden, and Hupei, together with Chang Tso-lin, were called to Peking. Ostensibly they were to report on their posts, but the real purpose of the gathering was to win the *tu-tus'* allegiance to the restoration of a monarchy.[5]

The monarchical movement came into the open when the Society for the Planning of Peace *(Ch'ou-an hui)* was founded on 23 August 1915. Its aim was to study *(yen-chiu)* the best form of government *(kuo-t'i)* for China.[6] The result of the 'study' however, was a foregone conclusion. The Society's manifesto was based on the views of Professor F. J. Goodnow, Yüan Shih-k'ai's former adviser who had in June presented a memorandum advocating monarchy as the best form of government for China.[7]

On 3 September Yüan Shih-k'ai sent his secretary-general, Liang Shih-i, to Jordan to discuss the principle of monarchy. Jordan believed that monarchy would, among other things, remove 'the vexed question of the succession', but he had grave misgivings as to the timing of the change. He feared that while Britain and the other Western powers were preoccupied with the European War, Japan would take advantage of the disorder which might arise out of the monarchical movement to further her ambitions in China. He concluded that the monarchy should be postponed until the war was over.[8]

At this point it is worth digressing to trace Jordan's attitude towards Japan throughout his career. Jordan was appointed as British consul-general at Seoul in 1896, and until 1905 he witnessed intense Russo-Japanese rivalry in Korea before the Russo-Japanese War (1904–5). He was unmistakably anti-Russian and pro-Japanese: Russia's influence over the corrupt Korean court was intolerable, especially during the three or four years before the war[9]; and Russian activities in Manchuria were nothing short of robbery. There were times when Jordan was highly critical of Japan for behaving with moderation, which Russia 'interpreted as a sign of weakness'.[10] Regarding Japan as the symbol of progress in the Far East,[11] Jordan found it difficult to understand why the Koreans should prefer Russia.

Then came the Russo-Japanese War which Jordan saw as 'a terrible struggle, the East against the worst part of the West, with the best part of the West's sympathies enlisted on the East's side'.[12] He admired the Japanese soldiers' discipline, precision of action, and foresight. The Russians, on the other hand, were intolerably ignorant and behaved immoderately.[13] For the interest of the Koreans, Jordan sincerely hoped that after putting aside her military burden Japan would concentrate on a large-scale reform programme in Korea.[14] He then thought that perhaps a Japanese protectorate over Korea might be more beneficial.[15]

Shortly after Jordan's arrival in Peking in 1906, a fairly intense anti-Japanese sentiment prevailed among the British communities at the treaty ports, particularly at Shanghai. British merchants were enraged by Japan's dishonest commercial dealings, the most outrageous of which was the piracy of British trademarks. From 1907 onwards it became apparent that Japan, as the Russian had done earlier, was discriminating against foreign goods in South Manchuria. For the next two years Japan's policy in the area was frustrated by the viceroy of Mukden, Hsü Shih-chang, and the governor of Fengtien, T'ang Shao-i, both of whom had been appointed to their posts through the influence of Yüan Shih-k'ai. Thus when Yüan was dismissed early in 1909, Jordan naturally suspected Japan's satisfaction with the sudden turn of events.[16]

Parallel with China's efforts, the United States also tried to halt Japan's takeover in Manchuria. American actions were mostly associated with Willard Straight, then American consul-general at Mukden, and later the Peking representative of the American group of the international consortium. Straight was eager to internationalize all railways in Manchuria before they fell into Japan's hands.[17] The United States, however, was denied British support. Sir Edward Grey, prepared to sacrifice British interests in Manchuria, did not wish to jeopardize Britain's relations with Japan who, with Russia's support, strongly opposed the American plans.[18] Jordan was uneasy about his government's uncooperative attitude towards the United States, though he still retained the good impression he had formed of Japan during his Korean days. In time he came to accept Japan's special position in Manchuria as long as Britain's treaty rights there were unviolated.[19]

The very gratifying outcome of the 1911 Revolution caused Jordan to forget temporarily the unpleasant differences between himself and Ijuin, and between his country and Japan. Jordan's absence from China during the 1913 Revolution produced similar results. At this time both the Japanese government and Japanese nationalists were involved in activities against Yüan Shih-k'ai.

It was late in 1913 and early in 1914 that Jordan found himself in the midst of an 'acute' Anglo-Japanese conflict for the 'first time'.[20] The Japanese were 'determined to make every effort to obtain a firm railway footing in the Yangtze Valley',[21] while the British, especially Jordan himself,[22] were 'determined to defend it'.[23] Jordan was strongly supported by Sir Edward Grey in keeping the Yangtze region as a British sphere.[24] Jordan protested to the Chinese government and Japanese legation against Japan's claim to build the Nanchang-Hankow and the Nanking-Hsiangtang lines. Britain was also anxious to block the plan for a Japanese railway from Fukien to a point on the Canton-Hankow line.[25]

There were other causes of dissension apart from railways. Jordan denounced Japan's loans to the Chapei Water Works, the Hupei Cement Works, the China Merchants Steam Navigation Company, certain mines in Anhui and, above all, the Hanyehping Iron Works as bearing political significance.[26] The situation intensified in March 1914, when a group of leading Japanese bankers and businessman founded the Japanese and Chinese Development Company for the purpose of guiding development in China, especially in the Yangtze area which centred on Kiangsi province. The company, though in name a private enterprise, clearly had the active support of the Japanese government.[27] The Japanese based most of their claims on China on the promises given by Sun Yat-sen and Li Lieh-chün in the summer of 1913 in return for Japan's assistance in their struggle against Yüan Shih-k'ai. Moreover, the Japanese were further encouraged by Yüan Shih-k'ai, who co-operated in the matter in the hope of gaining some personal benefit. Jordan was most dissatisfied with Yüan's behaviour and it was perhaps the time when he least respected Yüan.[28]

By the outbreak of World War I Jordan had become very wary of the marked increase of Japanese prestige in China, although he was confident that Britain was still the stronger and the more influential power in the Far East.[29]

Jordan's attitude towards Japan changed considerably during the war. Initially Sir Edward Grey had not intended to use the Anglo-Japanese Alliance to support Britain's war efforts in the Far East. Not long after the outbreak of war, however, the Foreign Office favoured Japanese aid for the protection of Hong Kong and Weihaiwei, and also Britain's naval position in the Far East. This decision though, did take into account the undesirability of Japan having complete freedom of action in the course of rendering assistance to Britain.[30]

By 8 August the Japanese cabinet had decided to comply with Britain's request for aid and to enter the war. Jordan was gravely concerned that Japan was interpreting Grey's request for help too widely. He told Grey that Japan's assistance was not imperative and, if Japan declared war, it would 'endanger the stability of the existing regime in China, to say nothing of the inevitable effect it would have upon our future political influence in this country and our prestige in Asia generally'.[31] Jordan's attitude was later known, and greatly resented, by Japan.[32]

Jordan's views on Japan's participation in the war were staunchly supported by the governor of Hong Kong, Sir Francis May.[33] Sir Edward Grey became even more uneasy when the United States and Australia expressed suspicion of Japan's designs. Anxious not to alienate the United States and the Dominions, Grey telegraphed the British minister at Tokyo, Sir Conyngham Greene: rather than allowing Japan absolute freedom of action, he would temporarily withdraw his request for Japan's assistance.[34] The move came too late. The same day Greene was officially informed by Baron Kato Komei of Japan's decision to declare war on Germany and to act against the German stronghold of Tsingtao, with or without Britain's consent.[35] Japan's threat of unilateral action was most effective. Grey quickly succumbed to it, although he tried to lay down geographical limits for Japan's military operations;[36] and Jordan now urged association with Japan in moving against Tsingtao. However, Jordan also suggested that France and Russia, Britain's allies in war, should take part in the expedition against Tsingtao, thus minimizing the importance of Japan's role.[37] It is therefore not surprising that Japan rejected the proposal.[38] Jordan moreover, insisted that Japan should make a public declaration to return Kiaochow, the area around Tsingtao, to China after the war. This demand, which Jordan repeated at least twice before Japan delivered her ultimatum to Germany on 15 August, elicited no response.[39]

Before the outbreak of war Jordan represented the country which had the largest interest in China. Now Britain's Far Eastern position was compromised by the Japanese, whom Jordan had come to distrust intensely.[40] Nevertheless, Jordan realized that if Britain was to win the war in Europe, sacrifices would have to be made elsewhere, notably in China.

For this reason Jordan tried to smooth Sino-Japanese relations over the Japanese occupation of Tsingtao. On 12 August Jordan received an emissary from Yüan Shih-k'ai: the president was tempted by a German offer of returning Kiaochow to China to avert Japanese occupation of the place. Jordan, aware of Japan's determination to enter the war and to act against Tsingtao, replied that there was little chance of the German offer materializing. However, Yüan was assured of British commitment to Tsingtao and that whatever the circumstances Chinese interests would be seriously considered.[41]

On 15 August Japan sent her ultimatum to Germany, demanding a reply by noon of 23 August. The Germans were to withdraw their armed vessels from Japanese and Chinese waters and surrender their leased territory of Kiaochow within a month. Expressly defying Sir Edward Grey,[42] the Japanese chargé d'affaires did not consult Jordan about informing the Chinese government of Japan's ultimatum. Yüan Shih-k'ai, having been assured by Jordan of joint Anglo-Japanese actions a few days before, was perturbed by the independent move of Japan. Jordan was both puzzled and enraged by Japan's behaviour as indeed was the Foreign Office. Nevertheless, he tried to convince Yüan that there was 'a complete understanding between the two governments'.[43]

On the expiry of the ultimatum on 23 August, Japan declared war on Germany. Japan's immediate concern after her declaration of war was the occupation of Tsingtao. In this matter Jordan adhered to his government's war-time Far Eastern policy, suppressing his intense dislike of it and trying to minimize China's ill feelings against Japan. On 2 September the first Japanese troops landed on Lungkow, on the northern coast of Shantung, about 150 miles outside the German leased territory. There was much haggling between Japan and China and embarrassment for Britain on the question of trespass over Chinese territory. China reluctantly agreed to establish a war zone over the adjacent territory of Kiaochow Bay, including Lungkow, Laichow, and Kiaochow. On 23 September a pitifully small British expeditionary force commanded by Brigadier-general Nathaniel Barnardiston, landed at Lao-shan-wan. This place was inside the German leased territory, and hence involved no violation of Chinese neutrality. The British soldiers were then put under the supreme command of the Japanese.

At the end of the month, Japanese troops proceeded to occupy the Kiao-Tsi Railway between Tsingtao and Tsinan, on the pretext that the siege of Tsingtao could not be effected without control of railroad communication.[44] As the greater part of the Kiao-Tsi Railway lay outside the prescribed war zone the Chinese were enraged at this encroachment on their country's sovereignty. Japan, however, was determined to keep her gain and justified it on the grounds that the railway was the property of the German government. The British Foreign Office supported the Japanese argument. Jordan by no means condoned Japan's behaviour, but tried to bring about a compromise between the two contending parties.[45] However, he advised the Foreign Office to adopt a more cautious approach. As a result, Grey informed the Japanese ambassador in London of his desire that the situation in China should be handled with tact and care.[46]

The occupation of Tsingtao was a depressing experience for British consular officials in China. The negligible size of their expeditionary force[47]—serving as a token of British presence to maintain Britain's prestige in the Far East—was in itself a cause of humiliation. Moreover, British soldiers complained of disrespectful treatment by their Japanese counterparts. Vice-consul R. H. Eckford at Tsingtao and Consul J. T. Pratt at Tsinan, the British officials nearest to the scene of the siege, deplored the indignities the British soldiers had to suffer. Jordan did not enclose Eckford's highly censorious report on the question in his regular official correspondence to the Foreign Office, but sent it along with a private letter to Langley. Moreover, he criticized Eckford and Pratt, who circulated the report, for acting contrary to 'high policy'.[48]

Not long afterwards, in the middle of January 1915, Japan presented to China the renowned 'Twenty-one Demands' under the threat of force. This episode once more revealed Britain's weakness in the Far East, since she was neither consulted nor informed before Japan made the demands. Furthermore, when Japan did inform the British Foreign Office a few days later, no mention was made of the fifth group of demands (called 'wishes'), while the other four groups were grossly understated. Finally, when Sir Conyngham Greene somehow learned of the existence of the 'wishes', including those for railway concessions in the Yangtze, he told Baron Kato that Sir Edward Grey, who was preparing a statement of British views on the demands, ought to be informed. Baron Kato rudely answered that Britain had not been invited to make observations on the matter.[49]

In China, Anglo-Japanese relations over the Twenty-one Demands were characterized by Japan's distrust of Jordan. It appears that Baron Kato was confident from the outset that his policy of power politics would result in China's quick acceptance of the Japanese demands. He only feared that Jordan's 'very pro-Chinese'[50] attitude might complicate the situation, and therefore tried to prevent him from knowing about the content of the demands. Kato hoped that by the time Jordan learned of the demands, their acceptance by the Chinese would have become a *fait accompli*.

Yüan Shih-k'ai was given the full list of the demands on 18 January. Four days later the London Foreign Office was presented with a summary of the list, with no reference to Group V of the so-called 'wishes', by the Japanese ambassador, Inouye Katsunosuke. Contrary to usual diplomatic practice, the Japanese foreign ministry instructed the Japanese minister in China, Hioki Eki, to refuse Jordan a copy of the summary given to the Foreign Office. Although he was not 'justified by his instructions', Hioki on 29 January translated orally to Jordan the principal points of what is commonly known as the released version of the demands.[51] Hioki's oral communication was almost invalidated when the Russian minister told Jordan of his belief that Japan had made more extensive demands than had been published.[52] The Russian communication was confirmed twice. On 6 February Jordan was given the gist of the full demands by Morrison, still political adviser to Yüan Shih-k'ai; and likewise on 9 February at an interview with Wellington Koo, then a councillor in the Chinese foreign ministry.[53] Hence it was not until some three weeks after Japan had first made her demands that Jordan saw the released version of them on paper for the first time.[54]

As in the occupation of Tsingtao, Jordan followed a policy of temporary effacement *vis-à-vis* Japan. On being told by Hioki of the four groups of demands, Jordan asured Grey that they did not seem to affect British interests seriously, and that they were the natural consequence of the current diplomatic situation in the Far East.[55] Commenting on the written form of the released demands nine days later, Jordan's chief concerns were that Britain's interests might be adversely affected and the stability of Yüan Shih-k'ai's regime jeopardized.[56] Even after Jordan had learned of Japan's 'wishes', which he found extremely distasteful, he was still remarkably self-restrained, resigning himself to the philosophy that 'weak states must pay the penalty of weakness'.[57]

Early in March, there was a split of opinion in the Foreign Office regarding Britain's future policy towards Japan. Beilby Alston believed that British interests in China would be protected if an agreement was reached with Japan, after which her actions could be restrained. Both Grey and Langley, however, feared that any negotiations with Japan might initiate another series of demands which Britain would be unable to resist, being so preoccupied with the war in Europe. The outcome of the discussion was a Foreign Office memorandum in mid-March, reaffirming the policy of temporary effacement *vis-à-vis* Japan.[58] Jordan received the memorandum shortly before an agreement was reached between Japan and China on the demands. He was indeed justified in asserting that, had the terms been sent to him months before, he could not have carried them out more carefully than he had done.[59]

As he had done during the siege of Tsingtao, Jordan urged the Chinese to be patient and tolerant. He assured them that their present losses and humiliation would be more than compensated when the war was over. Jordan's efforts in this direction were especially strenuous towards the end of the incident. One must recall that negotiations between China and Japan had begun on 2 February. The Japanese minister had been anxious to hurry the matter through, insisting that the representatives of both sides meet daily, and that China should comment on the demands group by group, instead of one by one. The newly appointed Chinese foreign minister, Lu Cheng-hsiang, on the other hand, was eager to bide his time: he agreed only to meet the Japanese twice a week, and was in favour of discussing the demands individually.[60]

The Japanese foreign ministry tried its utmost to avoid international attention—exactly what China aimed at through procrastination. In the course of the negotiations Yüan Shih-k'ai sent Ariga Nagao, his Japanese constitutional adviser, on a mission to the Japanese Elder Statesmen. These men were pacifists, and for this reason Yüan's adviser was instructed to advocate a policy of temporization. Moreover, China deliberately leaked out news of the negotiations to the foreign press to arouse international sympathy.

Meanwhile, the Japanese ambassador in London, Inouye Katsunosuke, the adopted son of Elder Statesman Marquis Inouye Kaoru, was most vexed by Kato's treatment of Britain.[61] Severely criticized by the Elder Statesmen, Kato was forced to act more reasonably and also soften his demands on China.[62] On 26 April China was given a revised version of the demands, in which the first four groups had been slightly modified; the fifth group was omitted altogether.[63]

However, these revised terms were still unacceptable to the Chinese government, and Jordan was informed accordingly.[64] On 1 May negotiations broke off after China had submitted her maximum concessions to Japan. She was prepared to go to war if these terms were rejected. Yüan Shih-k'ai even sent Liang Shih-i to ask Jordan what Britain's attitude would be if Japan declared war on China. Jordan emphatically denounced the idea of war, and urged China to comply with the modified terms.[65]

On 7 May Japan issued an ultimatum; China was to categorically reply to the revised demands by 6 p.m. on 9 May. On learning this, Jordan sent an urgent private message to Yüan Shih-k'ai, apparently through Lu Cheng-hsiang, emphasizing the 'necessity of giving an absolutely unconditional acceptance'.[66] Lu Cheng-hsiang later told Jordan that his advice did not go unnoticed, and had influenced Yüan Shih-k'ai, the members of the cabinet, and all those who took part in the meeting on 8 May, when the decision to defer to Japan's ultimatum was made.[67]

Jordan's official policy throughout the Twenty-one Demands incident was essentially the same as that during the capture of Tsingtao. There was, however, one significant difference; unlike what he had been doing since the beginning of the war, he now tried to dissociate Britain and himself from Japan. In urging China to be tolerant, he made it clear to the Chinese that his sympathy was with them and that he considered Japan's behaviour unforgivable. As the crisis developed, Jordan's private correspondence to the Foreign Office increasingly denounced Japan, as in the following instance: '[there can be] no reasoning with a highwayman well-armed and Japan's action towards China is worse than that of Germany in the case of Belgium'.[68]

Jordan confined his criticisms of Japan to his private letters, struggling to keep his resentment against his country's ally within limits and strictly on the personal level. He was only too aware that, as the official representative of Britain in China, his behaviour must not in any way jeopardize Anglo-Japanese war-time co-operation in the Far East. Indeed, Jordan's self-restraint was so remarkable that even Kato solicited his good offices to influence China to accept Japan's ultimatum.[69] The Foreign Office greatly appreciated Jordan's skilful handling of the delicate situation in Peking.[70]

There were, however, other reasons why Jordan's mounting anger towards Japan did not manifest itself during the incident of the Twenty-one Demands. It has already been mentioned that Jordan's main concerns were Britain's established interest in China and Yüan Shih-k'ai's political existence. Jordan had for some time been most worried that some of the demands might be detrimental to Britain's railway rights in the Yangtze area. Later on though, he realized, and informed the Foreign Office accordingly, that the question was purely an academic one; with or without the Japanese demands, British capital for railway construction in China would not be forthcoming for a long time after the war.[71]

For Yüan Shih-k'ai, the crisis turned out to be personally advantageous. The Japanese demands served as an unexpected rallying point of support for Yüan, the greatest he had enjoyed from his countrymen since the 1911 Revolution.[72] Moreover, Yüan was not displeased with the outcome of the negotiations, regarding it mainly as a victory of his own diplomacy.[73]

Jordan's considerations were based on the optimistic belief that the war would soon be over and that Japan would then be contained. But until that time came, there would always be the danger of mischief from Japan.[74] It was this fear which gave rise to Jordan's discouraging attitude at the beginning of September 1915 when he was first consulted on the monarchical movement.

For a while there was a lull, which Jordan interpreted as the result of his advice to Yüan Shih-k'ai regarding postponement of the monarchy. Examination of noteworthy dates, however, suggests that the cause of this apparent inactivity was the shift from the Society for the Planning of Peace, as the organ to prepare the monarchy, to the Association to Petition for a Monarchy (*Ch'ing-yüan lien-ho hui*), which was officially set up on 19 September under the auspices of Liang Shih-i.[75]

Thereafter the monarchical movement gathered momentum. The government was said to be innundated with petitions from merchants, educationalists, labourers, and women leaders for the republic to revert to a monarchy.[76] On 21 September Liang Shih-i tried to convince Jordan that public opinion *(min-i)* was overwhelmingly in favour of Yüan Shih-k'ai accepting the crown. Jordan's reply was blunt; he 'knew perfectly well that the whole agitation was engineered from Peking'. This vehement comment reflected Jordan's anxiety to discourage China from making any unwise change when 'international equilibrium, so essential to her safety', had been upset.[77]

While warning China of the likelihood of Japanese interference, Jordan was at the same time puzzled by Japan's apparent approval of the monarchical movement. It was much publicized that in early September the Japanese prime minister, Ōkuma Shigenobu, had made the informal statement that China was best suited for a monarchy and that Yüan Shih-k'ai would be the only qualified man for the Chinese throne. Moreover, Ōkuma stressed that if a change in the form of government was to take place, the Japanese government would regard it as China's domestic question and adopt a policy of non-interference, provided that Japan's interests would not be jeopardized in the process.[78] With the retrospective knowledge of Japan's later policies, historians have pointed out reservations in Ōkuma's statement.[79] In spite of his cautious nature, there was no reason for Jordan to misconstrue the statement as Japan's public profession of her approval of Yüan Shih-k'ai's monarchical plan.[80]

Moreover, eminent Japanese in China appeared to be advocating the restoration of a Chinese monarchy. Obata Torikichi, Japanese chargé d'affaires in Hioki's absence, gave Jordan the impression that he considered the monarchical movement entirely as China's domestic affair. Jordan also observed that Odagiri Masunosuke, director of the Yokohama Specie Bank who had played a key role in Japan's bid for industrial and economic control in the Yangtze early in 1914, was clearly encouraging Yüan Shih-k'ai in his monarchical ambition.[81]

At the end of September and the beginning of October, Jordan and Japan simultaneously changed their attitudes towards the monarchical movement. True to its name, the Association to Petition for a Monarchy had been responsible for hundreds of petitions from the provinces pouring into the capital. Early in October the Council of State *(Ts'an-cheng yüan)*, in its capacity as Legislative Chamber *(Li-fa yüan)*, passed a bill which put the monarchical question to a provincial referendum.[82] Japan then spoke officially for the first time: she opposed the change. In fact, on 29 September ambassador Inouye had been instructed to discuss with the British Foreign Office a joint Anglo-Japanese objection to the current Chinese political situation. A week later Inouye explained to Grey that Japan feared China's reversion to a monarchy might cause serious disorder in the country, particularly in the south.[83] Unlike Jordan, the Foreign Office was not too surprised by Japan's attitude, because Whitehall had not been informed of Ōkuma's informal statement allegedly made a month before.[84]

Meanwhile, Jordan now regarded the Chinese monarchy as 'the inevitable', and advised the Foreign Office 'to come to a close understanding with the Japanese Government as to the best course for minimising whatever risks the change may involve'. There were three reasons which caused his volte-face. In the first place Jordan was impressed by the massive popular support for Yüan, and concluded that outside opposition now would do more harm than good. Secondly, Yüan had by then somehow allayed Jordan's fears of internal trouble; it appears that he was most persuasive at his interview with Jordan on 2 October.[85] Thirdly, in spite of his wariness, even Jordan had been duped by the various Japanese utterances of approval. When he learned of Japan's real intention, his feeling of having been deceived was only natural.[86]

The Foreign Office, at variance with Jordan's changed views, instructed him 'to keep in close touch' with his Japanese colleague.[87] During the first half of October, a plan to frustrate the Chinese aim was quickly drawn up by a select group in the Japanese government. It was formally approved by the Japanese cabinet on 14 October, the day Ishii Kikujiro, newly returned from his post of ambassador to France, assumed the portfolio of foreign affairs.

On the following day Ishii instructed ambassador Inouye to inform the British government that the Allies and the United States should jointly advise China to give up the monarchical plan, which could cause internal unrest prejudicial to British and Japanese interests.[88] Ishii sent a second urgent telegram to Inouye later that day, pointing out that important Chinese officials such as Hsü Shih-ch'ang, Li Yüan-hung, Feng Kuo-chang, Tuan Chi-jui and Chou Hsüeh-hsi were passively resisting the change in the form of government.[89] Three days later Japan presented Britain with an official memorandum, which contained the proposal of joint advice and the rationale behind it.[90]

Grey sent a telegram to Jordan, asking him if he would object to Britain's acceptance of the proposal. The way the message was phrased, though, was more to inform than to consult; the intention of acceptance was obvious.[91] Nevertheless, Jordan twice called on Obata after he had received the telegram from Grey. On both occasions the British minister stressed that external interference would only embarrass Yüan Shih-k'ai and was therefore more likely to cause trouble.[92] In his reply to Sir Edward Grey, Jordan stated that the attitude of the Chinese officials need not be taken seriously.[93] Moreover, consular reports from the traditional revolutionary centres—Shanghai, the Yangtze ports, and Canton—did not apprehend disorder.[94] At the same time Jordan pointed out to Langley that only immediate foreign intervention would forestall the referendum which was being zealously organized in the provinces.[95]

While Jordan argued his case out with his government, he realized that ultimately it would not be acceptable to Japan. He told the Foreign Office that in any advice to be given to China, the participation of the United States, apart from that of the Allies, was vital. This statement was ostensibly to make the advice appear unanimous as well as to offset the memorandum of Professor Goodnow who was an American.[96] However, the real reason was Jordan's bitter awareness of the Allies' inability to deal with Japan. He naturally thought of the United States because of her liberty of action, and also her traditional anti-Japan and pro-Yüan attitude.

This time the Foreign Office was more sympathetic. Langley suggested that Britain should bide her time in complying with Japan's request; once the provincial referendum had resulted in the restoration of the Chinese monarchy, it would be too late for Japan's opposition.[97] But Japan would not be outwitted. On 24 October she suggested to Britain that the advice should be given immediately, without waiting for the replies from the powers.[98] In fact, the United States had not yet been informed of the move. The following day Obata informed Jordan of Japan's new proposal. The British minister reacted strongly against it,[99] but Sir Edward Grey instructed him to consult Obata about giving the advice at once.[100]

In the afternoon of 28 October Obata, Jordan and the Russian minister advised the Chinese to abandon their monarchical scheme. The Chinese foreign minister, Lu Cheng-hsiang, replied that the scheme was China's own affair in response to popular request and, therefore, would not lead to political turmoil. For Jordan the occasion was both distasteful and distressing; although he had been the chairman of the Diplomatic Corps in Peking since 1911, he declined to be the spokesman at the interview.[101] He felt strongly that his association with Obata was a personal betrayal of Yüan Shih-k'ai 'whose memory was a very long one'.[102]

Thereafter, Jordan's criticism of Japan became increasingly bitter and overt.

On 2 November China formally replied to the joint communiqué of Japan, Britain, and Russia, reiterating that while the constitutional change was being effected peace and order would be maintained. Japan, however, continued her pressure on the Chinese government during the following week.[103] To Jordan's relief, the Chinese foreign ministry informed him on 9 November that the monarchy would not be restored that year.[104] Two days later Lu Cheng-hsiang announced to the foreign ministers that the grand inauguration of the monarchy would be delayed.[105] Japan, still dissatisfied, was going to adopt 'an attitude of vigilance as to the further development of the situation'.[106]

China's promises to postpone the restoration of the monarchy proved to be mere lip service. Provincial voting continued and was completed by December.[107] The unsuccessful revolt staged by Ch'en Ch'i-mei in Shanghai on 5 December received scant attention and in no way daunted Yüan Shih-k'ai.[108] In Peking provincial delegates formed themselves into the so-called People's Representatives Convention *(Kuo-min ta-hui)* which was to take the final vote on the monarchical question. In the capital all non-conforming newspapers had by then been completely suppressed, so that public opinion appeared to favour the movement.[109] On 17 December the People's Representative Convention, consisting of 1,993 members, unanimously voted to restore the monarchy, and Yüan Shih-k'ai was twice petitioned to ascend the throne.[110] Yüan 'reluctantly' agreed to accept the crown the following day, although he would remain as president until the inaugural ceremony of the new dynasty.

The Japanese, feeling that they had been slighted, decided upon a new course of action. On 15 December Hioki, together with Jordan, and the Russian, French, and Italian ministers, warned China that the powers would intervene as soon as there was trouble in China.[111] As in the case of the first joint warning the Chinese response was ambiguous. Yüan Shih-k'ai told Hioki and Jordan that the formal inauguration of the *Hung-hsien* regime would not take place before Chinese New Year—a postponement of two months. Conversely, from 19 December onwards Yüan already acted like an emperor by conferring titles on his friends, high Peking officials, *tu-tus* of the provinces, and other personages.[112]

In spite of the second joint advice on 15 December the Allies had changed their stand on the monarchical question since Yüan Shih-k'ai's formal acceptance of the crown. The Allies were now anxious for China to join their own war efforts. For Britain this would mean the wholesale expulsion of the Germans from China, from the outset of the war many Germans had been engaged in underground activities in Tsingtao and Shanghai which threatened sedition in British India.[113] The Russians were hoping for larger supplies of arms and ammunition from China, and France needed Chinese coolies to replenish the depleted French labour force. Moreover, all the powers feared that if they further opposed the monarchy Yüan Shih-k'ai might be receptive to their enemies who had openly supported the monarchical movement from the outset.[114]

Even while Japan was clamouring to warn China a second time, Russia suggested that the Allies should recognize Yüan if he was formally proclaimed emperor.[115] France endorsed this proposal.[116] The British Foreign Office also recognized the monarchy as a *fait accompli* which could not be postponed until after the war.[117] Sir Edward Grey decided to confirm Jordan's opinion before holding any persuasive discussion with Japan.[118]

Grey's enquiry came as a pleasant surprise to Jordan who advocated immediate recognition of the Chinese monarchy.[119] Jordan believed that his view was shared by all the allied ministers in Peking, who nevertheless saw themselves as 'so many puppets pulled by Japanese strings'.[120]

At this point Japan's attitude became less intransigent. This was due to either a politic decision to humour the allies or the knowledge of an imminent revolt against Yüan in south China. On 19 December the Japanese minister informed Jordan that his country would probably recognize Yüan's monarchy after 'a postponement of three or four months unaccompanied by disturbances'.[121]

However, not even one week had passed before there was a revolt in Yunnan, the extreme south-western province. The rebels declared independence on Christmas Day, initiating what has commonly been referred to as the Movement to Protect the Republic *(Hu-kuo yün-tung)*. The uprising, unlike the 1911 Revolution, did not spread rapidly, and a whole month passed before there were similar activities in Kweichow. Jordan was not too concerned about the Yunnan outbreak, because after three weeks it still promised to be nothing more than 'an ordinary incident which marked the beginning of all dynasties in China'.[122]

Jordan's optimism largely was due to sanguine reports from Goffe, now the consul-general at Yunnanfu. According to Goffe, the rebellion had aroused little enthusiasm among the Yunnanese who seemed to prefer the peaceful inauguration of the monarchy to internal strife.[123]

More important, Yunnan could not boast much military might. The Yunnanese troops were grouped into three divisions under the respective commands of Ts'ai O, Li Lieh-chün, and T'ang Chi-yao, the *tu-tu* of the province.[124] Ts'ai's First Division was to enter Szechwan province, and then occupy strategic places such as Suchow, Luchow, and Chungking. Li's Second Division was to operate in Kwangsi, and T'ang's Third Division was to infiltrate Kweichow.[125] The military junta at Yunnanfu, however, lacked financial resources to effect the tripartite plan. Indeed, early in the movement T'ang Chi-yao was forced to negotiate with foreign representatives for use of the monthly subsidy derived from the salt revenue of the province.[126]

Jordan considered that Yüan Shih-k'ai's military arrangements could cope adequately with the Yunnanese rebel movement.[127] From the outset, Yüan Shih-k'ai had turned his attention to Ts'ai O's division, which he regarded as the greatest threat. To that end the Third and Seventh Divisions of the Northern Army, each consisting of 12,500 men, and under the command of Ts'ao Kun and Chang Ching-yao respectively, were mobilized to go to Szechwan where the main battles were expected to be waged. Before their arrival, however, Yüan had planned that Ts'ai O and his division of about 3,000 men would be engaged by the three mixed brigades of the Northern Army already in Szechwan. These brigades were under the command of the Szechwan *tu-tu*, Ch'en Huan, whom Yüan Shih-k'ai regarded as a close and faithful subordinate.[128]

Kweichow's declaration of independence on 27 January gave Jordan little cause to reappraise the strength of the anti-monarchical movement. He considered that the province was too poor to contribute significantly to the opposition.[129] During that first month Jordan genuinely believed that only Japan's opposition prevented Yüan Shih-k'ai from quelling the rebellion.

Indeed, the Yunnan revolt initially served to accelerate the monarchical movement. Peking was anxious to remove any diplomatic opposition to the new dynasty before concentrating on the internal problem. Early in January the government announced that the inauguration ceremony would take place during the next month at the time of the Chinese New Year. Russia, France, and especially the United States were anxious to recognize Yüan Shih-k'ai once he was officially enthroned. Jordan warned both his own government and the Japanese minister of the consequences if the Allies would not support Yüan when the United States, a neutral power, and the Central powers were prepared to do so. Such a juncture would not only encourage the rebels but also force Yüan to seek aid from Germany.[130] However, Japan was determined to eliminate Yüan Shih-k'ai. When Yüan argued against further delay in restoring the monarchy, Hioki made two suggestions: China should take a second, confirmatory vote on the issue, and for fairness, the national convention should be held at Nanking instead of Peking.[131] Jordan was meanwhile strongly censured by the Japanese press for urging his government to recognize Yüan Shih-k'ai's monarchy.[132]

On 12 January Jordan informed the Foreign Office of a volte-face: the Chinese vice-minister for foreign affairs had told Hioki that the inauguration ceremony would no longer take place at the Chinese New Year. Further developments hinged on the outcome of a Chinese mission, headed by Chow Tzu-ch'i, which was shortly to embark for Japan.[133] In spite of Yüan's anxiety to reach an agreement, the Japanese rejected an amicable settlement of the monarchical issue. On 12 January, too, an attempt was made on Ōkuma's life in protest against his weak China policy. Important Japanese political pressure groups such as the Black Dragon Society *(Kokuryukai)* and the army hoped to bring about Yüan Shih-k'ai's downfall by capitalizing on the Yunnan revolt.[134] Much to Yüan's chagrin, he was requested by the Tokyo government to cancel his special mission to Japan on the eve of its departure.

On 19 January the Japanese cabinet resolved not to recognize Yüan and his monarchy, irrespective of the views of the other Allied powers. At this point the Chinese minister at Tokyo, Lu Tsung-yü, repeatedly telegraphed the Chinese foreign ministry, urging that the monarchical plan be renounced immediately. Lu told Yüan Shih-k'ai that the Japanese had decided two days later on 'free action' *(tzu-yu hsing-tung)* in future, and that they intended to recognize the military government of Yunnan as a belligerent body.[135] On the same day Jordan was informed by Lu Cheng-hsiang that the enthronement was to be postponed, a move which the British minister regarded as the 'wisest decision in the circumstance'.[136]

It is significant to again note that by then the Kweichow uprising had still not occurred. Even after 27 January, Jordan was convinced that Yüan Shih-k'ai's hesitant behaviour did not result from the internal political and military situation. Unpredictably, on 23 February Yüan issued a mandate which postponed his monarchical role indefinitely. Once more, Jordan did not associate Yüan's drastic decision with the military development in the south.

But, by the beginning of February, the rebels had achieved a number of successes over the government troops. In Szechwan, Ts'ai O's forces were greatly strengthened at the end of January when the province's Second Brigade under the command of Liu Ts'un-hou, defected from the government. During the first week of February the insurgents rapidly occupied Chiang-an, Nan-chi, and Lan-t'ien-pa, and were intent on capturing the strategic post of Luchow. At the same time the Kweichow troops were also making some progress in Hunan.[137]

In Jordan's mind these setbacks for the government troops did not justify indefinite postponement of the monarchy. In fact, soon afterwards the first units of the Northern Army, under the command of Wu P'ei-fu, arrived in Szechwan and gained possession of Luchow.[138] By late February most of the northern government troops had reached Szechwan. Shortly before Jordan reported the indefinite postponement of the monarchy, he learned from Goffe that T'ang Chi-yao was very worried by the developments in Szechwan and that he had expressed doubts about the Kweichow troops fighting in Hunan in that their commander, Tai K'an, was a lawyer with little military experience.[139]

One week after the postponement of the monarchy, Yüan Shih-k'ai sent Richard Dane, the British inspector-general of the Salt Gabelle, to Jordan to ask if another mandate should be issued to cancel the monarchy altogether. The British minister raised strong objections, claiming that no such humiliating gesture was necessary. Jordan added that if Yüan seriously wanted to abandon the *Hung-hsien* dynasty, he should at least wait until an opportune victory, such as the recovery of Su-fu which had been lost to the rebels early in January.[140]

Meanwhile, government forces continued to have the upper hand in Szechwan, and by about the first week of March had succeeded in retrieving Su-fu, Nachi, the headquarters of Liu Ts'un-hou, and Chiang-an.[141] The rebels in Szechwan were so disheartened by the victories of the northern troops that at one stage T'ang Chi-yao in Yunnan was said to have been on the verge of deserting his post.

On 29 February Jordan received a telegram from Goffe concerning T'ang Chi-yao's imminent departure and suggesting that Jordan should ask Yüan Shih-k'ai to instruct the northern generals and general Lung Chi-kuang of Kwangtung, a faithful supporter of Peking, not to launch an attack on Yunnanfu.[142] Although Jordan was surprised by the news, he advised Goffe not to discourage T'ang's departure unless it would endanger the safety of British subjects.[143] At one point Goffe reported rumours of the Yunnanfu gentry plotting to prevent T'ang from leaving

the city and to hand him over to Yüan Shih-k'ai.[144] After these communications from the consulate-general at Yunnanfu to the legation in
Peking, Jordan informed the Foreign Office on 8 March that the rebellion
would 'shortly collapse were there no other influences at work to foster
opposition to present regime'.[145]

Both Jordan and Yüan identified those 'other influences' with Japan.
Ever since her decision not to recognize the Chinese monarchy on 19
January, Japan had instigated activities against Yüan Shih-k'ai and was
also involved in the rebellion itself. The Yunnanese troops were largely
equipped with Japanese arms and ammunition,[146] and Jordan learned
from reliable sources that Ts'ai O was assisted by retired Japanese
military officers.[147]

In addition to their military involvement, Japanese officials collabo-
rated with anti-Yüan elements. In Shanghai, for example, the Japanese
were in close communication with T'ang Shao-i and his group. Jordan
accordingly instructed the consul-general, Fraser, to ignore T'ang's
visits to the consulate-general, where he hoped to enlist British support
for the removal of Yüan Shih-k'ai.[148]

Besides utilizing Japanese officials already on the spot, Japan dispatched special agents to the various anti-Yüan centres. A certain major
Yamagata was sent to Yunnanfu to help the military government obtain
arms and other assistance from Japan via Tongking. General Aoki
Nobuzumi, who for eighteen years had been Japanese military attaché
in China, had been active in Shanghai since December 1915. According
to Jordan, this well-known Japanese nationalist 'was an expert in the
manipulation of Chinese political parties'. Together with a certain
Matsui, the general was instrumental in helping Li Tsung-huang, the
liaison representative of the Yunnan military government at Shanghai,
to establish contact with Feng Kuo-chang at Nanking.[149]

In the middle of March Yüan Shih-k'ai was troubled by more than
Japanese opposition. His military position in the south became suddenly
untenable with the defection of the *tu-tu* of Kwangsi, Lu Yung-t'ing.
This event precipitated the alienation of general Lung Chi-kuang in
Canton, whose allegiance was crucial both to Yüan's position in the
south and that of general Chien Huan in Szechwan.

Immediately after the outbreak of the Yunnan revolt it was Lung
Chi-kuang whom Yüan Shih-k'ai commissioned to quell the uprising.
Lung accordingly sent troops to Yunnan under the command of his
elder brother, Lung Chin-kuang. To ensure success, Lung also sent his
son, Lung T'i-chien, to bribe the local brigands to cause trouble for the

revolutionaries. After Kwangsi had declared independence, however, Lung Chi-kuang despondently told British consular officials at Canton that Lu Yung-t'ing's action came as a severe blow. Lung was not only apprehensive about the safety of his son but also his brother, who was then on the Kwangsi-Yunnan border.[150]

By this time Yüan Shih-k'ai realized that he could no longer cope with both Japan and the internal rebellion. He decided to renounce the monarchical scheme, and hold fast to whatever political power he was able to retain. Richard Dane was again sent to consult the British legation before Yüan Shih-k'ai publicly announced his intention. This time Jordan insisted that the abandonment of the monarchy must be irrevocable.[151] On 22 March Yüan Shih-k'ai issued the mandate which brought to an end the existence of the *Hung-hsien* regime after less than three months (the title was officially used from 1 January although the dynasty had not yet been formally instituted).

The mandate was definitive enough, but it came too late to be effective. During the following two months, Kwangtung, Chekiang, Shansi, Szechwan, and Hunan seceded from the central government one after another. The contentious question now was whether Yüan Shih-k'ai should be eliminated from Chinese politics altogether. During this period there was a distinct lack of unity among the 'non-Yüan'[152] and anti-Yüan elements over their treatment of Yüan,[153] although Japan (especially Ōkuma) was determined to overthrow Yüan once and for all. Jordan was convinced that Japan was instrumental in effecting the eventual downfall of his friend.

To Jordan the disunity in the anti-Yüan and non-Yüan camps was clearly noticeable. Of the provinces which seceded after Yüan Shih-k'ai had definitely renounced the monarchy, Kwangtung and Szechwan were his greatest losses. Both Lung Chi-kuang and Ch'en Huan, however, intrinsically supported Yüan even after their defection. In the case of Kwangtung, Lung had been forced to defect by the independence of Kwangsi and, later on, by the mutiny of the Kwangtung navy.[154] After Kwangtung had severed relations with Peking on 6 April it entered some kind of federation, with the other independent provinces, under the name of the Military Council *(Chün-wu yüan)*. Lung, however, was regarded as disloyal by the *tu-tus* of Yunnan, Kweichow, and Kwangsi, who were anxious to expel him from Canton.[155] By the end of May eight provinces had already broken away from the central government. With Jordan and Yüan in mind, Lung strongly hinted to Jamieson, that if Yüan took a strong stand, he would certainly revert his loyalty to the government.[156]

In the case of Szechwan, Ch'en Huan had held out for as long as he possibly could. Shortly after the independence of Kwangsi, the consul-general at Chengtu reported to Jordan that Ch'en had started negotiating with Ts'ai O. In doing so, Ch'en emphasized that his contact with the revolutionaries was not his own independent action, but had been made on the central government's behalf.[157] The emergence of an influential group called the Szechwan Party caused Chen's eventual defection. This party bitterly opposed the Yunnanese troops in the province, and argued that the pretext for their continued presence would be removed if Szechwan joined the rebellion.

Moreover, Ch'en Huan seems to have strongly resisted desertion. Even after severe pressure from the provincial gentry associated with the Szechwan Party, Ch'en still refused to declare independence. Instead, on 7 May, he telegraphed to Yüan Shih-k'ai, urging him to resign from the presidency. No response came from Peking, and on 22 May Ch'en declared independence. The British consul saw this as the painful outcome of Ch'en's lengthy vacillation between the Szechwan Party and his loyalty to Yüan Shih-k'ai.[158]

In May the Nanking conference was convened by generals Feng Kuo-chang, Chang Hsün, and Ni Ssu-ch'ung to consider the question of Yüan's presidency. Perhaps Jordan found that this conference epitomized the disunity of the opposition to Yüan Shih-k'ai. Of the generals named, Feng Kuo-chang played the most important role in calling the conference. Being one of the most influential military figures of the time, he was closely watched by Jordan throughout the anti-monarchical uprising. Frequent consular reports from Nanking gave Jordan the impression that Feng had no 'sympathy with the Yunnan rebellion, attributable though it be to the monarchical movement of which he disapproved'. In Jordan's view, Feng's attitude had been neutral and concentrated on maintaining law and order in his province, Kiangsu. For this purpose, he had taken actions equally against the anti-monarchical activists.[159]

The Nanking conference, held between 19 and 23 May, was attended by *tu-tus* of the still 'loyal' provinces. The basic issue concerning the treatment of Yüan Shih-k'ai was unresolved, despite the generals' ostensible view that he should unconditionally remain as president. For Jordan this outcome signified a rift between the generals in the north and the Military Council at Shiu-hing (transliteration from Cantonese

reading), Kwangtung, which had been formally established on 8 May.
In Jordan's opinion most military leaders in northern China, 'while
prepared if necessary to sacrifice Yüan-shih-k'ai to pressure of public
opinion, [were] not disposed to let political agitators have a large share
in future settlement'.[160] Jordan's observation proved to be accurate.
Several days later Liang Ch'i-ch'ao, one of the top office-bearers of the
Military Council, telegraphed Feng Kuo-chang from Shiu-hing insisting
on the removal of Yüan Shih-k'ai.[161] Moreover, many revolutionaries
in the south suspected Feng of using the Nanking conference to achieve
his personal ends. Feng was even sarcastically nicknamed 'Yüan Shih-
k'ai II', referring no doubt to Yüan's alleged duplicity in the 1911
Revolution.[162]

However, any benefit which Yüan Shih-k'ai might have gleaned from
the various political groups in China was overshadowed by Japan's
insistence on his downfall. The Japanese, Jordan was informed, had
been actively involved in the secession of Kwangtung.[163] At the end of
March the Foreign Office informed Jordan that Japan regarded any
support of Yüan as harmful to an early settlement of the crisis in China,
and that she herself would continue to watch the situation 'with
vigilance'.[164]

In brief, Japan wanted Britain's support to eliminate Yüan from
politics. Jordan could hold his peace no longer. He asked Sir Edward
Grey to tell the Japanese that their attitude was most unreasonable in
view of the indefinite postponement of the monarchy. Moreover, Jordan
was convinced that although Yüan had lost much prestige, his total
elimination would cause large-scale confusion.[165]

The Foreign Office was most embarrassed by such conflicting views.
Until then Jordan had never been so overtly anti-Japanese in official
correspondence. One British official analysed the situation thus:

'We are ill-armed to face a repetition of the 1912–1913 crisis. Then we had
the wherewithal at our disposal to finance a strong man, and in an extreme case
troops and ships. Now we have neither. . . . The only money that could be
forthcoming would be American money, but, if we avail ourselves of that for
the purpose of pursuing a policy with which the Japanese don't agree, we risk
raising one of the great questions of the future viz. our choice between the
U.S. and Japan'.[166]

The United States had for some time figured prominently in the Far
Eastern Department of the Foreign Office. Since the outbreak of World
War I there had been increasing polarization between the American and
Japanese attitudes *via-à-vis* China, especially towards Yüan Shih-k'ai.

To the discomfort of Britain President Woodrow Wilson had adopted a most friendly and helpful attitude towards Yüan throughout the monarchical movement.[167]

Sir Edward Grey resorted to one last compromise, by which Yüan Shih-k'ai would remain as president but with only constitutional powers.[168] On 8 April Ishii rejected the proposal.[169] The British government had expected the rebuff and was now resigned to abandoning Yüan Shih-k'ai to whatever fate was in store for him. Britain raised no objections to the United States' insisting on the *status quo* in China,[170] but the direction of British policy was reflected in a more favourable tone towards Britain in the Japanese press.[171]

Japan now intensified her campaign to eliminate Yüan. Jordan strongly suspected that the Japanese were financing the Military Council at Shui-hing. He had first learned of its establishment from the Japanese minister, Hioki, but the British consul-general at Canton had lacked official confirmation of the federation. Hioki must have received the news from the Japanese consul-general at Canton who had been actively involved 'in the matter of trying to create a South Republic'.[172]

Apart from being heavily involved in the south, Japan created fresh troubles for Yüan Shih-k'ai in the north. In the second week of May the British consul at Tsinan, capital of Shantung province, reported that the Japanese military authorities there were assisting the anti-Yüan elements and that the governor was under strong pressure to declare independence.[173] At the Nanking conference a fortnight later, Jordan was not at all surprised when the Shantung representatives opposed the retention of Yüan as president.[174] Meanwhile, in April Japan had obtained the approval of Britain, Russia, and France to suspend payment of the surplus salt revenue to Peking, despite strong protests from Jordan and Richard Dane. The government was now deprived of an important source of income, and its finances rapidly dwindled.[175]

The thorny problem of dealing with Yüan was unexpectedly solved by his death on 6 June. Jordan's reaction to this sudden event was highly emotional:

'As to Yüan Shih-k'ai, you will not expect a balanced opinion from me at this moment. I had a great personal liking for the man and feel both his loss and the manner of it acutely. The appreciation contained in my official dispatch is a very imperfect estimate of the loss we have sustained by his death . . . and to his last day he remained a firm friend of Great Britain. He could not speak a word of English, but he could repeat the names of all his English friends and often told me anecdotes of his association with them. Almost the last time I

saw him he said that he had been on very friendly terms with Englishmen
since his early manhood and that he had learned to trust and like them. Of this
he gave innumerable proofs. . . .
   I could go on indefinitely reciting acts to the credit of my dead friend—for
simply as a friend I shall always remember him. . . . He fell in an unequal
struggle and to me he was greater in his bitter adversity than he had been
even at the height of his power'.[176]

Both in this private letter and his official report on Yüan's demise,[177]
Jordan spoke of personal friendship rather than British interests. In
emphasizing Yüan's trust in Britain, Jordan implicitly blamed his
government for having betrayed Yüan. Jordan also reproached himself
for having failed Yüan when he most needed support. In fact he had
noted with sadness that towards the end Yüan had become much closer
to Paul Reinsch, the American minister, than to himself. Moreover,
Jordan learned that about a month previously Yüan had approached
Reinsch in the hope of finding asylum in the United States,[178] whereas
before he had often spoken of retiring in England where he had bought
properties.[179]

Most studies of this period in Chinese history have either concentrated
on the Movement to Protect the Republic or maintained that internal
and Japanese opposition contributed equally to Yüan Shih-k'ai's downfall. However, Jordan was convinced that the main instigators were the
Japanese, who initially encouraged the monarchical movement, then
opposed it at its height.

An objective study of the events during the last six months before
Yüan's death justifies Jordan's view. The uprising in the south would
have occured with or without Japan's intervention. The Yunnan revolt
appears to have resulted from the intricate plans of Liang Ch'i-ch'ao and
his Changsha student, Ts'ai O, and also of T'ang Chi-yao and his
associates in Yunnan. From the beginning the leaders of the uprising
had been aware of Yunnan's limited resources, and were anxious to
secure co-operation of the three neighbouring provinces, especially
Kwangtung and Kwangsi.[180]

However, Yüan Shih-k'ai had found it necessary to postpone the
monarchy before any of the three provinces joined the revolt. The main
cause of Yüan's timidity was the Japanese refusal in the middle of
January to receive his special envoy seeking approval of the monarchical
movement. The first act of weakness quickly led to the second, and to
the third. Yüan's increasing hesitation affected the morale of the

government troops fighting in the south; these men had hoped that their loyalty would be rewarded with titles and gold in the new dynasty.[181]

Some scholars are of the opinion that when Yüan Shih-k'ai chose to become emperor, he 'committed political suicide' because he had 'failed to harness the full support of his leading generals . . . and he aroused the wrath of Chinese intellectuals'.[182] More accurately, one could say that he was doomed because he chose to become emperor at the time when Japan, who was intent on his removal, was free to act in China. Had the Western powers been able to support Yüan to a greater extent the problem of internal opposition might well have been solved.

POSTSCRIPT

YÜAN Shih-k'ai's sudden death shattered Jordan's long-cherished dream for China; but for Japan, its dream was beginning to come true.[1] He could not forgive Japan for this, and from then on he 'saw behind every bush a Japanese'.[2] He now lost the sense of balance which had for so long enabled him to divorce personal feelings from national considerations. Since 1915 Whitehall had been continuously embarrassed by Jordan's overt bitterness towards Japan which was the cause of the virulent anti-British campaign in the Japanese press.[3] Jordan and his support for Yüan irked Japan as much as Yüan and his monarchy.

In May 1916 Jordan was shocked by the rumour that the Foreign Office was about to send Beilby Alston to Peking to replace him. On 12 May Sir Edward Grey telegraphed Jordan that he had the Foreign Office's 'entire approval and confidence'; and that he should publish a statement of his intention to remain in Peking. Moreover, Alston was only appointed to replace Ronald Macleay as acting councillor to the Peking legation. The Chinese minister in London was given the same explanation of Alston's appointment.[4]

This, however, was not the end of the episode. In July the Japanese press reported that there would be an 'impending change at British Legation in China'. A Japanese source interpreted the news as follows:

'Grey, fearing that Jordan had been stationed in China a long time, decided to recall him to London on long leave out of friendship for Japan. His intention was conveyed to the Japanese embassy most secretly. It goes without saying that for the British government to adopt such a friendly policy was due to the skill of Inoue. He immediately reported this news to the Tokyo government. Our Foreign Ministry officials imprudently published it to the press . . . : enlarging on the fact that Jordan had been given long leave, they said that the British Government had come round to dismissing him since his continuance at Peking was bad for Anglo-Japanese relations. . . .'[5]

In answer to Jordan's protests Grey reiterated what he had said in his telegram of 12 May, adding that Alston's appointment was intended to assist Jordan and not to shorten his stay in Peking.[6] Despite Grey's reassurances, Jordan was never reconciled to Alston's presence in Peking and made no effort to conceal his displeasure.[7]

From other sources, it seems that Alston was sent out on the assumption that Jordan, much upset by recent events, would ask to leave China and not return. Understandably, Jordan felt slighted and refused to discuss his future movements with his new colleague. Distressed and frustrated, Alston wrote to Eric Drummond, private secretary to Grey: 'I find Sir John much aged and depressed but he thinks it was a mistake that I came out before he was actually leaving—I asked him why he did not say so at once, he said "he wasn't asked" & it "wasn't his job"—so like him—but you know it was my idea too. I am afraid I have led myself in for a vast expediture of money & loss on sale of capital (over £900) which I might have avoided if we had known this and waited a little'. Alston must have been greatly relieved when Jordan at last went on leave in November 1916, with no intention of returning. Back in London however, he was asked by Balfour (Grey's successor) to return to China after a rest. And when Jordan 'showed reluctance because of his forty years' service there', Balfour said: ' "that is the reason" '.[8] Thus Jordan was back in China in the autumn of 1917, much to the disappointment of Alston[9] who had the full sympathy of Miles Lampson, acting first secretary of the legation who was to become minister ten years later.

Jordan came back to Peking a different man. He had left disheartened but returned hopeful, although Chinese politics were at their worst with the country split into two. The north was in the hands of military men who owed nominal allegiance to the Peking government, which was in effect dominated by Japan. The south was held in check by Sun Yat-sen and other nationalists who condemned the northern government as constitutionally illegal. Jordan was strangely undisturbed by China's chaos and Japan's growing encroachment. He believed that given time and freedom from outside intrusion, China would work out her salvation after the war. His private correspondence was now pervaded with his confidence of victory. There was something 'Wilsonian' about his concept of the 'New World' in the Far East after the war. It hinged on the subjection of the 'Power of Evil' [Japan] and the predominance of Anglo-American influence.[10] He was optimistic that the United States, 'a great disinterested Power', would remedy the situation in China when war was over. Anxious to promote Anglo-American solidarity Jordan devoted himself to bringing together the British and American communities in Peking, Shanghai, and Tientsin. He no doubt intended to point out to his government the futility of the Anglo-Japanese Alliance. The future of the Far East rested on the English speaking peoples, 'a much better foundation' than Britain's previous one.[11]

In December 1918 Jordan set out his views concerning British interests in China in a lengthy dispatch to the Foreign Office. The document was Jordan's final exposition, before his retirement, of what Britain's China policy should be. W. G. MaxMuller, in charge of the Far Eastern Department summarized Jordan's views:

'After a survey of the steps which have led up to the present political situation in China and of the reasons which render desirable a revision of the selfish policy of competition and mutual suspicion hitherto persued by the different Powers in China terminating in the far-reaching Japanese penetration of the past 4 years, Sir John proceeds to advocate a policy of reconstruction, based upon a firm adherence, in practice as well as in theory, to the principle of equal opportunity for all and upon the abolition of all special privileges.

1. First and foremost he advocates the unification, consolidation & neutralization of all railways under an International Committee of Administration.
2. A natural corollary of this is the abandonment of spheres of influence.
3. The finances of China must be put in order if bankrupcy [sic] is to be avoided. The only way to secure this and to abolish the existing widespread corruption is to appoint an International Finance Committee to control expenditure.

Other reforms advocated by Sir J. Jordan are:

4. Internationalization of Leased Territories and international concessions in Treaty Ports.
5. Reform of Customs Tariff.
6. Reform of Mining Laws.
7. Agreement for the conditional abolition of extra-territoriality including Consular jurisdiction.
8. Revision of Treaties and Protocol, including abandonment of Boxer Indemnity and Legation Guards'.

Jordan would never have adhered to such opinions before the war. However, despite its length and detailed content the dispatch reached the Foreign Office too late to influence the delegation at the Paris Peace Conference. Even if it had arrived in time, it would have been inconsequential. The Foreign Office regarded Jordan's views as 'idealistic and impracticable', but respected them as 'coming from one who had devoted his whole life to the study of the Problem of China'.[12]

Nevertheless, Jordan had the satisfaction of seeing his 'post war' ideals come to fruition after his retirement from China early in 1920. Immediately after the war Britain was too preoccupied with the pressing question of a European settlement to divert her attention elsewhere.

Meanwhile, events necessitated a reappraisal of the Far Eastern policy. Since the war the value of the Anglo-Japanese Alliance had been questioned in both countries. At the British Foreign Office a committee of four was formed by Victor Wellesley, assistant secretary of the Far Eastern Department, to analyse the question of the alliance. Apart from Wellesley the committee consisted of Sir William Tyrrell from the Foreign Office and Jordan and Sir Conyngham Greene who were both in retirement. After nearly five months of systematic investigation, the committee presented its report on 21 January 1921. It recommended that the Anglo-Japanese Alliance be replaced by a 'Tripartite Entente' between the United States, Japan, and Britain, consisting of a declaration of principles without 'the risk of embarrassing commitments'. Failing the consent of the United States, Britain might conclude an agreement with Japan, in harmony with the new spirit of the League of Nations, and 'so framed as not to exclude the eventual participation of the United States'. Unfortunately, the report was overlooked by the foreign secretary, Lord Curzon, the very person who had granted authorization to the alliance committee in the first place. The foreign secretary was more influenced by Sir Charles Eliot, ambassador at Tokyo, and Sir Auckland Geddes, ambassador to the United States, who favoured the continuation of the alliance.[13]

The report's primary recommendation, however, was more or less implemented within a year at the Washington Conference. Jordan, the only member of the alliance committee attending the conference, witnessed the signing of the Four Power Treaty between Britain, the United States, France, and Japan. The new treaty was designed to replace the Anglo-Japanese Alliance in the arena of Far Eastern international diplomacy. This outcome was the result of the complex and gradual adjustment of the views of Britain (including the British Dominions), Japan and the United States before and during the conference.[14] Unlike historians who denounce the treaty as weak, inadequate and unrealistic, Jordan wrote shortly after the conference: 'Though this is a very mild instrument as compared with the Anglo-Japanese Alliance which it ostensibly replaces, it does not follow that it will not be an equally effective means of preserving peace. It recognized the changed spirit of the time and, instead of holding out a threat of resort to force for the settlement of differences, it adopts by preference the reasonable alternative of meeting together and attempting to compose them by amicable discussion'.[15]

The Four Power Treaty did not cover all the ground of the Anglo-Japanese Alliance. The signatories concerned themselves with 'the preservation of the general peace and the maintenance of their rights in relation to their insular possessions in the region of the Pacific Ocean', and there was no reference at all to China. The alliance, however, 'had generally been understood to be as much continental as maritime'.[16] It is clear that the delegates at the conference sought to remedy this defect by signing two treaties and passing ten resolutions relating to China between 10 December 1921 and 6 February 1922. Jordan, with the assistance of Miles Lampson, was the British delegate responsible for the settlement of Chinese affairs. Although pressing family matters forced him to leave Washington in the middle of January, he had laid down the principles to be followed concerning China.

The most noteworthy of the two documents was the Nine Power Treaty between the British Empire, the United States, China, France, Italy, Japan, the Netherlands, Belgium, and Portugal, in which the powers, other than China, agreed:

1. To respect the sovereignty, the independence, and the territorial and administrative integrity of China;

2. To provide the fullest and most unembarrassed opportunity for China to develop and maintain for herself an effective and stable Government;

3. To use their influence for the purpose of effectually establishing and maintaining the principle of equal opportunity for the commerce and industry of all nations throughout the territory of China;

4. To refrain from taking advantage of conditions in China in order to seek special rights or privileges which would abridge the rights of subjects or citizens of friendly States, and from countenancing action inimical to the security of such States.

Jordan viewed these clauses with his characteristic post-war optimism, but Japanese aggression during the next fifteen years revealed the Nine Power Treaty to be weak and ineffectual.

By the other treaty signed by the nine powers, China was granted the right to levy a $2\frac{1}{2}$ per cent surtax, thus raising the import duty to $7\frac{1}{2}$ per cent *ad valorem,* in return for the abolition of *likin.* Other resolutions passed by the conference covered many topics concerning China: foreign postal agencies, extra-territoriality, radio stations, foreign troops in China, unification of railways, the reduction of Chinese military forces, and the Chinese Eastern Railway. As a whole, the two treaties and the resolutions closely resembled Jordan's memorandum of 1918 on foreign interests in China. Further satisfaction was derived from the treaty signed on 4 February 1922 between Japan and China. Japan agreed, on fixed terms, to restore to China the whole of the leased territory of Kiaochow together with the railway running from Tsingtao to Tsinanfu.[17] This treaty left Manchuria closed for Japan's exclusive exploitation and was the 'weakest point in the Conference'.[18]

The lesson learned from German aggression and its eventual collapse probably accounted for Jordan's change from a pragmatist to an idealist. In addition, Jordan admired the role played by the United States in the war, and the philosophy of Woodrow Wilson. Two other reasons may well have brought about Jordan's change: his realization of Britain's inability to compete with Japan in the use of force; and the fact that even Yüan Shih-k'ai, once the 'strong man' in China, had failed in the use of force and *realpolitik*.

Jordan's attitude towards Yüan Shih-k'ai was not unique among the foreigners who were associated with China early this century.[19] Jordan's predeccessor, Sir Ernest Satow, had already concluded that Yüan, 'with his faults', was 'the best man' China had. During Jordan's time as minister, most of his colleagues put their faith in Yüan, as did the representatives of the consortium. There was a close relationship between Jordan and Yüan Shih-k'ai which was based on mutual benefit and interests. The same kind of relationship does not appear to have existed between Yüan and any other foreign minister in Peking. There can be little doubt that Jordan truly regarded Yüan as a friend and respected him. Moreover, in supporting Yüan as China's only hope of salvation, Jordan sincerely believed he was helping the Chinese whom he repeatedly professed to love. For his part, Yüan Shih-k'ai was anxious to cultivate and maintain a friendship with Jordan who represented the power with whose support his political fortunes were inextricably linked.[20] No direct evidence indicates Yüan's real feelings towards Jordan, although it has been seen that he did not hesitate to make use of the British minister whenever it suited his purpose.

Jordan's unusually long career was fraught with contradiction and irony. During the 1911 Revolution he was forced to abandon the idea of a limited Manchu monarchy for a republic, which he had hitherto condemned as the most impracticable form of government for China. In 1915–16 he had to oppose Yüan Shih-k'ai's monarchy, the very event he had been most eager for. Jordan had also opposed the idea of international financial co-operation in China, and strongly denounced the consortium, for it severely restricted the expansion of British interests.[21] After the war, however, Jordan advocated internationalization in order to obstruct Japan's ambitious designs. As British minister, Jordan's burning passion for many years had been the extension of British railway interests in China—an attitude confirmin ghis position in the last generation of European imperialists. Before his retirement he had come to the conclusion that imperialism was a historical relic and China should be left to carry 'her own burdens and responsibilities in the family of nations'.[22] Until the death of Yüan Shih-k'ai, Jordan had always been on the side of the so-called 'north', first represented by the Manchu government and then by Yüan; the 'south' consisted of revolutionaries fighting the Ch'ing government and, later, the Kuomintang and other anti-Yüan elements. Yet after Yüan's death Jordan became increasingly hostile to the government because of its shameless reliance on Japan. Conversely, he was much less ill-disposed towards the Nationalists in the south. Perhaps the greatest irony of all was that, believing he had done his best for China as well as Britain, he has been uniformly condemned by Chinese writers as the arch-accomplice in Yüan Shih-k'ai's political crimes, and the agent of Britain's imperialist encroachment on China.[23]

NOTES

CHAPTER I BRITISH POLICY TOWARDS CHINA AND JORDAN'S CAREER BEFORE 1906
(pp. 1–9)

¹ J. S. Gregory, *Great Britain and the Taipings*, pp. 111, 155.

² For details of the Chinese reaction to the presence of missionaries, Britain's treatment of the missionary problem, and British missionaries' attitude towards their government, see P. A. Cohen, *China and Christianity;* E. S. Wehrle, *Britain, China, and the anti-missionary riots, 1891–1900;* and A. Hickling, 'The response of Protestant missionaries to the anti-missionary disturbances in China 1891–1907', M.A. thesis, University of Hong Kong, 1968.

³ Britain had other considerations in the crisis. For example, to offset Russia's naval influence in the north after her lease of Port Arthur, Britain decided to occupy Weihaiwei, regarding it as 'the last remaining port of any significance in north China'. Also, in view of her commitment to the military defence of Hong Kong, Britain took the opportunity to claim the 'New Territories' opposite to the colony. For British considerations and policies in relation to China in 1897–1899, see L. K. Young, *British policy in China 1895–1902*, pp. 43–99.

⁴ For the relative roles of the bank and the company in the corporation, see M. Collis, *Wayfoong, the Hongkong and Shanghai Banking Corporation*, p. 118.

⁵ Satow to Grey, no. 177, v. conf., 2 June 1906, FO 371/35; and Satow's entry in his journal, 19 July 1906, after a *tête à tête* with Grey that day shortly after his return to England, PRO 30/33/16/9. It is interesting that by 1905 the Germans had also found it extremely difficult to maintain their exclusive position in Shantung; see J. E. Schrecker, *Imperialism and Chinese nationalism*, pp. 140–209.

⁶ I. H. Nish, *The Anglo-Japanese Alliance*, p. 1.

⁷ P. Lowe, *Great Britain and Japan 1911–15*, p. 9.

⁸ The biography of Sir John Jordan given here is based, unless documented otherwise, on the following: *Dictionary of national biography, 1922–30*, pp. 461–463; *Foreign Office list and diplomatic and consular year book* for 1920, p. 408; *Hong Kong China Mail, Who's who in the Far East 1906–7*, p. 171; and the obituary notices in *The Times*, 15 September 1925, and *North China Herald*, 19 September 1925.

⁹ O'Conor to Sanderson, 4 February 1895, FO 17/1246 in which Jordan is referred to as 'our excellent Chinese secy.'; and O'Conor to Marquis of Salisbury, 10 October 1895, FO 17/1245.

[10] Jordan loved his work as Chinese secretary. Writing to his old friend Stewart Lockhart, 4 April 1899, he said: 'The work is congenial and intensely interesting—no position anywhere could be more so to me' (Letter is cited with the kind permission of Mrs Stewart Lockhart, daughter of the recipient). The main duties of the Chinese secretary were daily visits to the Chinese foreign ministry and being the language expert to the legation, see L. Marchant, 'Anglo-Chinese relations in the provinces of the West River and the Yangtze River basins 1889–1900', M.A. thesis, University of London, 1965, p. 64. Jordan's command of Chinese was reputable, see O'Conor to Marquis Salisbury, 10 October 1895, FO 17/1245; and *North China Herald*, 19 September 1925.

[11] Jordan, 'Some Chinese I have known', *Nineteenth century and after* LXXXVIII (December 1920), p. 947.

[12] See for example, Jordan to Walter Langley, then assistant under-secretary superintending the Far Eastern Department, private, 24 November 1914, FO 350/12.

[13] Foreign Office circular to British representatives abroad, 3 April 1905, FO 83/2027.

[14] Satow to Barrington, tel., private, 18 May 1905, FO 800/121.

[15] Barrington to Satow, tel., private, 19 August 1905, PRO 30/33/7/4; Lansdowne's note to Barrington, 29 August; and Barrington's reply, 30 August 1905, FO 800/121.

[16] Satow to Dickens, private, 17 July 1905, PRO 30/33/11/6.

[17] Satow to Barrington, tel., private, 23 August 1905; FO 800/121; and Satow to Barrington, private, 3 September 1905, PRO 30/33/14/16.

[18] Lansdowne to Satow, private, draft, 4 September 1905, FO 800/121.

[19] Satow's entry in his journal, 7 June 1906, PRO 30/33/16/9.

[20] C. Pearl, *Morrison of Peking*, pp. 158, 162.

[21] Balfour to Lansdowne, private, 23 August 1905, *Balfour papers,* British Museum Manuscript, 49729.

[22] Lansdowne to Balfour, private, 28 September 1905, *ibid.*

[23] MacDonald to Satow, private, 15 January 1906, PRO 30/33/9/15.

[24] See for example, Sir Cecil Clementi-Smith to Satow, private, 7 November 1905, PRO 30/33/10/8; and Walter Townley to Satow, private, 12 December 1905, PRO 30/33/9/15.

[25] Satow's entry in his journal, 7 November 1906, PRO 30/33/16/9.

[26] Pearl, *Morrison of Peking*, pp. 151, 165, 170; and Morrison to J. O. P. Bland in China, 31 May 1902 and 23 October 1903, *Bland papers*. See also Lo Hui-min, *The correspondence of G. E. Morrison 1895–1912*, p. 358.

[27] Jordan to Foreign Office, tel., unnumbered, 14 September 1905, and minute of F. A. Campbell, superintending under-secretary of the Far Eastern Department, on it, FO 17/1694.

[28] Campbell to Jordan, tel., private, 14 September; and Jordan to Campbell, tel., private, 15 September 1905, FO 17/1694.

[29] Cockburn to Satow, private, 28 December 1905, PRO 30/33/9/15.

[30] There is confirmation of the Department's reluctance. On being informed by the Japanese embassy that the Japanese resident-general in Korea would take up duties on 1 February, Campbell suggested, with Jordan who had arrived in London several days before, that there was no 'better man for the permanent post of Consul General than Mr. Cockburn if he were willing to remain on in that capacity'. The chief clerk, W. C. Cartwright, however, advised that Cockburn should be left as acting consul-general until another post could be offered to Jordan. See Campbell's and Cartwright's minutes on Tadasu Hayashi, Japanese ambassador, to Grey, 17 January 1906, FO 371/179.

[31] Grey to Satow, tel., private, 3 March 1906, PRO 30/33/7/5.

[32] Satow to Grey, tel., private, 4 March 1906, PRO 30/33/7/5. Between Tower and Townley, Satow preferred Townley. In retrospect, Satow concluded that early in 1906 'Peking lay between Townley and Jordan', see Satow's entry in his journal, 18 September 1906, PRO 30/33/16/9. It appears that Townley's desire had always been to return to Peking. Morrison records in his diary that before he left Peking for Europe in July 1905, he received a letter from Townley's wife, Susan, asking him to do what he could in England to secure her husband a post in Peking. On learning that Morrison had recommended Jordan instead, Townley wrote a letter of protest to Morrison; see Pearl, *Morrison of Peking*, pp. 157–58, 170. Satow preferred Townley to Jordan because the former had performed excellently as secretary of the legation, a rank above Chinese secretary, the highest Jordan had made so far in Peking. In addition the minister had to rule the China consular service, and Jordan was in the service junior to both Sir Pelham Warren, then consul-general at Shanghai, and Robert Mansfield, consul-general at Canton; see entry in Satow's journal, 24 April 1906, PRO 30/33/16/9.

[33] Hardinge to Edward VII, 6 March 1906, *Hardinge Papers*, IX.

[34] Foreign Office to Treasury, 14 March, draft, Treasury to Foreign Office, 16 March, and minutes of Walter Langley, then head of the Far Eastern Department, and Campbell on it, and Foreign Office to Treasury, 28 March 1906, draft, FO 371/179.

[35] Yeh Kung-cho, *T'ai-p'ing yang hui-i chien-hou Chung-kuo wai-chiao nei-mu chi ch'i yü Liang Shih-i chih kuan-hsi* [The inner history of China's diplomacy before and after the Washington Conference and its relations with Liang Shih-i], p. 7. Jordan was promoted to the Diplomatic Service only in 1912. Because of the transfer Jordan got a raise in salary from £4,500 to £5,000 per annum; see Grey to Treasury, 13 August 1912, FO 371/1348.

[36] Yüan K'e-wen, *Yüan-shang ssu-ch'eng* [Private history] in *YSH*, p. 2. On hearing of Jordan's death in 1925, T'ang Shao-i recalled that Jordan and Yüan had first met each other in Korea, *North China Herald*, 19 September 1925; and Yeh, *ibid.*, p. 7.

[37] See for example, *Dictionary of national biography, 1922–1930*, p. 462; Wu Hsiang-hsiang, 'Hai-wai hsin chien Chung-kuo hsien-tai shih shih-liao' [New materials seen abroad on modern Chinese history] in *CHT*, I, p. 62; and O. M. Green, *The foreigner in China*, p. 122.

38 J. Ch'en, *Yüan Shih-k'ai*, pp. 6, 44.

39 Lin Te-ming, *Yüan Shih-k'ai yü Chao-hsien* [Yüan Shih-k'ai and Korea], in Chung-yang yen-chiu yüan, *Chin-tai shih yen-chiu so tsun-k'an* [Monograph Series No. 26, Institute of Modern History], pp. 372, 375.

40 MacDonald to Marquis of Salisbury, no. 50, 23 July 1896, FO 17/1282.

41 Foreign Office to MacDonald, draft tel., 5 September 1896, FO 17/1281.

42 Jordan to Marquis of Salisbury, no. 38, 26 October 1896, FO 17/1284.

43 Jordan to Langley, private, 13 June 1916, FO 350/15.

44 Jordan to Grey, no. 535, conf., 21 December 1906, FO 371/221.

CHAPTER II JORDAN, YÜAN, AND CHINESE POLITICS, 1906–1911 (pp. 10–29)

[1] Jordan to Campbell, private, 29 November 1906, FO 350/4; and Jordan to Campbell, private, 23 December 1910, FO 350/7.

[2] For example, as early as the end of 1907 Jordan wrote, 'Wang [Ta-hsieh], the late Minister in London, Wu Ting-fang, who is going as Minister to Washington, and others whom I need not mention, tell me that they are glad to be out of the country, not knowing what may happen when the Empress Dowager dies', Jordan to Campbell, private, 12 December 1907, FO 350/5.

[3] Jordan to Grey, no. 14, conf., 6 January 1909, FO 405/190.

[4] Jordan to Campbell, private, 21 January 1909, FO 350/5; Jordan to Grey, annual report for 1909, FO 405/195. Tuan-fang was the governor of Shensi during the Boxer Uprising. Under him, the province, like Shantung under Yüan Shih-k'ai, passed through the crisis in peace and calm. Moreover, Tuan-fang and Yüan were good friends mainly because they both found an enemy in another official, Sheng Hsüan-huai, see Liu Hou-sheng, *Chang Chien ch'üan-chi* [The biography of Chang Chien], pp. 152–53.

[5] Jordan to Grey, no. 119, conf., 16 March 1909, FO 371/636.

[6] See text of the agreement in *Treaties*, I, pp. 387–409. For comments on terms of agreement, see Chang Kia-ngau, *China's struggle for railroad development*, p. 30.

[7] Sheng to Byron Brenan of the corporation, 24 May 1903, enclosure in Satow to Grey, no. 120, 17 March 1906, FO 371/22.

[8] British and Chinese Corporation to Foreign Office, 9 January 1906, FO 371/22. The imperial order was given at the instigation of Sheng to appease the provincial gentry.

[9] Acting consul Smith, Hangchow, to Satow in Satow to Lansdowne, no. 429, 11 December 1905; Satow to Grey, tel. 10, 13 January 1906; and British and Chinese Corporation to Foreign Office, 22 February and 1 March 1906, FO 371/22.

[10] Satow to Grey, no. 119, 17 March; and no. 163, 10 April 1906, FO 371/22.

[11] Carnegie to Grey, tel. 123, 11 June 1906, FO 371/22.

[12] Carnegie to Grey, tel. 166, 10 September 1906. This rescript was again made at the instigation of Sheng Hsüan-huai.

[13] Summary of events in Hangchow in November in Jordan to Grey, no. 507, 29 November 1906, FO 371/217.

[14] Jordan to Grey, no. 526, 12 December 1906, FO 371/220.

[15] Jordan to Grey, no. 150, 28 March 1907, FO 371/220.

[16] Monthly summary of events in Hangchow in Jordan to Grey, no. 74, 6 February 1907, FO 371/217; Jordan to Grey, no. 150, 28 March 1907, FO 371/220. The corruption of the gentry is confirmed by numerous Chinese sources, a good example of which is Ch'üan Han-hsing, 'T'ieh-lu kuo-yu wen-t'i yü hsin-hai ke-ming' [Nationalization of railways and the 1911 Revolution], in *CHT*, I, pp. 210–11, with reference to a number of authoritive Chinese sources on the question.

¹⁷ Memorandum to Hillier in Jordan to Grey, no. 370, 7 August 1907, FO 371/220.

¹⁸ Jordan to Grey, no. 370, *ibid;* and C. S. Chen, 'British loans to China 1860–1913', Ph. D. thesis, University of London, 1940, p. 114.

¹⁹ Jordan to Grey, no. 405, 20 August 1907, FO 371/220.

²⁰ Jordan to Grey, tel. 194, 12 November; and no. 513, 30 October 1907, FO 371/220. Also E-tu Zen Sun, 'The Shanghai-Hangchow-Ningpo Railway Loan of 1908', *Far Eastern Quarterly* X, no. 3 (February, 1951), p. 143. For contemporary records of the agitation, see, for example, *Cheng-lun* [Political discussion] (Shanghai), I, no. 2 (November, 1907), pp. 117–18.

²¹ Jordan to Grey, no. 553, 26 November, and no. 594, 24 December 1907, FO 371/409.

²² Jordan to Campbell, private, 28 November 1907, FO 350/5.

²³ Jordan to Grey, tel. 179, 16 October, tel. 190, 9 November, and tel. 213, 9 December 1907, FO 371/220.

²⁴ It was agreed at the last stage of the negotiations that the railway would start from Shanghai instead of Soochow.

²⁵ A comparison of the two agreements is seen in E-tu Zen Sun, *Chinese railways and British interests 1898–1911*, pp. 68–71.

²⁶ In fact, enough capital had been accumulated by the Chinese before the loan agreement was signed, and the railway was eventually built without having to resort to British loan funds.

²⁷ Jordan to Grey, tel. 37, 10 February 1908, FO 371/409.

²⁸ For details of the role of the American company until the redemption of the railway in 1905, see W. R. Braisted, 'The United States and the American Chinese Development Company', *Far Eastern Quarterly* XI, no. 2 (February, 1952), pp. 149–59. A full account of China's negotiations with the Americans to redeem the Hankow-Canton line is available in Lee En-han, 'Chung-Mei shou-hui yüeh-han t'ieh-lu ch'üan chiao-she' [Sino-American negotiations on the recovery of Canton-Hankow Railway rights] in Chung-yang yen-chiu yüan, *Chin-tai shih yen-chiu so chi-k'an* [Bulletin of the Institute of Modern History, Academia Sinica], I (August, 1969), pp. 149–215. See also Tseng K'un-hua, *Chung-kuo t'ieh-lu hsien-hsi t'ung-lung* [Railways in present day China], II, pp. 300–302.

²⁹ The Hong Kong government was anxious to keep the Canton-Hankow line free from the control of other powers because when the railway was built it would be connected with the Canton-Kowloon Railway.

³⁰ Chang's telegram to Fraser, in Chang Chih-tung, *Chang Wen-hsiang kung ch'üan-chi* [The complete work of Chang Chih-tung], chap. 200, telegraphic correspondence 80, pp. 8a–8b.

³¹ See for example, Jordan to Campbell, private, 29 October, and 24 December 1908, FO 350/5.

³² Jordan to Grey, tel. 33, 23 January 1909, FO 371/622; and Jordan to Campbell, private, 4 and 20 March 1909, FO 350/5.

[33] Jordan's displeasure can be seen in Jordan to Campbell, private, *ibid.*
Terms of the agreement are available in Addis to Grey, 17 May 1909, FO
371/624.

[34] Jordan to Campbell, private, 11 October 1909, FO 350/6.

[35] For text of the agreement, see *Treaties,* I, pp. 886–87.

[36] Fox to Jordan in Jordan to Grey, no. 303, 7 July 1908, FO 371/422.

[37] See translation of Chang's proclamation in Jordan to Grey, no. 455,
14 October 1908, FO 371/422.

[38] Jordan to Grey, no. 377, 13 October; and no. 423, 16 November 1909,
FO 371/626. Kwangtung was able to collect more capital for railway building
because its natives were more affluent than those of the two Hu provinces.
A sizeable number of them was engaged in overseas trade, and many were
receiving financial assistance from their relatives who had migrated abroad,
see Ch'üan, 'T'ieh-lu kuo-yu wen-t'i yü hsin-hai ke-ming', pp. 214–15. See
also Chang, *China's struggle for railroad development,* pp. 39–40; Tseng K'un-
hua, *Chung-kuo t'ieh-lu shih* [History of Chinese railways], p. 110; Hsü
T'ung-hsin, *Chang Wen-hsiang kung nien-p'u* [Chronology of Chang Chih-
tung], p. 213; and Yeh Kung-cho, *Hsia-an hui-kao* [Collected works of Yeh
Kung-cho], I, part 1, pp. 196–97.

[39] For the effect of Chang's death on the Hu provinces, see Jordan to Grey,
no. 468, 16 December; and no. 478, 22 December 1909, FO 371/851. The
release of the anti-loan sentiment in Hunan after Chang's death is vividly
illustrated in Lu Hun (pseud.), 'Tui yü Chang Chih-tung ssu-hou chih
Hu-nan jen' [Concerning the Hunanese after the death of Chang Chih-tung],
HHKM, IV, pp. 531–36. For the attitude of the local authorities, see, for
example, memorial of the governor of Hunan, Tsen Ch'un-hsüan, 23 November 1909, in Department of State of Manchukuo, *Ta-Ch'ing li-chao shih-lu*
[Records of the reigns of the Ch'ing dynasty], Hsüan-t'ung reign, ch. 25,
pp. 24b–25a. Jui-cheng, acting viceroy of the Hu provinces, also supported
the gentry, MaxMuller, chargé d'affaires in Jordan's absence, to Grey, no. 165,
25 May 1910, FO 371/851.

[40] See for example, H. A. Little to Jordan in Jordan to Grey, no. 6, 5
January 1910, FO 371/851. Szechwan was second only in raising capital for
railway building, Ch'üan, 'T'ieh-lu kuo-yu wen-t'i yü hsin-hai ke-ming',
pp. 214–15.

[41] Jordan to Grey, no. 51, 15 February 1910, FO 371/851.

[42] Jordan to Campbell, private, 16 March and 24 May 1911, FO 350/7.

[43] Sheng inspected Japanese industry and banking between September and
November in 1908. It appears that he based his policy of railway nationalization on the Japanese model which was put into practice about two years before
he visited the country, A. Feuerwerker, *China's early industrialisation : Sheng
Hsuan-huai and Mandarin enterprise,* pp. 79, 81–82. For Japan's railway
nationalization, see Japanese Railroad Ministry, *Nihon tetsudoshi* [History of
Japan's railways], pp. 797–830.

[44] According to Jordan, the rumours had a considerable effect on the banks' representatives and the foreign ministers concerned. The leader of the new combination appears to have been the Russo-Asiatic Bank, Jordan to Grey, no. 122, 17 March 1911, FO 371/1080.

[45] The exclusion of the branch particularly affected the Germans and the Americans. Jordan was not unhappy to see the Germans 'obliged to forego some of their ill-gotten gain after all', Jordan to Campbell, private, 16 March 1911, FO 350/7.

[46] Hillier to Addis, enclosed in Addis to Foreign Office, 13 April; and Jordan to Grey, tel. 99, 13 April 1911, FO 371/1080.

[47] Grey to Jordan, tel. 70, 19 April; and Addis to Foreign Office, 24 April 1911, FO 371/1080.

[48] Jordan to Grey, tel. 102, 20 April 1911, on which Campbell minutes: 'I dare say Sir J. Jordan is right', FO 371/1080.

[49] Jordan to Grey, tel. 103, 21 April 1911, FO 371/1080; and Jordan to Campbell, private, 22 April 1911, FO 350/7.

[50] Jordan to Campbell, private, 15 May 1911, FO 350/7.

[51] Jordan to Campbell, private, 24 May 1911, FO 350/7.

[52] Jordan to Grey, no. 594, 24 December 1907, FO 371/409; also Liu, *Chang Chien Ch'üan-chi*, pp. 152–53.

[53] Details of the Szechwan railway riot and the activities of the revolutionaries in controlling it are found in Ch'üan, 'T'ieh-lu kuo-yu wen-t'i yü hsin-hai ke-ming', pp. 230–71. Also see Tai Chih-li (ed.), *Ssu-ch'uan pao-lu yün-tung shih-liao* [Documents on the Szechwan railroad revolt].

[54] Jordan to Grey, tel. 242, 12 December, and tel. 244, 15 December 1906, FO 371/38. The risings were indeed suppressed within a week, and the chief instigator, Liu Tao-i, was executed on 31 December 1906. For Chinese accounts of the risings, see, for example, *Cheng-chih shih*, I, pp. 269–70; Wen Kung-chih, *Chung-hua min-kuo ke-ming shih* [History of the Chinese republic until the northern expedition], I, p. 25; and *HHKM*, II, pp. 463–75, 499–522.

[55] Jordan to Grey, no. 9, v. conf., 7 January 1907, enclosing a dispatch from the consul-general at Shanghai, FO 405/173. The state of official nervousness is confirmed in *Cheng-chih shih*, I, pp. 270–71.

[56] Jordan to Grey, tel. 100, 7 June, and tel. 101, 8 June 1907, FO 371/231. For details of the risings, see Feng Tzu-yu, *Ke-ming i-shih* [Reminiscences of the 1911 Revolution], V, pp. 99–116; Lo Chia-lun, *Kuo-fu nien-p'u ch'u-kao* [Draft chronological biography of Sun Yat-sen], I, pp. 177–82; and *The Times*, 30 May, 1–3 June 1907.

[57] Details of the Anking incident and its aftermath can be found in, for example, Lo Chia-lun (ed.), *Ke-ming wen-hsien* [Materials on the 1911 Revolution], I, pp. 96–132; Lo, *Kuo-fu nien-p'u ch'u-kao*, I, pp. 182–86; and Chung-hua min-kuo k'ai-kuo wu-shih nien wen-hsien p'ien-tsuan wei-yüan hui, *Chung-hua min-kuo k'ai-kuo wu-shih nien wen-hsien* [Collection of materials on the origin of the Chinese republic on its 50th anniversary], XIII, pp. 167–89.

⁵⁸ Jordan to Grey, no. 332, 10 July 1907, FO 371/231; and no. 392, 20 August 1907, FO 371/217.

⁵⁹ These attempts were the Fang-ch'eng revolt of September 1907, the Chen-nan-kuan revolt of December 1907, the Ch'in-lien-chou revolt of late March 1908, the Ho-k'ou revolt of November 1908, and the Canton uprising of February 1910. Examples of references to these events are Feng Tzu-yu, *Chung-kuo ke-ming yün-tung erh-shih-liu nien tsu-chih shih* [Organization of the Chinese revolutionary movement], pp. 146–47; Huang Fu-luan, *Hua-chiao yü Chung-kuo ke-ming* [The overseas Chinese and the revolution], pp. 151–60; *HHKM*, III, pp. 217–28, 259–322; and Tsou Lu, *Chung-kuo kuo-min tang shih-kao* [Draft history of the Nationalist Party], III, pp. 753–63, 766–69.

⁶⁰ Accounts of the incident are given in Tsou Lu, *Kuang-chou san-yüeh erh-shih-chiu ke-ming shih* [The uprising of April 1911 in Canton], pp. 1–77; Hsü Shih-shen, *Kuo-fu ke-ming yüan-ch'i hsiang-chu* [Detailed commentary on texts selected to illustrate the revolutionary career of Sun Yat-sen], pp. 155–68.

⁶¹ Jordan to Grey, no. 151, 11 April 1911, FO 405/204.

⁶² Jordan to Grey, tel. 111, 3 May 1911, FO 371/1090.

⁶³ Jordan to Grey, tel. 207, 7 November; and tel. 211, 10 November; no. 476, 14 November 1906, FO 371/31; and Jordan to Grey, annual report for 1906, FO 371/231. Details of the reforms stated in these decrees are given in Chang Chih-pen, *Hsien-fa lun* [Constitutional law], p. 143.

⁶⁴ Jordan to Grey, no. 336, 11 July 1907, FO 371/224.

⁶⁵ Jordan to Grey, no. 474, 3 October, and no. 501, 17 October 1907, FO 371/224.

⁶⁶ A succint record of the actions of the court since the return of the constitution mission from its study tour is given in Ku Tun-jou, *Chung-kuo i-hui shih* [A History of the Chinese Parliament], pp. 25–27. For the text of the edict promulgated on 27 August 1908 which decreed the nine years' plan, see Liu Chen-k'ai, *Chung-kuo hsien-cheng shih-hua* [History of the Chinese constitution], pp. 29–31.

⁶⁷ Jordan to Grey, no. 408, 14 September 1908, FO 405/183.

⁶⁸ Y. C. Wang, *Chinese intellectuals and the West 1892–1949*, pp. 255–56.

⁶⁹ There is also the view that the constitutionalists consisted of three groups: reformists under the leadership of K'ang and Liang, the provincial gentry and the entrepreneurs, see, for example, Poon Chun-kau, 'The constitutional movement of the late Ch'ing period, 1905–1911', M.A. thesis, University of Hong Kong, 1969, pp. 178–98. The second and the third groups, however, overlapped a great deal. For instance, well-known constitutionalists such as Chang Chien (Kiangsu), T'ang Shou-ch'ien (Chekiang), T'an Yan-k'ai (Hunan), and P'u Tien-chün belonged to both groups, Chūzo Ichiko, 'The role of the gentry: an hypothesis', in M. C. Wright (ed.), *China in revolution : the first phase 1800–1913*, pp. 311–12; and Marie-Claire Bergère, *La bourgeoisie chinoise et la révolution de 1911*, pp. 33–34.

⁷⁰ Jordan to A. W. Moore, private, 16 December 1907, FO 350/5.

[71] Jordan to Grey, no. 474, 20 December 1909, FO 405/199, enclosing a report on the origin, governing rules, composition, franchise and powers of the assemblies. The rules governing election meant almost that only the gentry could have the right to elect and be elected. Also see Table 3.2., entitled 'Proportion of gentry to other members in five provincial assemblies', in Chang P'eng-yüan, 'The Constitutionalists', in Wright, *China in revolution: the first phase 1900–1913*, p. 151.

[72] Jordan to Campbell, private, 10 December 1908, FO 350/5.

[73] For information on the activities of the gentry constitutionalists between September 1906 and August 1908, see Ku, *Chung-kuo i-hui shih*, pp. 27–28; S. C. Chu, *Reformer in modern China, Chang chien, 1853–1926*, pp. 64–66; and Li shih-yüeh, *Chang Chien ho li-hsien p'ai* [Chang Chien and the constitutionalists], pp. 50–51.

[74] The boycott is described in C. F. Remer, *A study of Chinese boycotts*, pp. 40–45; and Feng, *Ko-ming i-shih*, IV, pp. 188–94. For the role of the Kwangtung Self-government Association in the boycott, see Chang Yu-fa, *Ch'ing-chi chih li-hsien t'üan-t'i* [Constitutionalists of the Ch'ing Period], in *Chin-tai shih yen-chiu so tsun-k'an*, p. 376; and E. J. M. Rhoads, *China's Republican Revolution: the case of Kwangtung, 1895–1913*, pp. 135–41.

[75] Jordan to Grey, tel. 1, 2 January, and no. 4, 4 January 1909, FO 371/613. See also Chang, *ibid.*, pp. 376–77. For details of the boycott which was later extended to Butterfield & Swire, see Rhoads, *China's Republican Revolution: the case of Kwangtung, 1895–1913*, pp. 141–43.

[76] Fox to Jordan in Jordan to Grey, no. 83, 19 February 1909, FO 371/634.

[77] See for example, Jordan to Grey, no. 409, 10 November 1909, FO 405/191; Jordan to Grey, no. 423, 16 November, and no. 441, 30 November 1909, FO 371/626; and Jordan to Grey, no. 474, 20 December 1909, FO 405/199. See also *North China Herald*, 16 October, 11 December 1908, and 18 February 1910.

[78] For details of the petitions, see Wang, *Chinese intellectuals and the West 1892–1949*, pp. 256–61; Chang, 'The Constitutionalists', pp. 160–65; Li Shou-k'ung, 'Ko sheng tzu-i chü lien-ho hui yü hsin-hai ke-ming' [The Association of Provincial Assemblies and the 1911 Revolution] in *CHT*, III, pp. 328–43; and MaxMuller to Grey, no. 237, 22 July, and tel. 176, 27 October 1910, Fo 371/858.

[79] Jordan to Grey, annual report for 1910, FO 405/201. Similar details are available in Poon, 'The constitutional movement of the late Ch'ing period, 1905–1911', pp. 248–49. See also Wang, *Chinese intellectuals and the West 1892–1949*, p. 261.

[80] For regulations governing the membership and duties of the national assembly, see H. M. Vinacke, *Modern constitutional development in China*, pp. 83–84; L. R. O. Bevan, *Constitution building in China*, pp. 48–57; translation of the first instalment of regulations of the assembly in Jordan to Grey, no. 337, 22 July 1908, FO 405/183; and Jordan to Grey, annual report for 1910, FO 405/201.

[81] MaxMuller to Grey, tel. 176, 27 October 1910, FO 371/858. See also Chang, *Ch'ing chi ti li-hsien t'üan-t'i*, pp. 440–41.

⁸² Campbell's minute on MaxMuller to Grey, tel. 181, 5 November 1910, FO 371/858.

⁸³ Jordan to Grey, annual report for 1910, FO 405/201; and Jordan to Campbell, private, 6 December 1910, FO 350/7. According to Chang Peng-yüan, whose research on the constitutional movement is reputable, many of the appointed members held a neutral attitude because even they found it difficult to defend many of the corrupt policies of the government. A few of them were openly critical, particularly Marquis Tseng Kuang-luan. On the other hand, there were quite a few forthright characters among the provincial representatives, the most prominent of whom were Lei Fen of Kiangsu, I Tsung-k'uei and Lo Chieh of Hunan, and Liu Ch'un-lin of Chihli, see Chang Peng-yüan, *Li-hsien p'ai yü hsin-hai ke-ming* [The Constitutionalists and the 1911 Revolution], pp. 84–86.

⁸⁴ Jordan to Alston, private, 15 December 1910; and Jordan to Grey, private, 11 January 1911, FO 350/7.

⁸⁵ Vinacke, *Modern constitutional development in China,* pp. 86–87; Jordan to Grey, annual report for 1910, and Jordan to Grey, no. 458, conf., 20 December 1910, FO 405/204; *HHKM,* IV, pp. 69–71; and Chang, *Li-hsien p'ai yü hsin-hai ke-ming,* pp. 86–101.

⁸⁶ Poon, 'The constitutional movement of the late Ch'ing period, 1905–1911', pp. 227, 234–35, 240. Many people believe that Yüan was not sincerely sympathetic with the idea of constitutionalism. He committed himself to the reforms insofar as to maintain a prominent position in the political sphere of the time, see for example, Shen Yün-lung, 'Chang I-lin yü Yüan Shih-k'ai' [Chang I-lin and Yüan Shih-k'ai] in *Hsien-tai cheng-ch'ih jen-wu shu-p'ing* [The political figures in modern China], II, pp. 275–76.

⁸⁷ Jordan, 'Some Chinese I have known', p. 955. Jordan to Grey, no. 535, conf., 21 December 1906, FO 371/221; and Jordan to Grey, no. 14, conf., 6 January 1909, FO 405/190. Full details of Yüan's administration in Chihli are available in Kan Hou-t'zǔ (ed.), *Pei-yang kung-tu lei-tsuan* [Collection of correspondence of Yüan Shih-k'ai as viceroy of Chihli] in *YSH.*

⁸⁸ Jordan to Grey, no. 579, conf., 11 December 1907, FO 371/409.

⁸⁹ Jordan to Grey, tel. 13, conf., 8 January; and Jordan to Grey, no. 14, conf., 16 January 1909, FO 405/190.

⁹⁰ See Far Eastern Department, General Memorandum, December 1908, FO 405/187.

⁹¹ This is according to the representative of the Yokohama Specie Bank in Peking, see Wu Hsiang-hsiang, 'San-Han Fu-sang so chien Yüan Shih-k'ai kuan-hsi shih-liao' [Materials relating to Yüan Shih-k'ai in Korea and Japan] in *CHT,* IV, pp. 446–47.

⁹² Jordan to Grey, tel. 3, 2 January 1909, FO 405/190.

⁹³ Jordan to Grey, tel. 5, 3 January, and Campbell's minute on it; and Grey's minute on Jordan to Grey, tel. 26, 15 January 1909, FO 371/612.

⁹⁴ Jordan to Grey, tel. 17, 9 January; and MacDonald to Grey, tel. 3, 10 January 1909, FO 405/190.

[95] Liang Tun-yen, who filled Yüan's vacancy in the Ministry of Foreign Affairs, firmly believed that the Japanese had actively encouraged the Manchu faction, headed by Prince Ch'un, to depose Yüan, Jordan to Grey, tel. 20, 11 January; MacDonald to Grey, tel. 5, 14 January; and no. 11, conf., 23 January 1909, FO 405/190.

[96] Jordan to Campbell, private, 19 January 1909, FO 350/5. Details of Hsü Shih-ch'ang's activities in Manchuria 1907–1909 are available in the twelve-volume work of Hsü Shih-ch'ang, *Tung-san sheng cheng-lüeh* [Policies in Manchuria]; and Hara Takemichi, 'Chinese policy in Manchuria', M.A. thesis, University of Hong Kong, 1971, pp. 125–49, 197–239. For the turn of British opinion, see P. Lowe, *Great Britain and Japan 1911–15*, pp. 18–21; annual reports from the British embassy in Tokyo for 1909 and 1910, FO 405/195; FO 405/201; the Rt. Hon. Earl Stanhope, 'Great Britain and Japan in the Far East', in *Nineteenth century and after*, LXVII (1910), p. 534; and F. Coleman, *The Far East unveiled*, p. 12.

[97] Grey's minute on Jordan to Grey, tel. 26, 15 January 1909, FO 371/612.

[98] James Bryce, British ambassador to the United States, to Grey, tel. 8, 10 January 1909, FO 405/190.

[99] Jordan to Grey, tel. 26, 15 January 1909, FO 371/612.

[100] Jordan to Grey, tel. 3, 2 January 1909, FO 405/190.

[101] See for example, Jordan to Campbell, private, 11 November 1909, FO 350/6; Jordan to Grey, no. 458, conf., 20 December 1910, FO 405/204; and *The Times*, 6, 8 September 1910, and 29, 30 September 1911.

[102] Jordan to Grey, annual report for 1910, FO 405/201.

CHAPTER III THE 1911 REVOLUTION (pp. 30–54)

[1] Jordan to Grey, tel. 225, 14 October 1911, FO 371/1093.

[2] For the actual working of the British policy of neutrality during the revolution, see Chan Lau Kit-ching, 'British policy of neutrality during the 1911 Revolution in China', *Journal of Oriental Studies* VIII, no. 2 (July 1970) 357–79.

[3] Details relating to the Manchu and Yüan's requests for financial assistance are available in Chan, 'British policy of neutrality during the 1911 Revolution in China', pp. 363–67.

[4] Jordan to Grey, no. 444, conf., 16 November 1911, FO 371/1096.

[5] Jordan to Grey, tel. 225, 14 October 1911, 371/1093.

[6] For details of the mutiny, see *HHKM*, VI, pp. 331–39; for the twelve articles, see *Cheng-chih shih*, pp. 251–52.

[7] Jordan to Grey, tel. 259, 2 November 1911, FO 371/1094.

[8] Jordan to Campbell, private, 3 November 1911, FO 350/7.

[9] For details of events at Shih-chia-chuang, see *HHKM*, VI, pp. 329–31, 360–62, 371. Details of the revolution in Shansi are available in Yen Hsi-shan, who was the well-known warlord of Shansi in the warlord period, *Yen Hsi-shan tsao-nien hui-i lu* [Yen Hsi-shan's reminiscences of his early years], pp. 13–28.

[10] Many Chinese historians think that Wu Lu-chen was assassinated by Yüan Shih-k'ai who found Wu a threat to his power in the north, for example, *HHKM*, VI, p. 272; Wen Kung-chih, *Tsui-chin san-shih nien chung-kuo chün-shih shih* [The military history of China of the last thirty years] in *CHST*, II, p. 5; and *Cheng-chih shih*, I, p. 313. A detailed hypothetical analysis as to who the murderer of Wu was is found in Appendix 5 to Chu ten-chia, 'Wu Lu-chen yü Chung-kuo ke-ming' [Wu Lu-chen and the revolution in China], in *CHT*, VI, pp. 218–23.

[11] Jordan to Grey, tel. 256, 30 October 1911, 371/1093.

[12] Jordan to Grey, tel. 258, 2 November 1911, FO 371/1093.

[13] Details of these particular sessions of the assembly are available in *Peking Daily News*, 3, 8, 9 November 1911. For the constitution drawn up by the assembly, known as the Nineteen Articles *(Shih-chiu hsin-t'aio)*, see W. L. Tung, *The political institutions of modern China*, pp. 18–19.

[14] Jordan to Grey, tel. 256, 30 October 1911, FO 371/1093.

[15] Jordan to Campbell, private, 3 November 1911, FO 350/7; and *Peking Daily News*, 14 November 1911.

[16] Jordan to Grey, no. 427, 6 November 1911, FO 371/1095.

[17] Jordan to Grey, tel. 274, 12 November 1911, FO 371/1095.

[18] Campbell's minute to Grey, 26 October 1911, FO 371/1093.

[19] Jordan to Grey, tel. 249, 29 October 1911, FO 371/1094.

[20] Jordan to Grey, tel. 302, 26 November 1911, FO 371/1096.

[21] Goffe to Jordan in Jordan to Grey, tel. 307, 27 November 1911, FO 371/1096; see also Pearl, *Morrison of Peking*, p. 232.

[22] Jordan to Grey, tel. 314, 1 December 1911, FO 371/1096.

[23] See for example, Goffe to Jordan, tel. 103, 11 December; and tel. 111, 15 December 1911, FO 228/1802.

[24] Nicolson's minute on Jordan to Grey, tel. 314, 1 December 1911, FO 371/1096.

[25] Campbell's minute on Jordan to Grey, tel. 314, *ibid.*

[26] Grey's minute on Jordan to Grey, tel. 314, *ibid.*

[27] Jordan to Grey, no. 495, 12 December 1911, FO 371/1310.

[28] Jordan to Admiral Winsloe in Jordan to Grey, no. 480, 5 December 1911, FO 371/1098.

[29] For example, E. P. Young, 'Yüan Shih-k'ai's rise to the presidency' in Wright, *China in revolution : the first phase 1900–1913,* pp. 424–25 and note 16, referring to the remarks made by contemporary American diplomatic and consular officials; and Sih-Gung Cheng, *Modern China,* pp. 15–16. Even the British commander-in-chief of the China Station was considerably impressed by the equipment, organization, and discipline of the government troops fighting in the Hanyang campaign which he observed on the spot; see Admiral Winsloe to Admiralty in Admiralty to Foreign Office, 13 January 1912, FO 371/1311.

[30] Jordan to Grey, tel. 97, 24 February 1912, FO 371/1315.

[31] Fraser to Jordan in Jordan to Grey, tel. 352, 20 December 1911, FO 371/1097.

[32] Fraser to Jordan in Jordan to Grey, tel. 357, 21 December 1911, FO 371/1097.

[33] For British opinion in Shanghai on the revolution and its influence on Jordan, see Chung-hua min-kuo k'ai-kuo wu-shih-nien wen-hsien p'ien-tsuan wei-yüan-hui, *Chung-hua min-kuo k'ai-kuo wu-shih-nien wen-hsien,* I, p. 380; *HHKM,* VIII, p. 439; and J. O. P. Bland, *Recent events and present policies in China,* p. 267.

[34] H. Croly, *Willard Straight,* p. 412; Pearl, *Morrison of Peking,* p. 231; and a report on an interview between Yüan and Morrison in *North China Daily News,* 9 December, 1911.

[35] Jordan to Grey, tel. 258, 2 November 1911, FO 371/1094. It is an established fact that Yüan had written to Li Yüan-hung twice before Yüan's representatives, Liu Cheng-en and Ts'ai T'ing-kan, reached Wuhang on 11 November to negotiate with Li. Chinese historians interpret these actions of Yüan as evidence of his disloyalty to the Manchus, for example, Wu Hsiang-hsiang, 'Yüan Shih-k'ai mou-ch'ü lin-shih ta-tsung-t'ung chih ching-kuo' [The way in which Yüan Shih-k'ai plotted for the provisional presidency], in *CHT,* I, p. 6; and Chü Cheng, *Hsin-hai cha-chi* [Notes on the 1911 Revolution], p. 75.

[36] Jordan to Grey, tel. 281, 15 November 1911, FO 371/1095.

[37] See for example, Jordan to Grey, no. 502, 17 December 1911, FO 371/1310; and Wu, 'Yüan Shih-k'ai mou-ch'ü lin-shih ta-tsung-t'ung chih ching-kuo', p. 8.

[38] Jordan to Campbell, private, 27 November 1911, FO 350/7.

[39] Jordan to Grey, no. 495, 12 December 1911, FO 371/1310.

[40] Jordan to Campbell, private, 4 January 1912, FO 350/8.

[41] The intimate relationship between Miyazaki Torazo and Sun Yat-sen until the 1911 Revolution can be seen in Miyazaki's autobiography, *Sanjū sannen no yume* [Thirty-three years' dream]; also in Jansen, *The Japanese and Sun Yat-sen*, pp. 49–51, 64–153; and P'eng Tse-chou, 'Kung-ch'i t'ao-t'ien yü Chung-kuo ke-ming' [Miyazaki Torazo and the revolution in China], in *CHT*, V, pp. 23–50.

[42] M. Ikei, 'Japan's response to the Chinese Revolution of 1911', in *JAS* XXV, p. 214; for the Manchu request of 13 October, see Ijuin to Hayashi Tadasu, the communications minister holding the post of foreign minister pending the arrival of Uchida, no. 261, secret, 13 October 1911, *NGB*, XLIV–XLV, pp. 134–35; and Lowe, *Great Britain and Japan 1911–1915*, p.62.

[43] Ikei, 'Japan's response to the Chinese Revolution of 1911', pp. 214–15; and Lowe, *Great Britain and Japan 1911–1915*, pp. 62–63.

[44] Ijuin to Uchida, nos. 398, 401, 1 November 1911, *NGB*, XLIV–XLV, pp. 54–56. See also P'eng, 'Hsin-hai ke-ming yü Jih-pen Hsi-yüan-szu nei-ko' [The 1911 Revolution and the Saionji cabinet of Japan], in *CHT*, VI, p. 16.

[45] Uchida to Ijuin, no. 299, 17 November 1911, *NGB*, XLIV–XLV, pp. 164–66.

[46] Ijuin to Uchida, no. 548, v. conf., 18 November 1911, *NGB*, XLIV–XLV pp. 380–82.

[47] For greater details, see Lowe, *Great Britain and Japan 1911–1915*, p. 71.

[48] Memoranda communicated by Yamaza in Grey to MacDonald, no. 244, 1 December 1911, FO 371/1096.

[49] Grey to Jordan, tel. 195, 5 December 1911, and Jordan to Grey, tel. 318, 3 December 1911, FO 371/1096.

[50] Jordan to Grey, tel. 323, 5 December, and tel. 329, 8 December 1911, FO 371/1096. Also Ijuin to Uchida, no. 648, 8 December 1911, *NGB*, XLIV–XLV, pp. 403–4.

[51] Grey to MacDonald, tel. 58, 8 December 1911, FO 371/1096; and MacDonald to Grey, tel. 56, 9 December 1911, FO 371/1097. Also Uchida to Ijuin, no. 372, 13 December 1911, *NGB*, XLIV–XLV, p. 410.

[52] Lowe, *Great Britain and Japan 1911–1915*, pp. 67–68.

[53] Jordan to Grey, tel. 340, 13 December 1911, FO 371/1097.

[54] Ijuin to Uchida, no. 668, v. conf., urgent, 12 December 1911, *NGB*, XLIV–XLV, pp. 405–9.

[55] Uchida to Ijuin, no. 380, 15 December 1911. In fact, earlier that day Uchida had instructed Ijuin and the Japanese consul-general at Shanghai to co-operate with their respective British counterparts at the forthcoming peace conference at Shanghai; see Uchida to Ijuin, no. 379, 15 December; and Uchida to Ariyoshi (Akira?), no. 146, v. conf., 15 December 1911, *NGB*, XLIV–XLV, pp. 410–13.

56 Jordan to Grey, tel. 351, secret, 17 December 1911, FO 371/1097.

57 Jordan to Grey, tel. 223, 18 December 1911, FO 371/1097.

58 MacDonald to Grey, tel. 62, 20 December 1911, FO 371/1098.

59 Ijuin to Uchida, no. 711, 20 December 1911, *NGB,* XLIV–XLV, pp. 432.

60 Ariyoshi to Uchida, no. 429, 20 December 1911, *NGB,* XLIV–XLV, pp. 435–36.

61 Ijuin to Uchida, no. 715, urgent, 22 December 1911, *NGB,* XLIV–XLV, pp. 437–39.

62 Memorandum communicated to the Foreign Office, 24 December 1911, FO 371/1098.

63 Jordan to Grey, tel. 366, 25 December 1911, FO 371/1098.

64 Confidential clause of MacDonald to Grey, tel. 64, 26 December 1911, FO 371/1098.

65 Jordan to Grey, tel. 360, 22 December 1911, FO 371/1098.

66 Ijuin to Uchida, no. 720, v. urgent, *NGB,* XLIV–XLV, pp. 449–52.

67 *The Times,* 23 December 1911.

68 Jordan to Grey, tel. 364, 23 December 1911, FO 371/1098.

69 Grey to Jordan, tel. 236, 24 December 1911, FO 371/1098.

70 The quotation is from Croly, *Willard Straight,* p. 431; see also Pearl, *Morrison of Peking,* p. 242.

71 Jordan to Grey, tel. 367, 26 December 1911, FO 371/1098.

72 Croly, *Willard Straight,* p. 431.

73 Translation of the terms is taken from Ch'en, *Yüan Shih-k'ai,* p. 95; and details of the conference are available in Li Yün-han, 'Huang K'e-ch'iang hsien-sheng nien-p'u kao' [Draft chronology of Huang Hsing], in *CHT,* IV, pp. 283–84. The negotiations took place in the Wen-ming Bookstore because it was under the management of a revolutionary, Yü Fu, who also took part in the negotiations; see *HHKM,* VIII, p. 104.

74 Hu O-kuang, *Hsin-hai ke-ming pei-fang shih-lü* [The 1911 Revolution in north China], pp. 103–4; and Wu, 'Yüan Shih-k'ai mou-ch'ü lin-shih ta-tsung-t'ung chih ching-kuo', pp. 9–10.

75 Pearl, *Morrison of Peking,* pp. 235–36. See also Lin, *Yüan Shih-k'ai yü Chao-hsien,* pp. 2, 4.

76 Jordan to Grey, tel. 365, 24 December 1911, FO 371/1098.

77 Ijuin to Uchida, no. 726, 25 December 1911, *NGB,* XLIV–XLV, p. 459.

78 The Japanese cabinet was unanimously in favour of abandoning the demand for a Chinese constitutional monarchical government on 22 December. On 24 December, however, the Elder Statesmen, notably Yamagata Aritomo, put pressure on the cabinet to have further talks with Britain and Yüan about a constitutional monarchy; see Ikei, 'Japan's response to the Chinese revolution of 1911', p. 223; and Uchida to Ijuin, no. 405, 24 December 1911, *NGB,* XLIV–XLV, pp. 454–55.

⁷⁹ Afterwards, Yüan even complained to Ijuin that he was being forced to abandon the dynasty because Japanese aid was not forthcoming, and Ijuin seemed to believe it; see Ijuin to Uchida, no. 738, 27 December 1911, *NGB*, XLIV–XLV, pp. 472–77.

⁸⁰ Bland, *Recent events and present policies in China*, p. 167. The edict was 'the death warrant of the dynasty' in that the assembly would certainly vote for a republic since of all the Chinese provinces only Kansu, Sinkiang, Manchuria, Shantung, Chihli, and Honan were still nominally under imperial rule.

⁸¹ Fraser to Jordan in Jordan to Grey, tel. 372, 30 December 1911, FO 371/1310.

⁸² For minutes of the meetings see *HHKM*, VIII, pp. 85–95.

⁸³ Jordan to Grey, tel. 1, secret, 1 January 1912, FO 371/1310.

⁸⁴ Details of Sun's return and inauguration are available in *Cheng-chih shih*, I, pp. 334–35; and Lo Kang, *Lo p'ien Kuo-fu nien-p'u chiu-miu* [Correction of errors in the chronology of Sun Yat-sen compiled by Lo Chia-lun], pp. 282–84. For translation of Sun's speech, see H. F. MacNair, *Modern Chinese history*, p. 719.

⁸⁵ Jordan to Grey, tel. 13, conf., 12 January 1912, FO 371/1310; and Jordan to Grey, no. 29, 16 January 1912, FO 371/1312.

⁸⁶ Jordan to Grey, tel. 17, 14 January 1912, FO 371/1310.

⁸⁷ Ijuin knew of Liang's visit to Jordan from Jordan; see Ijuin to Uchida, urgent, no. 28, 12 January 1912, *NGB*, XLIV–XLV, pp. 543–44. It appears, however, that Ijuin was ignorant of Ts'ai's visit to Jordan.

⁸⁸ For these details, see *Cheng-chih shih*, p. 337; *HHKM*, VIII, p. 111; and Kao Yin-tsu, *Chung-hua min-kuo ta-shih chi* [Chronology of important events of the republican period], p. 2.

⁸⁹ Jordan called personally on Yüan to congratulate him on his escape; see Jordan to Grey, tel. 18, conf., 19 January 1912, FO 371/1311.

⁹⁰ The role played by Wu, Chao, and Liang in persuading the court to abdicate on Yüan's behalf is recorded in Ts'en Hsüeh-lü, *San-shui Liang Yen-sun hsien-sheng nien-p'u* [Chronology of Liang Shih-i], in *CHST*, pp. 105–11.

⁹¹ For the two conferences, see *Cheng-chih shih*, I, pp. 338–39.

⁹² Jordan to Grey, tel. 18, conf., 19 January 1912, FO 371/1311.

⁹³ Grey to Jordan, tel. 14, 21 January 1912, FO 371/1311.

⁹⁴ Such details are available in *HHKM*, VIII, pp. 112–13; Ch'en, *Yüan Shih-k'ai*, p. 99; and Aisin Gioro P'u-i, *Wo-ti ch'ien pan-sheng* [Autobiography of the last Ch'ing emperor], p. 43.

⁹⁵ Jordan to Grey, tel. 21, 23 January 1912, FO 371/1311.

⁹⁶ Langley's minute on Jordan to Grey, tel. 21, 23 January 1912, *ibid.*

⁹⁷ Langley to Jordan, private, 25 January 1912, FO 350/1; and the minutes of Grey and Nicolson on Jordan to Grey, tel. 21, 23 January 1913, FO 371/1311.

[98] Jordan to Grey, no. 47, 27 January 1912, FO 371/1312.

[99] Wilkinson to Jordan, no. 73, 20 January 1912, FO 228/1836. For the terms in question, see *Cheng-chih shih,* I, pp. 339–40.

[100] Jordan to Grey, no. 40, conf., 22 January 1912, FO 371/1312.

[101] Wilkinson to Jordan, no. 6, 24 January 1912, FO 228/1836.

[102] Jordan to Grey, tel. 20, 22 January 1912, FO 371/1311.

[103] Jordan to Grey, no. 71, 10 February 1912, FO 371/1314. See also Tsou, *Chung-kuo kuo-min tang shih-kao,* p. 953; and *Cheng-chih shih,* I, pp. 341–42. According to Chang P'eng-yüan, the idea was from Chang Chien who had definitely changed from being a constitutionalist to a republican by early November and who saw in Yüan Shih-k'ai China's only hope; see *Li-hsien p'ai yü hsin-hai ke-ming,* pp. 223–25. For details of Chang Chien's change, see Lu Yao-tung, 'Hsin-hai ke-ming ch'ien-hou Chang Chien ti kai-pien' [Chang Chien before and after the 1911 Revolution], in *CHT,* V, pp. 213–29.

[104] Jordan to Grey, tel. 30, 1 February 1912, FO 371/1311.

[105] Wilkinson to Jordan, no. 6, 24 January 1912, FO 228/1836.

[106] *Lin-shih cheng-fu kung-pao,* 29 January 1912.

[107] *Lin-shih cheng-fu kung-pao,* 31 January 1912.

[108] Jordan to Grey, no. 47, 27 January 1912, FO 371/1312; and Jordan to Grey, no. 50, 29 January 1912, FO 371/1313. According to the plan of Huang Hsing, commander-in-chief of the army in the Nanking government, the revolutionaries were to march on to Peking along six different routes. For details of Huang's plan see Li, 'Huang K'e-ch'iang hsien-sheng nien-p'u kao', pp. 295–96.

[109] Jordan learned from Fraser, who had been told by Wu T'ing-fang, that the revolutionaries had no means to pay the troops; see Jordan to Grey, no. 50, 29 January 1912, FO 371/1313. Wilkinson also reported the same difficulty of the revolutionaries from Nanking; Wilkinson to Jordan, no. 11, 3 February 1911, FO 228/1836. Huang Hsing is said to have been greatly tormented by the financial difficulty; see Li, 'Huang K'e-ch'iang hsien-sheng nien-p'u kao', p. 296. For another enlightening account of the financial exigencies of the revolutionaries, see G. Lanning, *Old forces in new China,* pp. 359–61.

[110] Jordan to Grey, no. 71, 10 February 1912, FO 371/1314. This is an important document which not only portrays the events which occurred in the days immediately before the abdication, but summarizes Jordan's attitude since his definite rejection of the monarchical cause from about 20 December 1911.

[111] Pearl, *Morrison of Peking,* p. 250.

[112] Jordan to Grey, no. 13, 6 January 1911, FO 371/1311.

[113] Jordan to Campbell, private, 27 November 1911, FO 350/7; Jordan to Grey, tel. 278, 14 November 1911, the confidential clause in Jordan to Grey, tel. 289, 20 November 1911, FO 371/1095; Jordan to Langley, private, 6 September 1912, and Jordan to Campbell, private, 4 January 1912, FO 350/8.

[1] The following discussion on the reorganization loan is essentially based on the author's article, 'British policy in the reorganisation loan to China 1912–1913', *Modern Asian Studies* V, part 4 (October 1971) 355–72.

[2] The description of the Yüan-T'ang relationship is based on Jordan to Grey, annual report for 1919, FO 405/229. See also C. T. Sigel, 'T'ang Shao-yi (1860–1938): the diplomacy of Chinese nationalism', Ph.D. thesis, Harvard University, 1972.

[3] T'ang, after all, had had seven years of American education. For Jordan's recognition of T'ang's ability compared with most Chinese, see, for example, Jordan to Langley, private, 7 February 1907, FO 350/4.

[4] Jordan to Campbell, private, 24 December; and 17 September 1908, FO 350/5.

[5] Jordan to Cambell, private, 21 January 1909, FO 350/5.

[6] Jordan to Campbell, private, 19 January 1911, FO 350/7.

[7] Wilkinson to Jordan in Jordan to Grey, no. 163, 3 April 1912, FO 405/208, enclosing the text of the provisional constitution in English. The original Chinese text is available in Ku, *Chung-kuo i-hui shih,* pp. 63–68. For an analysis of its shortcomings see Huang Kung-chüeh etc., *Chung-kuo chih-hsien shih* [History of the constitution in China], I, pp. 41–44.

[8] *Cheng-chih shih,* II, pp. 374–75; T'ao Chü-yin, *Pei-yang chün-fa t'ung-chih shih-chih shih-hua* [China under the warlords], I, pp. 132–33; and Wu Hsiang-hsiang, *Sung Chiao-jen,* pp. 166–67.

[9] It is true that the minister of finance, Hsiung Hsi-ling who was close to Yüan, strongly opposed T'ang's transactions with an outside group. See, for example, Chiang Chün-chang, *Chung-hua min-kuo chien-kuo shih* [History of the establishment of the Chinese Republic], p. 108.

[10] Ch'en, *Yüan Shih-k'ai,* p. 118.

[11] Jordan to Langley, private, 25 March 1912, FO 350/8. Here Jordan was obviously alluding to T'ang's attitude at the Shanghai peace conference in the 1911 Revolution.

[12] Details of the incident are obtainable in T'ao, *Pei-yang chün-fa t'ung-chih shih-chih shih-hua,* I, pp. 134–35; and Ts'en, *San-shui Liang Yen-sun hsien-sheng nien-p'u,* I, p. 121. Both assert with certainty that the telegram from the Chihli military leaders was Yüan's doing. For T'ang's letter of resignation, see Hsü Yü-p'eng (ed.), *Yüan-ta tsung-t'ung shu-tu hui-p'ien* [Correspondence of president Yüan Shih-k'ai], in *CHST,* chap. 4, pp. 4–5.

[13] Jordan to Langley, private, 21 May, and 25 June 1912, FO 350/8; and Jordan to Grey, no. 276, 28 June 1912, FO 371/1320.

[14] Jordan to Grey, no. 276, 28 June 1912, *ibid.*

[15] It has been said that Lu's personality was what Yüan liked to find best in his subordinates; see Ch'eng Ts'ang-po, 'Lu Cheng-hsiang yü t'ien-chu chiao' [Lu Cheng-hsiang and Catholicism] in *Li-shih wen-hua yü jen-wu* [History, culture, and personalities], p. 82.

[16] It has been asserted that Yüan executed Chang, who was bitterly hated by the vice-president Li Yüan-hung, and Fang, Chang's subordinate, to secure the loyalty of Li who had by then become a popular public figure; see F. Farjenel, *Through the Chinese revolution*, p. 231; T'ao, *Pei-yang chün-fa t'ung-chih shih-chih shih-hua*, I, pp. 138–41; and Shen Yün-lung, *Li Yüan-hung p'ing-chüan* [Analytical biography of Li Yüan-hung], pp. 39–47.

[17] See political principles of the Kuomintang in Yu Jun-t'ang etc., *Chung-kuo tang-tai cheng-tang lun* [Political parties in present-day China], p. 30; Wu Hsiang-hsiang, 'Sung Chiao-jen wei hsien-fa hsi-sheng' [Sung Chiao-jen's sacrifice for constitutionalism] in *Min-kuo cheng-chih jen-wu* [Political figures of the Chinese republic], pp. 15–16; Wu, *Sung Chiao-jen*, pp. 174–75; and *Min-li pao*, 23 March 1913. For the history of the founding of the party, refer to Wu, *ibid.*, pp. 199–205.

[18] Apparently, Sung had attacked Yüan's government even before he founded the Kuomintang. For example, in a large gathering in Peking on 21 July 1912, Sung denounced the existing government as useless and said that it should be replaced by another organized by the T'ung-meng hui; see S. K. Hornbeck, *Contemporary politics in the Far East*, p. 73. About half a month before his death, Sung was heard criticizing the government as degenerate and unpopular; see Li, 'Huang K'e-ch'iang hsien-sheng nien-p'u kao', p. 359.

[19] Jordan to Grey, annual report for 1912, FO 405/229.

[20] Fraser to Jordan, tel. 13, conf., 28 March, and dispatch, conf., 28 March 1913, FO 228/1875. Later, in a telegram to Grey, Jordan explained that the evidence consisted of a private code given to Ying by Hung, and telegrams between them in the same code. Among the telegrams was one from Ying to Hung sent after the assassination, reporting that the 'arch criminal had been removed'. There was also a letter from Hung to Ying which promised a large reward if the 'great object' was fulfilled; see Jordan to Grey, no. 143, conf., 3 April, and no. 183, 3 May 1913, FO 371/1623. See also telegram from Cheng Te-ch'üan, *tu-tu* in Shanghai, received on 27 April, in Li Yüan-hung to Yüan Shih-k'ai, 27 April 1913, in I Kuo-kan (ed.), *Li fu tsung-t'ung cheng-shu* [Official documents of vice-president Li Yüan-hung], in *CHST*, pp. 230–31.

[21] Fraser to Jordan, tel. 14, 31 March 1913, FO 228/1875.

[22] Jordan to Grey, no. 143, conf., 3 April; and no. 149, 9 April 1913, FO 371/1624.

[23] For the dissension and weakness of the Kuomintang in Shanghai and the provinces, the special court, and Chao Ping-chün, who had been on 'sick leave' after Sung's death and eventually resigned on 1 May, see Chün-tu Hsüeh, *Huang Hsing and the Chinese Revolution*, pp. 154–55; Chün-tu Hsüeh, *Revolutionary leaders of modern China*, p. 148; Shen I-yün, wife of Huang Fu, *I-yün hui-i* [Reminiscences of Shen I-yün], I, pp. 82–84; P'an Kung-chan, *Ch'en Ch'i-mei*, pp. 57–58; and Chin Wen-ssu etc. (ed.), *Huang Ying-po hsien-sheng ku-chiu kan-i lu* [Memorial volume of Huang Fu], in *CHST*, pp. 164–65. Chao Ping-chün died of poison early in the following spring while he was *tu-tu* of Chihli. Almost all Chinese historians assert that he was poisoned by Yüan so that he could never disclose Yüan's guilt in Sung's death,

for example, *Cheng-chih shih,* II, p. 389. Jordan, however, said that Chao's death was caused by Kuomintang members; see Jordan to Grey, no. 88, 2 March 1914, FO 405/214.

²⁴ Tsou Lu, then a member of parliament from Kwangtung, *Hui-ku lu* [Memoir], pp. 53–54; Tsou Lu, *Tsou Lu wen-ts'un* [Collections of Tsou Lu], part 5, p. 10; and Huang, *Yüan-sheng i-chü,* II, p. 101.

²⁵ Jordan to Grey, tel. 104, v. conf., 29 April 1913, FO 371/1624.

²⁶ Grey to Jordan, tel. 122, 1 May 1913, FO 371/1624.

²⁷ Jordan talks at length about the 'root cause' of the revolution in his telegram to Grey, no. 211, 19 May 1913, FO 371/1624.

²⁸ Fraser to Jordan, tel. 27, 1 May 1913, FO 228/1875.

²⁹ Fraser to Jordan, tel. 29, 6 May 1931, FO 228/1875.

³⁰ Fraser to Jordan, tel. 33, 16 May 1913, FO 228/1875. Fraser, however, thought that this request for mediation was the Kuomintang's test of the attitude of the powers whom it suspected of having promised Yüan their unqualified support.

³¹ Jordan to Fraser, tel. 20, 17 May 1913, FO 228/1875.

³² Jordan to Grey, no. 217, conf., 23 May 1913, FO 371/1624.

³³ See for example, Ch'en Po-ta, *Ch'ieh-kuo ta-tao Yüan shih-k'ai* [Yüan Shih-k'ai—destroyer of the republic], p. 21, quoting *Shih Pao,* 24 May 1913. For Ts'en's attitude, see Shen, *I-yün hui-i,* I, p. 121.

³⁴ See record of the interview in Jordan to Grey, no. 234, 5 June 1913, FO 371/1624.

³⁵ Pearl, *Morrison of Peking,* p. 286.

³⁶ Actually China got less than £21 million after various bank charges were deducted; see Liu Ping-lin, *Chin-tai Chung-kuo wai-tsai shih-kao* [History of foreign debts of modern China], p. 106; and Hsü I-sheng, *Chung-kuo chin-tai wai-tsai shih t'ung-chi tzu-liao 1853–1927* [Statistical materials relating to foreign debts of modern China], p. 109.

³⁷ *Treaties,* II, p. 1013; and Chia Shih-i, *Min-kuo ch'u-nien ti chi jen ts'ai-cheng tsung-chang* [Ministers of finance of the early Chinese republic], p. 26.

³⁸ It is not possible to be more definite without having full details of the expenditure of the reorganization loan.

³⁹ Chou Shu-chen, grandaughter of Chou Hsüeh-hsi, *Chou Chi-an hsien-sheng pieh-ch'uan* [Biography of Chou Hsüeh-hsi], p. 81. Chou is said to have hoped that the loan would, if spent as designed, rehabilitate China's finances in a matter of six months; see Chia, *Min-kuo ch'u-nien ti chi jen ts'ai-cheng tsung-chang,* pp. 27–28.

⁴⁰ Jordan to Grey, annual report for 1913, FO 405/229.

⁴¹ Quite a number of Kuomintang generals at Nanking were bribed. The biographer of Huang Hsing attributes Huang's defeat largely to this; see Li, 'Huang K'e-chiang hsien-sheng nien-p'u kao', p. 377.

⁴² Tyler, *Pulling strings in China,* pp. 230–37.

[43] During the war a number of foreign, particularly English naval men were employed in the Chinese navy; see Chung-kuo chin-tai ching-chi shih tzu-liao ts'ung-k'an p'ien-chi wei-yüan hui, *Chung-kuo hai-kuan yü Chung-Jih chan-cheng* [The Chinese Customs and the Sino-Japanese War], in the series *Ti-kuo chü-i yü Chung-kuo kai-kuan* [Imperialism and the Chinese Customs], pp. 88–111. Tyler's own narrative of his service in the war and as adviser is enclosed in Satow to Lansdowne, private, 3 October 1905, FO 800/121.

[44] Fulford to Alston, no. 93, conf., 19 July 1913, FO 671/357.

[45] Stephen to Hillier, 17 July 1913, FO 228/2498.

[46] Alston to Fulford, tel. 20 July 1913, FO 228/1498; and Alston to Grey, tel. 164, 20 July 1913, FO 371/1624.

[47] Tyler, *Pulling strings in China,* pp. 240–41; Shao Yüan-ch'ung, *Ch'en Ying-shih hsien-sheng ke-ming hsiao-shih* [Brief history of the revolutionary career of Ch'en Ch'i-mei], pp. 10–11; and Alston to Grey, no. 320, draft, 15 August 1913, FO 228/1500.

[48] Alston to Grey, no. 367, 22 September 1913, FO 371/1625.

[49] Jordan to Langley, private, 8 February 1914, FO 350/12.

[50] For details of Yüan's autocratic measures between July 1913 and December 1914, see Hornbeck, *Contemporary politics in the Far East,* pp. 48–58; F. W. Houn, *Central government of China 1912–1928,* pp. 86–92; Li Shou-k'ung, *Min-ch'u chih kuo-kui* [The parliament in the early republican years], pp. 118–44; Liu, *Chung-kuo hsien-cheng shih-hua,* pp. 48–51; and Ch'ien Tuan-sheng etc., *Min-kuo cheng-chih shih* [History of the administrative system of the Chinese republic], I, pp. 66–103.

[51] Jordan to Langley, private, 20 April 1914, FO 350/12.

[52] Jordan to Langley, private, 30 November 1913, 4 May, 25 October, and 24 November 1914, FO 350/12. According to Ou Tsung-yu, *Chung-kuo yen-cheng hsiao-shih* [A brief history of the Chinese salt administration], pp. 74–75, annual income from salt to the central government during the late Ch'ing period had never exceeded 13 million yüan (Chinese dollar), but in 1914 it was 69,494,915 yüan. See also Ho Wei-ning, *Chung-kuo yen-cheng-shih* [History of the Chinese salt administration], II, p. 428; W.R.S., 'The Chinese Salt Administration', in C. F. Remer, *Readings in economics for China,* p. 289; and S. A. M. Adshead, 'The reform of the Chinese Salt Administration (1913–1918)', in East Asian Research Centre, Harvard University, *Papers on China* XVIII (December 1964), pp. 55–89.

[53] Jordan to Langley, private, 6 April 1914, FO 350/12.

[54] Jordan to Langley, private, 28 October 1914, FO 350/12.

CHAPTER V THE MONARCHICAL MOVEMENT (pp. 76-100)

¹ Huang I, *Yüan-shih tao-kuo chi* [History of the stealing of the republic by Yüan Shih-k'ai], in *CHST*, p. 21; and T'ao, *Pei-yang chün-fa t'ung-chih shih-chih shih-hua*, II, pp. 90-94. Jordan also refers to the Imperialist Restoration Movement *(Fu-pi yün-tung)* in his private letter to Langley, 2 December 1914, FO 350/12.

² *Cheng-chih shih,* II, p. 419. Soon after the Monarchical Movement had formally begun, Liang publicly denounced it in an article entitled 'I-tsai so-wei kuo-t'i wen-t'i che' [What strangeness, the so-called question of the form of government]. Liang refused to withhold publication of the article, even when offered $20 thousand; see Liang Ch'i-ch'ao, *Tun-pi chi* [Collected cables, documents, articles etc. in support of the Yunnan declaration of independence against the regime of Yüan Shih-k'ai in 1916], in *CCST*, part 4, p. 80; and J. R. Levenson, *Liang Ch'i-ch'ao and the mind of modern China,* p. 179.

³ This allegation has been both endorsed and repudiated. For support see, for example, Putnam Weale (pseud.), *The fight for the Republic in China,* pp. 123-24, 146; Liu Yen, *Chung-kuo wai-chiao shih* [History of China's foreign relations], p. 446; Liu Yen, *Ti-kuo chü-i ya-pe Chung-kuo shih* [China under the oppression of imperialism], p. 66; and Pai Chiao, *Yüan Shih-k'ai yü Chung-hua min-kuo* [Yüan Shih-k'ai and the Chinese republic], in *CHST*, p. 139.

For refutation of the statement. see Chang Chung-fu, *Chung-hua min-kuo wai-chiao shih* [History of China's foreign relations], p. 180; Wang Yün-sheng, *Liu-shih nien lai Chung-kuo yü Jih-pen* [Documents on Sino-Japanese relations for the last sixty years], VII, pp. 1-2; and Shih Chün-min, *Chung-Jih kuo-chi shih* [Sino-Japanese diplomatic history], pp. 149-50. In my opinion, it is not likely that Yüan had accepted such a bribe from Japan, even if it had in fact been offered. The Sino-Japanese negotiations over the demands lasted for four months, during which time there were over twenty conferences. Yüan seemed to have done his best to minimize Japan's demands, and he allowed the long-censored press to agitate against Japan, see Chow Ts'e-tsung, *The May Fourth Movement,* p. 21. The revolutionary Huang Hsing, in exile abroad, telegraphed to Yüan, pledging his support; see Hsüeh, *Huang Hsing and the Chinese Rrevolution,* p. 53. After the Sino-Japanese treaty was signed, Yüan expressed to Jordan his pride in having successfully rejected the fifth group of Japan's demands; see Jordan to Langley, private, 10 June 1915, FO 350/13. Moreover, according to Jansen, *The Japanese and Sun Yat-sen,* p. 194, Japan's hatred of Yüan intensified after the incident and Tokyo became determined to oust him from the Chinese scene. Following this line of argument is also P. Lowe, 'Great Britain, Japan and the fall of Yüan Shih-k'ai, 1915-1916', *The Historical Journal* XIII, 4 (1970), pp. 719-20. However, the allegation, true or otherwise, has gained popular belief.

⁴ Liang Ch'i-ch'ao, *Yin-ping shih wen-chi* [Collected works and essays of the ice-drinker's studio], LVI, p. 14b; T'ao, *Pei-yang chün-fa t'ung-chih shih-chih shih-hua,* II, p. 99; and Putnam Weale, *The fight for the Republic in China,* p. 137, note 1.

[5] T'ao, *Pei-yang chün-fa t'ung-chih shih-chih shih-hua*, II, pp. 103–4. For an analysis of Chang Tso-lin's intention in giving his support, see Sonoda Ikki, *Kaiketsu Chō saku-rin* [Biography of Chang Tso-lin], p. 88–90.

[6] Hence the title of Liang Ch'i ch'ao's article mentioned in note 2. The society was sponsored by well-known figures of the day: Yang Tu, who was the leader of the group, Sun Yün-yu, Liu Shih-pei, Wu Ying, Yen Fu and Li Hsieh-ho. Together they were called the 'six gentlemen' *(liu chün-tzu)*. Details about them are available in T'ao Chü-yin, *Liu chün-tzu ch'uan* [Biography of the six gentlemen], pp. 238–40. For Yen Fu's rationale in supporting the movement, see B. Schwartz, *In search of wealth and power, Yen Fu and the West*, pp. 223–28.

[7] For the full text of Goodnow's memorandum, see *Peking Gazette*, 17 August 1915, enclosed in Jordan to Grey, no. 214, 25 August 1915, FO 371/2338.

[8] Jordan to Langley, private, 19 August, and 7 September 1915, FO 350/13; and Jordan to Grey, no. 234, 10 September 1915, FO 371/2338. As far as Jordan's approval of the principle of monarchy in China is concerned, it has even been alleged that he had told Yüan before the war broke out that Britain welcomed the idea of his becoming emperor, see for example, Liu Yü-sheng, *Shih-ts'ai t'ang tsa-i* [Reminiscences of Liu Yü-sheng], p. 174.

[9] See for example, Jordan to Campbell, private, 11 January 1904, FO 350/3.

[10] Jordan to Satow, then minister at Peking, private, 16 December 1903, FO 350/3.

[11] Jordan to Satow, private, 17 January 1904, FO 350/3.

[12] Jordan to Campbell, private, 9 February 1904, FO 350/3.

[13] See for example, Jordan to Campbell, private, 15 February, 22 February, 16 March, and 7 June 1904, FO 350/3.

[14] Jordan to Campbell, private, 15 February, and 17 June 1904, Fo 350/3.

[15] Jordan sided with the Japanese in preventing the Korean court from appointing a new minister to London—a step towards converting Korea into a Japanese protectorate; see Jordan to Campbell, private, 23 November, and 2 December 1904, FO 350/3. For Russo-Japanese relations in East Asia during the period when Jordan was British representative in Seoul, see G. A. Lensen (ed.), *Korea and Manchuria between Russia and Japan 1895–1904*.

[16] See chapter II, pp. 27–28.

[17] See for example, Li Tze-fun, *Chung-Jih kuan-hsi shih* [History of Sino-Japanese relations], pp. 477–82; and Li Yu-shu, *Chung-Jih erh-shih-i t'iao chiao-she* [Sino-Japanese negotiation over the Twenty-one Demands], pp. 49–57.

[18] The most authoritative work on this subject is certainly E. W. Edwards, 'Great Britain and the Manchurian railway question, 1909–10', *English Historical Review* LXXXI (1966), pp. 740–69. The article contains several references to Jordan's attitude towards the matter. See also Li, *ibid.*, pp. 57–58; and Huang Cheng-ming, *Chung-kuo wai-chiao shih* [Diplomatic history of China], pp. 240–42.

[19] See for example, Jordan to Campbell, private, 18 February 1909, FO 350/5.

[20] Jordan to Langley, private, 23 February 1914, FO 350/12.

[21] Jordan to Grey, no. 269, 27 July 1914, FO 371/1942.

[22] The Foreign Office was, at first, not averse to the idea of co-operation with the Japanese in the Yangtze area; see Lowe, *Great Britain and Japan 1911–15*, p. 152.

[23] Jordan to Grey, tel. 31, 19 February 1914, FO 371/1941.

[24] See for example, Jordan to Grey, no. 63, conf., 10 February 1914, FO 371/1940; Jordan to Grey, tel. 31, 19 February 1914, in which Jordan urged a definite and firm policy, no. 77, 21 February, and Grey to Jordan, tel. 32, 25 February 1914, FO 371/1941. See also J. O. P. Bland, 'The future of China', *Edinburgh Review* CCXX (October, 1914), p. 443.

[25] Materials relating to these railway plans of Japan are found in abundance in FO 371/1941, 1942. See also Kajima Morinosuke, *Nihon gaiko seisaku no shiteki kosatsu* [A historical study of Japan's foreign policy], pp. 454–56; and Lowe, *Great Britain and Japan 1911–15*, pp. 148–68, 171–76.

[26] Jordan to Grey, tel. 38, 25 February, no. 89, 28 February, tel. 47, 5 March, no. 96, 7 March 1914, FO 371/1941; and Jordan to Langley, private, 23 February 1914, FO 350/12.

[27] For details of the company's programme, see Conyngham Greene, British ambassador in Tokyo, to Grey, tel. 17, 13 March 1914, FO 371/1941; and no. 79, conf., 19 March 1914, FO 371/1942. See also Lowe, *Great Britain and Japan 1911–15*, pp. 169–70.

[28] See for example, Jordan to Langley, private, 23 February 1914, FO 350/12.

[29] See for example, Jordan to Grey, no. 135, conf., 30 March 1914, FO 371/1942.

[30] Nihon kokusai seiji gakukai, *Nihon gaikoshi kenkyu—daiichi sekai daisen* [Studies on diplomatic history of Japan—the World War I], p. 3.

[31] Jordan to Grey, tel. 146, secret, 9 August 1914, FO 371/2016.

[32] Greene to Grey, tel. 71, 10 August 1914, FO 371/2016. It appears that it was Greene who told the Japanese of Jordan's attitude; see Kajima Morinosuke, *Nihon gaikoshi* [Diplomatic history of Japan], p. 790.

[33] May to Jordan, tel., 9 August 1914, FO 228/2306.

[34] Lowe, *Great Britain and Japan 1911–15*, pp. 185–86; and Nihon Kokusai seiji gakukai, *Nihon gaikoshi kenkyu—daiichi sekai daisen*, p. 5.

[35] Greene to Grey, tel. 72, 10 August 1914, and Japanese memorandum to the Foreign Office of the same date, FO 371/2016.

[36] Grey to Greene, tel. 47, 11 August 1914, FO 371/1016.

[37] Jordan to Grey, tel. 153, secret, 11 August 1914, FO 371/2016.

[38] Greene to Grey, tel. 94, 19 August 1914, FO 371/2017.

[39] Jordan to Grey, tel. 153, secret, 11 August, tel. 162, 13 August 1914. In this Jordan says that without a public statement 'we should be making a false start'. Also tel. 163, 14 August 1914, FO 371/2016.

[40] As soon as Britain had agreed to Japan's participation in the war on 10 August, Admiral Jerram of the China Station was instructed to leave the Japanese navy to defend the China seas north of Hong Kong. During the war, the station was increasingly depleted of strength; see I. H. Nish, 'Admiral Jerram and the German Pacific fleet 1913–15', *The Mariner's Mirror* LVI, no. 4 (1970), p. 421.

[41] Jordan to Grey, tels. 156 and 158, secret, 12 August 1914, FO 371/2016. Besides Japan, Jordan seemed to have another reason for objecting to a direct German restoration of Kiaochow to China. Since the outbreak of war, Jordan had been extremely irritated by the fact that Tsingtao was used by the Germans as a base for antagonistic activities in the Far East. In the case of a direct restoration, German influence in the place could not be eradicated; see T'ao, *Pei-yang chün-fa t'ung-chih shih-chih shih-hua*, II, pp. 46–47. T'an T'ien-k'ai says in his work that Yüan thought of using his own military strength to take Tsingtao back. He is certainly incorrect in asserting that Yüan's plan had the support of Jordan, in *Shan-tung wen-t'i shih-mo* [The Shangtung question], p. 31. Also see Feng-djen Djang, *The diplomatic relations between China and Germany since 1898*, p. 174.

[42] Grey to Jordan, tel. 140, and Grey to Greene, tel. 50, 12 August 1914, FO 371/2016.

[43] Jordan to Grey, tel. 165, 17 August 1914, FO 371/2016. For an explanation of Japan's action, see Greene to Grey, tel. 100, conf., 20 August 1914, FO 371/2017.

[44] A lucid account of the Japanese and British landing in Shantung and the steps by which the Japanese occupied the Kiao-Tsi Railway, together with a sketch, is found in Li, *Chung-Jih kuan-hsi shih*, p. 492.

[45] For example, Jordan to Grey, tel. 205, 29 September, and tel. 208, 30 September 1914, FO 371/2017.

[46] Lowe, *Great Britain and Japan 1911–15*, p. 796.

[47] Japanese troops involved in the event were about 20 thousand as opposed to about 1,000 British soldiers, Li, *Chung-Jih kuan-hsi shih*, p. 492.

[48] Lowe, *Great Britain and Japan 1911–15*, pp. 197–98.

[49] Details of Anglo-Japanese relations in the incident up to this stage are available in Lowe, *Great Britain and Japan 1911–15*, pp. 229–32.

[50] Jordan was aware of Kato's opinion of him for some time before the event; see Jordan to Langley, private, 2 October 1914, FO 350/12.

[51] Jordan to Grey, tel. 19, 29 January 1915, FO 371/2322. According to Morrison, Jordan complained to him on 29 January, apparently before Hioki made the oral communication: 'The Japanese have kept him in entire ignorance of the demands have said nothing to him at all . . . and he knows nothing more than the man in the street. He presumes only that the F.O. may know something but he is not sure'; see Pearl, *Morrison of Peking*, p. 308.

[52] Lowe, *Great Britain and Japan 1911–15*, p. 231.

[53] Lowe, *Great Britain and Japan 1911–15*, p. 231; and Jordan to Langley, private, 15 February 1915, FO 350/13.

[54] The Foreign Office, and particularly Alston, believed that Kato was deliberate in concealing the terms from Jordan, see Alston's minute on Greene to Grey, tel. 78, 22 February 1915, FO 371/2322. However, one is left with the question why the Foreign Office did not send Jordan a copy of the demands given it by Japan.

[55] Note 51 to this chapter.

[56] Jordan to Grey, tel. 27, 8 February 1915, FO 371/2322.

[57] Jordan to Langley, private, 15 February 1915, FO 350/13.

[58] Events prior to the writing of the memorandum are recorded in Lowe, *Great Britain and Japan 1911–15*, pp. 238–40.

[59] Alston to Jordan, private, 19 March 1915, FO 350/14; and Jordan to Alston, private, 6 May 1915, FO 350/13.

[60] Lo Kuang, *Lu Cheng-hsiang ch'üan* [Biography of Lu Cheng-hsiang], pp. 101–2; and Li, *Chung-Jih erh-shih-i t'iao chiao-she*, I, pp. 350–52.

[61] Lowe, *Great Britain and Japan 1911–15*, pp. 235, 246.

[62] For attitude of the *Genro*, see, for example, Shinobu Seizaburō, *Taisho seijishi* [Political history of the Taisho period], p. 254.

[63] To compare the original and revised versions of the demands, see texts in Li, *Chung-Jih kuan-hsi shih*, pp. 493–501.

[64] Jordan to Grey, tel. 102, 29 April 1915, FO 371/2323.

[65] Jordan to Grey, tel. 110, 5 May 1915, FO 371/2324.

[66] Jordan to Grey, tel. 119, conf., 8 May 1915, FO 371/2324. According to the biography of Lu, Jordan said something more. He urged China to accept Japan's modified terms since, militarily speaking, she was in no position to do otherwise. But China should spend the next ten years on military reorganization after which she could deal squarely with Japan; see Lo, *Lu Cheng-hsiang ch'uan*, p. 104.

[67] Jordan to Grey, tel. 122, 8 May 1915, FO 371/2324; and Lo, *Lu Cheng-hsiang ch'uan*, p. 104. According to another source, however, Tuan chi-jui, the minister of war, advocated armed resistance, see Wang, *Liu-shih nien lai Chung-kuo yü Jih-pen*, VI, pp. 310–11. For a lucid account of the Sino-Japanese negotiations throughout the crisis over the demands, see M. Chi, *China diplomacy, 1914–1918*, pp. 41–43, 50–59.

[68] Jordan to Alston, private, 6 May 1915, FO 350/13.

[69] Greene to Grey, tel. 175, 8 May 1915, on which Alston minutes sarcastically: 'Contrast Baron Kato's desire for Sir John Jordan's good offices at the eleventh hour with his mistrust of him at the first!', FO 371/2324; also *The Times*, 24 May 1915.

[70] See for example, Alston's and Langley's minutes on Jordan to Grey, no. 83, conf., 7 April 1915, FO 371/2324.

[71] Jordan to Grey, tel. 106, conf., 3 May 1915, FO 371/2324.

[72] Many revolutionaries were willing to renounce their differences so that Yüan could concentrate entirely on dealing with Japan. As mentioned in note 3 to this chapter, Huang Hsing, still in exile on account of the 1913 Revolution, publicly declared his support for Yüan. See also Li, *Chung-Jih kuan-hsi shih*, pp. 497, 505.

[73] According to the biographer of Lu Cheng-hsiang, Yüan studied the demands laboriously and minuted on each of them as to how the Chinese negotiators should allow it to be discussed; see Lo, *Lu Cheng-hsiang ch'üan*, p. 102. See also Jordan to Langley, private, 10 June 1915, FO 350/13; T. E. La Fargue, *China and the World War*, pp. 76–78; and Shih, *Chung-Jih kuo-chi shih*, pp. 149–50.

[74] Jordan to Langley, private, 13 May 1915, FO 350/13.

[75] A vivid comparison between the two organizations and the circumstances under which they were formed is given in Li Tsung-huang etc., *Yün-nan ch'i-yi yung-hu kung-ho wu-shih chou-nien te-k'an* [Special issue on the 50th anniversary of the Yunnan uprising 1915–1916], p. 84. For the correspondence of the Society for the Planning of Peace from 22 August to 29 September 1915, see Ch'ou-an hui (ed.), *Chün-hsien wen-t'i wen-t'ien hui-p'ien* [Correspondence relating to the monarchical movement], in *CCST*, pp. 3–57. Liang Shih-i has frequently been accused as the arch-sinner in the monarchical plot. Some works, however, suggest that Liang objected to the move at the beginning, for example, Huang, *Yüan-shih tao-kuo chi*, pp. 24–26; and Ts'en, *San-shui Liang Yen-sun hsien-sheng nien-p'u*, I, pp. 267–71. Ts'en in his anxiety to defend the hero of his biography, implies on p. 280 that Liang had still not been involved by 19 September. This view is negated, however, by Jordan's account of the interview on 3 September in which Liang wanted to find out Jordan's reaction to the monarchical plan, see note 8 to this chapter.

[76] A list of the organizations in Peking associated with the Association to Petition for a Monarchy is given in Huang, *Yüan-shih tao-kuo chi*, pp. 31–32; and Ch'en, *Ch'ieh-kuo ta-tao Yüan Shih-k'ai*, p. 50.

[77] Jordan to Langley, private, 23 September 1915, FO 350/13.

[78] Jordan enclosed Ōkuma's statement in his letter to Langley, 23 September 1915, FO 350/13.

[79] See for example, Kwanha Yim, 'Yüan Shih-k'ai and the Japanese', in *Journal of Asian Studies* XXXIV, no. 1 (November 1964), p. 64.

[80] Jordan to Langley, private, 23 September 1915, FO 350/13.

[81] Jordan to Grey, tel. 30, 12 February 1915, FO 371/2322; and Jordan to Langley, private, 20 October 1915, FO 350/13.

[82] A report of the movement at this stage is found in Jordan to Grey, no. 253, 1 October 1915, 371/2338.

[83] Grey to Jordan, tel. 214, 8 October 1915, FO 371/2338.

[84] The letter, Jordan to Langley, private, 23 September, in which Jordan enclosed Ōkuma's statement, had still not reached the Foreign Office; see Grey to Jordan, tel. 217, 12 October 1915, FO 371/2338; and Langley to Jordan, private, 14 October 1915, FO 350/14. Greene, treating Ōkuma's statement as 'one of His Excellency's usual irresponsible utterances', sent it to the Foreign Office by ordinary mail; see Greene to Grey, tel. 397, 13 October 1915, FO 371/2338.

[85] Jordan to Grey, tel. 251, 11 October 1915, FO 371/2338. According to the Japanese archives, Jordan again, as in the 1911 Revolution, fell a prey to the manipulating and scheming skill of Yüan. At this particular meeting,

Jordan appeared to have been more than usually convinced by Yüan's arguments and assurances. On the following day it was said in the Chinese press that Jordan had explicitly pledged support to the monarchy. Although the Chinese foreign ministry corrected the statement afterwards, the desired effect was achieved; see Obata to Kato, no. 550, 8 October 1915, *NGB*, LXXXI (1915), pp. 68–72, enclosing the cuttings of a dialogue which was supposed to have passed between Yüan and Jordan from *The Peking Daily News* of 7 October and the Chinese corrective statement from *The Asiatic Daily News*, which was the propaganda organ of Yüan. For the role of *The Asiatic Daily News* in the monarchical movement, see Ko Kung-chen, *Chung-kuo pao-hsüeh shih* [History of journalism in China], pp. 241–42, 245. See also Li Nai-han, *Hsin-hai ke-ming yü Yüan Shih-k'ai* [The 1911 Revolution and Yüan Shih-k'ai], pp. 119–20.

⁸⁶ See for example, Jordan to Langley, private, 20 October 1915, FO 350/13.

⁸⁷ Grey to Jordan, tel. 217, 12 October 1915, FO 371/2338.

⁸⁸ Ishii to Inouye, no. 265, urgent, 15 October 1915, *NGB*, LXXXI, pp. 74–76. In his recollection Ishii writes that at that time he felt that 'the Allies were too preoccupied on the European fronts . . . and consequently the duty of nipping the Chinese upheaval in the bud fell entirely on the shoulders of Japan'; see Ishii Kikujiro (W. R. Langdon trs.), *Diplomatic commentaries*, p. 94.

⁸⁹ Ishii to Inouye, no. 266, urgent, 15 October 1915, *NGB*, LXXXI, p. 76. The description of the attitude of the officials named is generally a correct one, see *Cheng-chih shih*, II, pp. 432–34; Ching-min (pseud.), *Hsü Shih-ch'ang*, in *CCST*, pp. 28–31; Chia, *Min-kuo ch'u-nien ti chi jen ts'ai-cheng tsung-chang*, p. 30; Shen, *I-yün hui-i*, I, p. 130; Shen, *Li Yüan-hung p'ing-ch'uan*, pp. 67–69; Lai-chiang cho-wu (pseud.), *Tuan Ch'i-jui pi-shih* [Secret history of Tuan Ch'i-jui], pp. 14–15; and Fei Ching-chung, *Tuan ch'i-jui*, in *CCST*, pp. 43–44.

⁹⁰ Paper communicated by ambassador Inouye, 18 October 1915, FO 371/2338.

⁹¹ Grey to Jordan, tel. 221, 18 October 1915, FO 371/2338.

⁹² Obata to Ishii, no. 570, 18 October, and no. 576, urgent, 20 October 1915, *NGB*, LXXXI, pp. 81–83.

⁹³ Jordan to Grey, tel. 260, 19 October 1915, FO 371/2338.

⁹⁴ Jordan to Grey, tel. 262, 21 October 1915, FO 371/2338.

⁹⁵ Jordan to Langley, private, 20 October 1915, FO 350/13.

⁹⁶ Jordan to Langley, private, 20 October 1915, FO 350/13; and Jordan to Grey, tel. 262, 21 October 1915, FO 371/2338.

⁹⁷ Langley's minute on Jordan to Grey, tel. 262, 21 October 1915, FO 371/2338.

⁹⁸ Japanese memorandum, 24 October 1915, FO 371/2338.

⁹⁹ Jordan to Grey, tel. 265, 25 October 1915, FO 371/2338.

¹⁰⁰ Grey to Jordan, tel. 225, 25 October 1915, FO 371/2338.

¹⁰¹ Jordan to Grey, tel. 272, 28 October 1915, FO 371/2338.

¹⁰² Jordan to Langley, private, 4 November 1915, FO 350/13.

[103] Telegrams from the Chinese minister in Tokyo, Lu Tsung-yü, show that during that time Japanese warships were being mobilized, a second warning was being prepared, and Lu was repeatedly threatened by the Japanese foreign ministry; see Wang, *Liu-shih nien lai Chung-kuo yü Jih-pen*, VII, pp. 14–15.

[104] Jordan to Grey, tel. 287, 9 November 1915, 371/2338.

[105] Jordan to Grey, tel. 294, 11 November 1915, FO 371/2338.

[106] Inouye to Foreign Office, 18 November 1915, FO 371/2338.

[107] Yüan has always been accused of having forged the result, see Huang, *Yüan-shih tao-kuo chi*, pp. 90–91; Liang, *Tun-pi chi*, part 4, pp. 23–43; and a booklet entitled *Yüan Shih-k'ai wei-tsao min-i chi shih* [The people's will: an exposure of the political intrigues at Peking against the Republic of China].

[108] Li Tsung-huang, 'Yün-nan chi-i yü Shang-hai chih kuan-hsi' [The Yunnan uprising and Shanghai], in *Chung-kuo ti-fang tzu-chih* [Chinese local self-government], XII, no. 10 (January, 1960), p. 19.

[109] The only exception was the *Shun-t'ien shih-pao*, a Chinese newspaper in Peking run by the Japanese, which was outspokenly against the monarchy; see Ku, *Chung-kuo pao-hsüeh shih*, pp. 110, 241; Huang Shao-hung, *Wu-shih hui-i* [Memory of fifty years], pp. 28–29. For Yüan's censorship of the press, see Ma Yin-liang, *A brief history of the press*, p. 18; Tseng Hsü-pai, *Chung-kuo hsin-wen shih* [History of mass communication in China] in *Ta-hsüeh hsin-wen hsüeh ts'ung-shu* [Series on mass communication at university level], pp. 266–67, 273, 275, 281, 293–96; and Chang Ching-lu (ed.), *Chung-kuo chin-tai ch'u-pan shih-liao* [Materials relating to the history of publication in China], II, p. 304.

[110] For details of the convention, see Huang, *Yüan-shih tao-kuo chi*, pp. 68–83.

[111] Jordan to Grey, tel. 346, 15 December 1915, FO 371/2338.

[112] For details of awards, see *Cheng-fu kung-pao*, the official daily publication of the government in Peking, from date to about the end of the year.

[113] A piece of enjoyable and interesting reading which throws some light on German activities in Shanghai is found in L. Thomas, *Lauterback of the China Sea*, pp. 203–8.

[114] See for example, Jordan to Grey, tel. 354, 21 December 1915, FO 371/2338.

[115] Buchanan to Grey, tel. 1874, 14 December 1915, FO 371/2338.

[116] Bertie to Grey, tel. 1032, 21 December 1915, FO 371/2338.

[117] Alston's and Langley's minutes on Buchanan to Grey, tel. 1874, 14 December 1915, FO 371/2338.

[118] Grey to Jordan, tel. 293, conf., 16 December 1915, FO 371/2338.

[119] Jordan to Grey, tel. 347, conf., 17 December 1915, FO 371/2338.

[120] Jordan to Langley, private, 21 December 1915, FO 350/13.

[121] Jordan to Grey, tel. 351, conf., 19 December 1915, FO 371/2338.

[122] Jordan to Langley, private, 14 January 1916, FO 350/15.

[123] Goffe to Jordan in Jordan to Grey, tel. 6, 5 January 1916, FO 371/2644.

[124] Ts'ai O was the leader in the 1911 Revolution in Yunnan. With the establishment of the Chinese republic, Ts'ai became the first *tu-tu* of the province. However, being suspected and feared by Yüan Shih-k'ai, he was soon transferred from Yunnan to Peking where he was kept under strict surveillance. As the monarchical movement became more and more apparent, Ts'ai, to divert Yüan's attention, feigned wantonness by frequenting the dissolute quarters in the city and becoming conspicuously intimate with the well-known prostitute Little Balsam *(Hsiao Feng-hsien)*. At the end of November he succeeded in slipping away from Peking, and arrived in Tientsin from where he left for Japan at the beginning of December. He sailed from Japan and on 19 December arrived in Yunnan where he still retained much of his former popularity with the troops. For details of Ts'ai's activities in Yunnan in the 1911 Revolution, see Chung-kuo ko-hsüeh yüan li-shih yen-chiu so ti san so, *Yün-nan Kuei-chou hsin-hai ke-ming tzu-liao* [Materials relating to the 1911 Revolution in Yunnan and Kweichow], pp. 97–120. For the rest, see T'an Hsi-k'ang, *Ts'ai Sung-po ku-shih* [The story of Ts'ai O], pp. 6–16.

[125] A detailed description of the military plan is given in Yü En-yang, an important official in the military government of Yunnan, *Yün-nan shou-i yung-hu kung-ho shih-mo chi* [History of the Yunnan uprising of 1916 against Yüan Shih-k'ai] in *YSH,* pp. 125–29. It appears, however, that T'ang did not lead troops into Kweichow as planned, but remained to oversee matters in Yunnan. See also Tung-nan p'ien-chi she, *T'ang Chi-yao,* in *CCST,* pp. 63–64.

[126] See for example, Goffe to Jordan, tel. 66, 27 December 1915, FO 228/1952.

[127] Jordan to Grey, no. 6, 5 January 1916, FO 371/2644. Yüan himself considered these steps adequate to meet the Yunnan exigency. According to Ts'ao Ju-lin, who had by then become Yüan's trusted subordinate, Yüan was not the least disturbed at the beginning of the uprising; see his *I-sheng chih hui-i* [Reminiscences], p. 154.

[128] Details of Yüan's military arrangements against Ts'ai are available in Chang Chün-ku, *Wu P'ei-fu ch'uan* [Biography of Wu P'ei-fu], I, p. 158. Wu P'ei-fu was the commander of the Sixty Brigade of the Third Division which was ordered to Szechwan. The strength of the government forces is attested by General Feng Yü-hsiang, commander of one of the three mixed brigades originally in Szechwan, who recalls in his autobiography that although he was in sympathy with Ts'ai O and his movement he could do nothing because he was hemmed in by government troops; see his *Wo-ti sheng-huo* [My life], part 2, pp. 1–21. This is confirmed in Ts'ai's telegram from Szechwan to T'ang Chi-yao, see Ts'ai O, *Sung-po chün-chung i-mo* [Writings of Ts'ai O while fighting against Yüan Shih-k'ai's monarchy], in *CCST,* pp. 30–31.

[129] Jordan to Grey, tel. 49, 30 January 1916, FO 371/2644.

[130] Jordan to Grey, tel. 10, 7 January 1916, FO 371/2644. Also Jordan to Grey, tel. 21, 13 January, and confidential clause of tel. 35, 19 January 1916, FO 371/2644.

131 Jordan to Grey, tel. 8, conf., 6 January, and tel. 10, 7 January 1916, FO 371/2644.

132 See for example, Jordan to Langley, private, 14 January 1916, FO 350/5.

133 Jordan to Grey, tel. 20, 12 January 1916, FO 371/2644.

134 Yim, 'Yüan Shih-k'ai and the Japanese', p. 70.

135 Lu's telegrams are available in Wang, *Liu-shih nien lai Chung-kuo yü Jih-pen,* VII, pp. 34–37.

136 Jordan to Grey, tel. 37, 21 January 1916, FO 371/2644.

137 Details of fighting in the period from the points of view of the government and rebel troops are available respectively in Chang, *Wu P'ei-fu ch'uan,* I, pp. 161–65; and Liu Ts'un-hou, *Hu-kuo ch'uan-chün chan-chi* [The record of fighting of the Szechwan army to protect the republic], pp. 12–18. See also Chien Lu (pseud. ?), 'Min-kuo Ssu-ch'uan ta-shi chi (18)' [Important happenings in Szechwan during the Chinese republican period], in *Ssu-ch'uan wen-hsien* [Materials relating to Szechwan], no. 47 (September, 1962), pp. 25–27.

138 For accounts of the government capture of Luchow, see Chang, *Wu P'ei-fu ch'uan,* I, pp. 165–71; and Liu, *Hu-kuo ch'uan-chün chan-chi,* pp.18–21.

139 Goffe to Jordan, no. 10, 16 February 1916, FO 228/1985.

140 Jordan to Grey, tel. 80, conf., 1 March 1916, FO 371/1645.

141 J. L. Smith, consul-general at Chengtu, to Jordan, no. 11, 5 March, tel. 19, 8 March, and tel. 20, 10 March 1916, FO 228/2736. Also Yü, *Yün-nan shou-i yung-hu kung-ho shih-mo chi,* pp. 383–84.

142 Goffe to Jordan, tel. 44, v. conf., 29 February 1916, FO 228/1736.

143 Jordan's minute on Goffe to Jordan, tel. 44, v. conf., 29 February 1916, *ibid;* and Jordan to Goffe, tel. 21, v. conf., 2 March 1916, FO 228/2736.

144 Goffe to Jordan, tel. 46, 2 March 1916, FO 228/2736.

145 Jordan to Grey, tel. 87, secret, 8 March 1916, FO 371/2645.

146 See for example, Goffe to Jordan, tel. 50, 4 March 1916, FO 228/2736.

147 Postscript of Jordan to Grey, no. 67, 8 March 1916, draft, FO 228/2736.

148 Jordan to Grey, tel. 87, secret, 8 March 1916, FO 371/2645.

149 Jordan to Langley, private, 1 February 1916, FO 350/15; Jordan to Grey, tel. 87, secret, 8 March 1916, *ibid;* and Jordan to Grey, no. 70, conf., draft, 13 March 1916, FO 228/2736. For details of Aoki, see Yim, 'Yüan Shih-k'ai and the Japanese' p. 68; and Jordan to Langley, private, 12 September 1916, FO 350/15. A lucid description of anti-Yüan activities carried out in and from Shanghai and the role of Aoki and his Japanese colleagues in them is available in Li, *Yün-nan chi-i yung-hu kung-ho wu-shih chou-nien chi-nien te-k'an,* pp. 23–25. See also Li, 'Yün-nan chi-i yü Shang-hai chi kuan-hsi', p. 19.

150 Wilton, acting consul-general, to Jordan, tel. 29, 16 March, tel. 36, 23 March, and Jamieson to Jordan, no. 60, 3 April 1916, FO 228/2736. As a result of the independence of Kwangsi, the Kwangtung troops became sandwiched between Yunnan and Kwangsi. As it turned out, the Yunnan and

Kwangsi troops joined forces and Lung Chin-kuang was forced to telegraph
his brother to declare independence in Canton; see Yü, *Yün-nan shou-i
yung-hu kung-ho shih-mo chi,* pp. 394–95, 418–19. For Lung T'i-ch'ien's
activities in Yunnan, see *ibid;* and Liu, *Hu-kuo ch'uan-chün chan-chi,* p. 30.

[151] Jordan to Grey, tel., private and secret, 20 March 1916, FO 371/2645.

[152] This adjective applies to all those who were not basically against Yüan
but were forced by circumstances to take such a stand.

[153] For a lucid analysis of the non-Yüan and anti-Yüan elements, see Li Chu,
Hsin-hai ke-ming ch'ien-hou ti Chung-kuo cheng-ch'ih [Chinese politics before
and after the 1911 Revolution], pp. 130–35.

[154] Jamieson to Jordan, tel. 42, 6 April 1916, FO 228/2736. For the immediate circumstances of Kwangtung's independence see Kao Lao etc., *Ti-chih
yün-tung shih-mo chi* [History of the monarchical movement], pp. 33–35.

[155] Jamieson to Jordan, tel. 51, 19 April, and tel. 53, 20 April 1916, FO
228/2736. On the other hand, distrust of Lung was justified in that he main-
tained an extremely hostile attitude towards the other generals and the
Military Council which was officially established early in May. According to
Li Ken-yüan, commissioner for the northern expedition of the Military
Council, Lung threatened to murder him and Liang Ch'i-ch'ao, who was also
holding an important position in the council; see Li, *Hsüeh-sheng nien-lu*
[Chronology of Li Ken-yüan], in *CCST,* p. 70. Liang Ch'i-ch'ao also describes
Lung's hostility in *Tun-pi chi,* part 4, pp. 83–84. For details of the formation
of the Military Council, see Li, *Yün-nan chi-i yung-hu kung-ho wu-shih chou-
nien chi-nien te-k'an,* pp. 32–33; Yu Yün-lung, *Hu-kuo shih-kao* [History of
the anti-monarchical movement], pp. 37–40; and Jamieson to Jordan, no. 76,
9 May 1916, FO 228/2738.

[156] Jamieson to Jordan, tel. 63, 30 May 1916, FO 228/2738.

[157] Smith to Jordan, tel. 23, 4 April 1916, FO 228/2736.

[158] Smith to Jordan, no. 24, 13 May 1916, FO 228/2738. For Ch'en and the
Szechwan Party, see Feng, *Wo ti sheng-huo,* part 2, p. 5; Liu, *Hu-kuo ch'uan-
chün chan-chi,* p. 38. See also Huang Chi-lu, *T'ao Yüan shih-liao* [Materials
on activities against Yüan Shih-k'ai's monarchy], in Chung-kuo kuo-min tang
chung-yang wei-yüan hui tang-shih shih-liao p'ien-tsuan wei-yüan hui,
Ke-ming wen-hsien [Materials on revolutions in China], II, pp. 271–74.

[159] See for example, Giles to Jordan in Jordan to Grey, no. 62, 28 February
1916, FO 371/2645.

[160] Jordan to Grey, tel. 141, 9 May 1916, FO 371/2645.

[161] Liang, *Tun-pi chi,* part 3, pp. 26–27.

[162] See for example, Giles to Jordan, no. 63, 17 May, and Kirke to Jordan,
no. 28, 30 May 1916, FO 228/2738.

[163] See for example, secret and confidential clause of Jamieson to Jordan,
tel. 34, 19 March 1916, FO 228/2736.

[164] Grey to Jordan, tel. 61, 31 March 1916, FO 371/2645.

[165] Jordan to Grey, tel. 107, 3 April 1916, FO 371/2645.

[166] Gregory's minute on Jordan to Grey, tel. 107, 3 April, FO 371/2645.

[167] Tien-yi Li, *Woodrow Wilson's China policy, 1913–1917,* pp. 146–158; and Chi, *China diplomacy 1914–1918,* p. 68.

[168] Grey to Greene, no. 97, 5 April 1916; and Grey to Jordan, no. 90, 13 April 1916, FO 371/2645.

[169] Grey to Jordan, tel. 69, 8 April; and paraphrase of Ishii's telegram in Grey to Greene, no. 106, 11 April 1916, FO 371/2645.

[170] Grey to Spring-Rice, tel. 923, 11 April, repeated to Peking, and tel. 926, 12 April 1916, FO 371/2645.

[171] Greene to Grey, no. 176, 20 April 1916, FO 371/2645.

[172] Jamieson to Jordan, no. 79, 10 May, and Jordan to Grey, no. 122, draft, 10 May 1916, FO 228/2738.

[173] Pratt to Jordan in Jordan to Grey, tel. 142, 9 May 1916, FO 371/2645.

[174] Giles to Jordan, tel. 10, 22 May 1916, FO 228/2738. However, it appears that Jordan was little concerned about the separatist movements instigated by Japan in South Manchuria and Inner Mongolia. Details of these movements are available in Tanaka Giichi denki kankokai, *Tanaka Giichi denki* [Biography of Tanaka Giichi], I, pp. 629–30; and Iwanami Shoten, *Nihon Rekishi* [A course in Japanese history], XIX, pp. 73–75.

[175] Chi, *China diplomacy 1914–1918,* pp. 82–83.

[176] Jordan to Langley, private, 13 June 1916, FO 350/15.

[177] Jordan to Grey, no. 154, conf., 12 June 1916, FO 371/2646.

[178] Jordan to Grey, tel. 162, 26 May 1916, conf., FO 371/2645; P. Reinsch, *An American diplomat,* p. 192; and Li, *Woodrow Wilson's China policy, 1913–1917,* p. 157.

[179] See for example, T'ao, *Pei-yang chün-fa tung-ch'ih shih-chih shih-hua,* II, p. 99.

[180] Liang, *Tun-pi chi,* part 4, pp. 81–82; Levenson, *Liang Ch'i-ch'ao and the mind of modern China,* pp. 181–82; and Pa Chih-han, 'Yünnan hu-kuo chien-shih' [Brief history of the anti-monarchical movement in Yunnan], in *Chung-kuo ti-fang tzu-chih,* XIV, no. 9 (January, 1962), pp. 24–25.

[181] The prospect of being rewarded was a great incentive to the northern troops. For example, when Yüan received news of the government capture of Luchow he immediately sent to the front large quantities of food, wine, silk and other luxuries. He also instituted a medal/annual payment system of reward whereby a person awarded a class I medal would at the same time be entitled to 3,000 dollars annually, apart from his normal salary, for life. A class II medal was equal to 2,000 dollars; class III medal 1,000 dollars; class IV medal 500 dollars; and class V medal 250 dollars. At that time 250 dollars would enable any family to live comfortably for a year. And all these were only for a small victory; see Chang, *Wu P'ei-fu ch'uan,* I, pp. 174–75.

[182] A. A. Altman and H. Z. Schiffrin, 'Sun Yat-sen and the Japanese: 1914–16', *Modern Asian Studies* VI, no. 4 (1972), p. 399.

POSTSCRIPT (pp. 101–107)

[1] In his private letter to Langley, 29 May 1918, Jordan writes: 'Two years ago Yüan Shih-k'ai died. Before his death he had brought the provinces into a state of order and the writ of the Central Government ran from Peking to the borders of Tibet in the west and to Canton in the south. Now not a farthing of revenue, not even salt revenue, is received from Szechwan, Yunnan, or Canton and all the country south of the Yangtze is a law unto itself. As in Yüan's time, we have a military autocracy at Peking, the great difference being that the present one is supported by foreign money and is as inefficient as his was efficient', FO 350/16.

[2] E. Teichman, *Affairs of China,* p. 46.

[3] *London and China Telegraph,* 20 March 1916. The Japanese declared that the anti-British campaign was 'aimed against the English in the Far East [notably Jordan] rather than against Britain as a power', see Coleman *The Far East unveiled,* pp. 21–23; and I. H. Nish, *Alliance in decline,* p. 188.

[4] Grey to Jordan, tel., private, 12 May 1916, FO 800/44.

[5] Inouye Kaoru-ko denki hensankai, *Segai Inouye-ko den* [Biography of Inouye Kaoru], V, pp. 245–46. The translation quoted is given in Nish, *Alliance in decline,* p. 188.

[6] Grey to Jordan, 7 July 1916, draft, FO 800/44.

[7] Alston to Eric Drummond, private secretary to Grey, private, 16 August 1916, FO 800/44.

[8] Nish, *Alliance in decline,* p. 189.

[9] Alston to Drummond, private, 6 August 1917, FO 800/30.

[10] References to the end of the war are found in, for example, Jordan to Langley, private, 6 March, 15 April, 29 May, and Jordan to Macleay, who had become acting head of the Far Eastern Department, 3 June 1918, private, FO 350/16.

[11] See for example, Jordan to Langley, private, 6 March, and Jordan to Macleay, private, 3 June 1918, *ibid.*

[12] Jordan to Balfour, no. 564, 23 December 1918, and MaxMuller's minute on it, FO 371/3693. Also W. R. Louis, *British strategy in the Far East 1919–1939,* p. 20.

[13] Nish, *Alliance in decline,* pp. 310–13.

[14] For a masterly account and analysis of the feelings of the three principal actors, Britain, Japan, and the United States, during the year or so prior to the treaty, see Nish, *Alliance in decline,* pp. 313–82.

[15] Jordan, 'The Washington Conference and Far Eastern questions', *Quarterly Review* CCXXXVIII (1922), p. 105.

[16] Nish, *Alliance in decline,* pp. 376, 380.

[17] The vexed question of Shantung was not put on the formal agenda of the conference. Japan endeavoured her utmost to prevent this and Charles Evans Hughes, the American secretary of state, was of the same mind for fear that difficulties over this question might jeopardize the success of the conference.

It was eventually decided that China and Japan would negotiate on the matter between themselves in the presence of American and British representatives. The British representatives were Jordan and Lampson, and it was Jordan, together with J. V. A. MacMurray, head of the Far Eastern Division of the American Department of State and an American witness of the Sino-Japanese negotiations, who acted as mediators on the many occasions when a deadlock occurred; see Chia Shih-i, a member of the Chinese delegation to the conference, *Hua-hui chien-wen lu* [Reminiscences of the Washington conference], pp. 143–55.

[18] Jordan's detailed analysis of the decisions of the conference with regard to China is found in his article 'The Washington conference and Far Eastern questions', pp. 106–16.

[19] See, for example, the extremely pro-Yüan attitude of the French minister, Jacquin de Margerie, and of the French government generally during the 1911 Revolution in Ch'en San-ching, 'Fa-kuo yü hsin-hai ke-ming', in *Chin-t'ai shih yen-chiu so chi-k'an*, II, pp. 250–52.

[20] Yüan's special feelings towards Britain, as opposed to other powers, dated back to his Korean days when Britain, anxious to curb Russian influence in the Far East, strongly supported China to exert her sovereignty in Korea, see Lin, *Yüan Shih-k'ai yü Chao-hsien*, pp. 291–92, 299.

[21] Jordan to Campbell, private, 9 October 1911, FO 350/7; and Jordan to Langley, private, 22 October 1912, FO 350/8.

[22] Jordan to Balfour no. 564, 23 December 1918, FO 371/3693.

[23] When the news of his death reached China, 'not a single Chinese newspaper . . . contained any appreciation' of him, see *North China Herald*, 19 September 1925. In contrast, Jordan's death 'cast a pall' over the China Association, see Louis, *British strategy in the Far East 1919–1939*, p. 146.

SELECT BIBLIOGRAPHY

A. OFFICIAL PAPERS

I. *British Foreign Office records*

These are all in the Public Record Office, London. They are classified into various categories, which uniformly carry the letters FO followed by different index numbers.

Foreign Office general correspondence, political (China, before 1906). FO, 17.

Although the book begins essentially with Jordan's arrival in China in 1906, the following volumes of FO 17 were used:

FO 17/1245–46,	1281–82,
1284,	1694.

Foreign Office general correspondence, political (China, after 1906). FO, 371.

This series of materials is of primary significance in that it contains the official correspondence between Jordan and the Foreign Office for the years 1906 to 1920. In it are also available the Foreign Office officials' minutes which clearly indicate the attitude of the Foreign Office towards Jordan's service and specific happenings in China. The following volumes were consulted:

FO 371/22,	35,
38,	213,
217,	220–21,
223–24,	229–31,
233,	409,
422,	425,
612–13,	622,
624,	626,
634,	636,
851,	858,
1080,	1093–98,
1310–25,	1348,
1590–93,	1620,
1623–25,	1940–42,
2322–24,	2338,
2644–45,	2655–56.

Foreign Office general correspondence, political (Japan, after 1906). FO, 371.

It is of little significance because it contains little about Sino-Japanese relations which is not available in the above-mentioned FO 371 volumes. Volumes 2016–2017, however, are the exception in that they contain information on Japan's entry into World War I which are not obtainable in the China series.

Foreign Office confidential print, China. FO, 405.

Although being a valuable guide to the most important Foreign Office records, the following volumes of the *Confidential print,* under the index FO 405, are, however, no adequate substitute for the FO 371 China volumes in that in them the officials' minutes are omitted.

FO 405/183,	190,
195,	199,
201,	204,
208,	214,
229.	

Foreign Office consular and embassy archives, China. FO, 228, 671, 233.

The official, and sometimes private, correspondence between Jordan and consular officials is available here. However, much of what have been referred to in the following files appear as enclosures in the official correspondence of Jordan to the Foreign Office.

FO 228/1081–82,	1084–86,
1836,	1841,
1952,	1966,
1985,	2306,
2348–49,	2500,
2736–37,	2338.
FO 671/336,	339,
357.	
FO 233/133.	

Foreign Office political: Japanese policy in Korea: case 306. FO, 371.

FO 371/179.

Foreign Office Great Britain and general. FO, 83.

Only FO 83/2027 is relevant.

II. *Chinese records*

Cheng-fu kung-pao 政府公報. This is the official gazette of the Chinese republican government during the presidency of Yüan Shih-k'ai.

Hsü Yu-p'eng (ed.) 徐有朋, *Yüan ta tsung-t'ung shu-tu hui-p'ien* 袁大總統書牘彙編, in *CHST*, series 1. This is the collection of the official documents of Yüan Shih-k'ai while he was president.

I Kuo-kan (ed.) 易國幹, *Li fu tsung-t'ung cheng-shu* 黎副總統政書, in *CHST*, series 1. This is the collection of the official papers of Li Yüan-hung when he was vice-president, 1912–16.

Kan Hou-tz'u (ed.) 甘厚慈, *Pei-yang kung-tu lei-tsuan* 北洋公牘類纂, 3 vols., in *YSH*. This is a collection of the official papers of Yüan Shih-k'ai as viceroy of Chihli.

——, *Pei-yang kung-tu lei-tsuan hsü-p'ien* 北洋公牘類纂續編, 3 vols., in *YSH*. This is the continuation to the above collection.

Lin-shih cheng-fu kung-pao 臨時政府公報. This is the official gazette of the provisional Chinese republican government in Nanking which existed during the first quarter or so of 1912.

Wu Yen-yün (ed.) 吳硯雲, *Huang Liu-shou shu-tu* 黃留守書牘, in *CHST* series 1. This is the collection of Huang Hsing's official papers when he was generalissimo in Nanking in 1912.

III. *Japanese Records*

Japanese Foreign Ministry, *Nihon gaiko bunsho* 日本外交文書. This is the collection of documents on Japan's diplomacy. Those volumes particularly devoted to the 1911 Revolution and the years 1915 and 1916 are of extreme importance for the present study.

B. PRIVATE PAPERS, COLLECTIONS, AND MEMOIRS

I. IN ENGLISH

Alston papers. Public Record Office, FO 800/244–48. They contain the originals of most of the letters from Jordan. Especially valuable are letters in which Alston portrays Jordan's conditions during the short period between Yüan Shih-k'ai's death and Jordan's departure from China in 1916.

Balfour papers, British Museum. A large collection, but only volume 49729 is cited here.

[*J. O. P.*] *Bland papers.* Thomas Fisher Rare Book Library, University of Toronto.

Grey papers. Public Record Office, FO 800/35–114. A vast and valuable collection but contains little on the Far East. Volumes 43, 44 and 106 are of particular value in this context.

Jordan papers. Public Record Office, FO 350/1–16. A most important and valuable source. The collection contains copies of most of Jordan's private letters to Foreign Office officials and the consular staff in China. It also includes many letters from Grey, Tyrrell, Campbell, Langley, and Alston. Jordan wrote much more candidly in his private letters than in his official correspondence.

Langley papers. Public Record Office, FO 800/29, 31. They contain little that is not available either in the Alston or the Jordan papers.

Lansdowne papers. Public Record Office, FO 800/115–46. Only FO 800/121 is of use in connection with Jordan's appointment to Peking.

Satow papers. Public Record Office, PRO/30/33. This is a huge collection of Sir Ernest Satow's private papers. The following volumes are invaluable in giving the background to Jordan's appointment as minister to China:

PRO 30/33 7/4,	7/5,
9/15,	10/8,
11/6,	14/16,
16/9.	

Ishii Kikujiro, *Diplomatic commentaries,* Baltimore, 1936. This memoir has to be used with care because it contains a great deal of misleading information.

II. In Chinese and Japanese

Aisin Gioro P'u-i 愛新覺羅溥儀, *Wo-ti ch'ien pan sheng* 我的前半生. Peking, 1964. The author was the last emperor of the Ch'ing dnyasty.

Feng Yü-hsiang 馮玉祥, *Wo-ti sheng-huo* 我的生活. 3 vols., 1944.

Huang Shao-hung 黃紹竑, *Wu-shih hui-i* 五十回憶. Hong Kong, 1969.

Huang Yüan-yung 黃遠庸, *Yüan-sheng i-chu* 遠生遺著, 2 vols., in *CHST*, series 1. Huang was an extremely resourceful newspaperman during the first few years of the Chinese republic.

Li Ken-yüan 李根源, *Hsüeh-sheng nien-lu* 雪生年錄, in *CCST*.

Liang Ch'i-ch'ao 梁啓超, *Tun-pi chi* 盾鼻集, in *YSH*.

———, *Yin-ping shih wen-chi* 飲冰室文集. 80 vols., Shanghai, 1925.

Liu Yü-sheng 劉禺生, *Shih-ts'ai t'ang tsa-i* 世載堂雜憶. Peking, 1960. The author was a revolutionary and had wide contact with political personages in the early republican years. The book, however, has to be used with care.

Miyazaki Torazo 宮崎寅藏, *Sanju sannen no yume* 三十三年の夢. Tokyo, 1926, 1943. This is the memoir of the well-known Japanese adventurer who was deeply involved in China's revolutionary movement in the early twentieth century. The Chinese version is *San-shih-san nien lo-hua meng* 三十三年落花夢. Shanghai, 1934.

Shen I-yün 沈亦雲, *I-yün hui-i* 亦雲回憶. 2 vols., Taipei, 1968. The author was the wife of Huang Fu, a well-known Kuomintang member.

Ts'ai O 蔡鍔, *Sung-po chün-chung i-mo* 松坡軍中遺墨, in *CCST*.

———, *Ts'ai Sung-po hsien-sheng i-chi* 蔡松坡先生遺集, in *CHST*.

Ts'ao Ju-lin 曹汝霖, *I-sheng chih hui-i* 一生之回憶. Hong Kong, 1966. The book suffers from too much self-justification.

Tsou Lu 鄒魯, *Hui-ku lu* 回顧錄. n.p., 1943.

———, *Tsou Lu wen-ts'un* 鄒魯文存. Peking, 1930.

Yen Hsi-shan 閻錫山, *Yen Hsi-shan tsao-nien hui-i lu* 閻錫山早年回憶錄. Taipei, 1968.

Yüan K'e-wen 袁克文, *Yüan-shang ssu-ch'eng* 洹上私乘, in *YSH*. The author is a son of Yüan Shih-k'ai.

C. NEWSPAPERS AND PERIODICALS

I. In English

London and China Telegraph, August 1915—June 1916.

North China Daily News, Shanghai, October—December 1911.

North China Herald and Supreme Court and Consular Gazette, Shanghai.

Peking and Tientsin Times, 1918.

Peking Daily News, 1911.

The Times.

II. In Chinese

Cheng-lun 政論, no. 2, Shanghai, November 1907.

Chia-yin tsa-chih 甲寅雜誌, Tokyo, 1914.

Chung-kuo ti-fang tzu-chih 中國地方自治, Taipei, XII, no. 10 (January, 1960), and XIV, no. 9 (January, 1962).

Min-li pao 民立報, Shanghai, 1913.

Ssu-ch'uan wen-hsien 四川文獻, Taipei, no. 47 (September, 1962).

Wai-chiao pao 外交報, Shanghai, 1908.

D. UNPUBLISHED THESES

I. In English

Chen, C. S., 'British loans to China, 1860–1913'. Ph.D. thesis, University of London, 1940.

Hara, Takemichi, 'Chinese policy in Manchuria, 1905–1911'. M.A. thesis, University of Hong Kong, 1971.

Hickling, A., 'The response of Protestant Missionaries to the anti-missionary disturbances in China, 1891–1907'. M.A. thesis, University of Hong Kong, 1968.

Marchant, L., 'Anglo-Chinese relations in the provinces of the West River and the Yangtze River basins, 1889–1900'. M.A. thesis, University of London, 1965.

Sigel, L. T., 'T'ang Shao-yi (1860–1938): the diplomacy of Chinese nationalism'. Ph.D. thesis, Harvard University, 1972.

II. In Chinese

Poon, Chun-kau 潘鎮球, 'The constitutional movement of the late Ch'ing period, 1905–1911' 晚清之憲政運動. M.A. thesis, University of Hong Kong, 1969.

E. BOOKS AND ARTICLES

I. In English and French

Adshead, S. A. M., 'The reform of the Chinese Salt Administration (1913–1918)', in East Asian Research Center, Harvard University, *Papers on China,* XVIII (December 1964).

Altman, A. A., and Schiffrin, H. Z., 'Sun Yat-sen and the Japanese: 1914–16', *Modern Asian Studies* VI, no. 4 (October, 1972).

Bland, J. O. P., *Recent events and present policies in China.* London, 1912.

——, 'The future of China', *Edinburgh Review* CCXX (October 1914).

Bevan, L. R. O., *Constitutional building in China.* Shanghai, 1910.

Bergère, Marie-Claire, *La bourgeoisie chinoise et la revolution de 1911.* Paris, 1968.

Braisted, W. R. 'The United States and the American Chinese Development Company', *Far Eastern Quarterly* XI (February 1952).

Cameron, M. E., *The reform movement in China*. Stanford, 1931.

Chang, Kia-ngau, *China's struggle for railroad development*. New York, 1943.

Chan, Lau Kit-ching, 'British policy in the Reorganisation Loan to China 1912–1913', *Modern Asian Studies* V, no. 4 (October 1971).

——, 'British policy of neutrality during the 1911 Revolution in China', *Journal of Oriental Studies* VIII, no. 2 (July 1970).

Ch'en, Jerome, *Yüan Shih-k'ai*. Stanford, 1972.

Cheng, Shih-Gung, *Modern China*. Oxford, 1919.

Chi, M., *China diplomacy 1914–1917*. Cambridge, Mass., 1970.

Chow, Ts'e-tsung, *The May Fourth Movement*. Cambridge, Mass., 1960.

Cohen, P. A., *China and Christianity*. Cambridge, Mass., 1967.

——, etc. (ed.), *Reform in nineteenth century China*. Cambridge, Mass., 1976.

Coleman, F., *The Far East unveiled*. London, 1918.

Chu, S. C., *Reform in modern China, Chang Chien, 1853–1926*. New York, 1965.

Collis, M., *Wayfoong, the Hongkong and Shanghai Banking Corporation*. London, 1965.

Croly, H. D., *Willard Straight*. New York, 1925.

Dictionary of national biography, 1922–30. Oxford, 1937.

Djang, Feng-djen, *The diplomatic relations between China and Germany since 1898*. Shanghai, 1936.

Edwards, E. W., 'Great Britain and the Manchurian railway question 1909–1910', *English Historical Review* LXXXI (1966).

Esherick, J. W., *Reform and revolution in China : the 1911 revolution in Hunan and Hupei*. Berkeley, 1976.

Farjenel, F., *Through the Chinese revolution,* translated from French by M. Vivian. London, 1915.

Feuerwerker, A., *China's early industrialisation, Sheng Hsuan-huai (1844–1916) and Mandarin enterprise*. Cambridge, Mass., 1958.

Foreign Office list and diplomatic and consular year book for 1920.

Green, O. M., *The foreigner in China*. London, 1943.

Gregory, J. S., *Great Britain and the Taipings*. London, 1969.

Hornbeck, S. K., *Contemporary politics in the Far East*. London, 1916.

Hong Kong China Mail, *Who's who in the Far East, 1906–7*.

Houn, F. W., *Central government of China 1912–1928*. Wisconsin, 1959.

Hsüeh, Chün-tu, *Huang Hsing and the Chinese revolution*. Stanford, 1961.

—— (ed.), *Revolutionary leaders of modern China*. New York, 1971.

Ikei, Masaru, 'Japan's response to the Chinese revolution of 1911', *Journal of Asian Studies* XXV, no. 2 (February 1966). A useful article based largely on Japanese sources.

Jansen, M. B., *The Japanese and Sun Yat-sen*. Cambridge, Mass., 1954.

Jordan, J. N., 'Some Chinese I have known', in *Nineteenth century and after* LXXXVIII (December 1920). This is Jordan's frank revelation of his attitude toward a number of important political figures in early twentieth century China.

La Fargue, T. E., *China and the World War*. Stanford, 1937.

Lanning, G., *Old forces in new China*. Shanghai, 1912.

Lensen, G. A. (ed.), *Korea and Manchuria between Russia and Japan 1895–1904*. Florida, 1966.

Levenson, J. R., *Liang Ch'i-ch'ao and the mind of modern China*. London, 1965.

Lewis, C. M., *Prologue to the Chinese revolution: the transformation of ideas and institutions in Hunan province 1891–1907*. Cambridge, Mass., 1976.

Li, T'ien-yi, *Woodrow Wilson's China policy, 1913–1917*. New York, 1952.

Lo, Hui-min, *The correspondence of G. E. Morrison 1895–1912*. Cambridge, 1996.

Louis, W. R., *British strategy in the Far East 1919–1939*. Oxford, 1971.

Lowe, P., *Great Britain and Japan 1911–15*. London, 1969. A most valuable work for illuminating Anglo-Japanese relations in the early twentieth century which centred largely on China.

——, 'Great Britain, Japan and the fall of Yüan Shih-k'ai, 1915–1916', *The Historical Journal* XIII, no. 4 (1970). A useful article.

Ma, Yin-liang, *A brief history of the Chinese press*. Shanghai, 1937.

MacMurray, J. V. A., *Treaties and agreements with and concerning China*. 2 vols., New York, 1921.

MacNair, H. F., *Modern Chinese history*. Shanghai, 1927.

Nathan, A. J., *Peking politics, 1918–1923: factionalism and the failure of constitutionalism*. Berkeley, 1976.

Nish, I. H., 'Admiral Jerram and the German Pacific fleet 1913–15', *The Mariner's Mirror* LVI, no. 4 (1970).

——, *Alliance in decline*. London, 1972. Besides being a piece of superb research on Anglo-Japanese relations 1908–1923, it sheds much light on Jordan in China.

——, The *Anglo-Japanese alliance*. London, 1966.

Pearl, C., *Morrison of Peking*. Sydney, 1967. Made up mainly of extracts from the *Morrison papers*.

Putnam Weale (pseud.), *The fight for the republic in China*. London, 1919.

Reinsch, P., *An American diplomat*. London, 1922.

Remer, C. F., *A study of Chinese boycotts*. Reprinted in Taipei, 1966.

——, *Readings in economics for China*. Shanghai, 1922.

Rhoads, E. J. M., *China's Republican Revolution: the case of Kwangtung, 1895–1913*. Cambridge, Mass., 1975.

Schrecker, J. E., *Imperialism and Chinese nationalism*. Cambridge, Mass., 1971.

Schwartz, Benjamin, *In search of wealth and power, Yen Fu and the West,* Cambridge, Mass., 1964.

Sheridan, J. E., *China in disintegration.* New York, etc., 1975.

Stanhope, Rt. Hon Earl, 'Great Britain and Japan in the Far East', in *Nineteenth century and after* LXVII (1910).

Sun, E-tu Zen, *Chinese railways and British interests 1898–1911.* New York, 1954. A helpful guide for understanding the intricate problem of British railway investment in China in the early twentieth century.

——, 'The Shanghai-Hangchow-Ningpo Railway Loan of 1908', *Far Eastern Quarterly* X, no. 3 (February 1951).

Teichman, E., *Affairs of China.* London, 1938.

Thomas, L., *Lauterback of the China Sea.* London, 1930.

Trevor-Roper, H. R., *Hermit of Peking : the hidden life of Sir Edmund Backhouse.* New York, 1977.

Tung, W. L., *The Political institutions of modern China.* The Hague, 1964.

Tyler, W. F., *Pulling strings in China.* London, 1929. The author's eyewitness account confirms the significance of the reorganization loan in enabling Yüan Shih-k'ai to crush the 1913 Revolution.

Vinacke, H. M., *Modern constitutional development in China.* Princeton, 1920.

Wang, Y. C., *Chinese intellectuals and the West 1892–1949.* Chapel Hill, North Carolina, 1966.

Wehrle, E. S., *Britain, China, and the anti-missionary riots, 1891–1900.* Minneapolis, 1966.

Wright, M. C. (ed.), *China in revolution : the first phase 1900–1913.* New Haven, 1968. A most valuable collection of essays on the topic.

Yim, Kwanha, 'Yüan Shih-k'ai and the Japanese', *Journal of Asian Studies* XXIV, no. 1 (November 1964). A most useful article.

Young, E. P., *The presidency of Yüan Shih-k'ai : liberalism and dictatorship in early Republican China.* Ann Arbor, 1977.

Young, L. K., *British policy in China 1895–1902.* Oxford, 1970.

II. IN CHINESE AND JAPANESE

Ch'ai Te-keng 柴德賡 (ed.) etc., *Hsin-hai ke-ming* 辛亥革命. 8 vols., Shanghai, 1957.

Chang Chih-pen 張知本, *Hsien-fa lun* 憲法論. Shanghai, 1946.

Chang Chih-tung 張之洞, *Chang Wen-hsiang kung ch'üan-chi* 張文襄公全集. 6 vols., reprinted in Taipei, 1963.

Chang Ching-lu 張靜廬, *Chung-kuo chin-tai ch'u-pan shih-liao* 中國近代出版史料. 2 vols., Shanghai, 1953–1954.

Chang Chün-ku 章君穀, *Wu P'ei-fu ch'uan* 吳佩孚傳. Taipei, 1968.

——, *Yüan Shih-k'ai ch'uan* 袁世凱傳. Hong Kong, 1970.

Chang Chung-fu 張忠紱, *Chung-hua min-kuo wei-chiao shih* 中華民國外交史. Shanghai, 1957.

Chang Peng-yüan 張朋園, *Li-hsien p'ai yü hsin-hai ke-ming* 立憲派與辛亥革命. Taipei, 1969.

Chang Yu-fa 張玉法, *Ch'ing-chi chih li-hsien t'uan-t'i* 清季之立憲團體. Taipei, 1971, in Chung-yang yen chiu yüan 中央研究院, *Chin-tai shih yen-chiu so tsun-k'an* 近代史研究所專刊, no. 28.

Ch'en Po-ta 陳伯達, *Ch'ieh-kuo ta-tao Yüan Shih-k'ai* 竊國大盜袁世凱. Peking, 1954.

Ch'en San-ching 陳三井, 'Fa-kuo yü Hsin-hai ke-ming' 法國與辛亥革命, in Chung-yang yen-chiu yüan 中央研究院, *Chin-tai shih yen-chiu so chi-k'an* 近代史研究所集刊, II, Taipei, 1970.

Ch'ien Tuan-sheng etc. 錢端升, *Min-kuo cheng-chih shih* 民國政制史. Shanghai, 1946.

Ch'eng Ts'ang-po 程滄波, *Li-shih wen-hua yü jen-wu* 歷史文化與人物. Taipei, 1954.

Chia Shih-i 賈士毅, *Hua-hui chien-wen lu* 華會見聞錄. Shanghai, 1924.

——, *Min-kuo ch'u-nien ti chi jen ts'ai-cheng tsung-chang* 民國初年的幾任財政總長. Taipei, 1967.

Chiang Chün-chang 蔣君章, *Chung-hua min-kuo chien-kuo shih* 中華民國建國史. Taipei, 1957.

Chin Wen-ssu 金問泗, *Huang Ying-po hsien-sheng ku-chiu kan-i lu* 黃膺白先生故舊感憶錄, in *CHST*, series 4.

Ching Min (pseud.) 警民, *Hsü Shih-ch'ang* 徐世昌, in *CCST*.

Ch'ou-an hui 籌安會 (ed.), *Chün-hsien wen t'i wen-t'ien hui-p'ien* 君憲問題文電彙編, in *CCST*.

Chou Shu-chen 周叔楨, *Chou Chi-an hsien-sheng pieh-ch'uan* 周止菴先生別傳. Shanghai, 1947.

Chü Cheng 居正, *Hsin-hai cha-chi* 辛亥箚記. Taipei, 1965.

Chu Yen-chia 朱炎佳, 'Wu Lu-chen yü Chung-kuo ke-ming' 吳祿貞與中國革命, in *CHT*, VI.

Ch'üan Han-hsing 全漢昇, 'T'ieh-lu kuo-yu wen-t'i yü hsin-hai ke-ming' 鐵路國有問題與辛亥革命, in *CHT*, I.

Chung-hua min-kuo k'ai-kuo wu-shih nien wen-hsien p'ien-tsuan wei-yüan hui 中華民國開國五十年文獻編纂委員會, *Chung-hua min-kuo k'ai-kuo wu-shih nien wen-hsien* 中華民國開國五十年文獻. 5 vols., Taipei, 1964.

Chung-kuo chin-tai ching-chi shih tzu-liao ts'ung-k'an p'ien-chi wei-yüan hui 中國近代經濟史資料叢刊編輯委員會, *Chung-kuo hai-kuan yü Chung-Jih chan-cheng* 中國海關與中日戰爭, in *Ti-kuo chü-i yü Chung-kuo hai-kuan* 帝國主義與中國海關. Peking, 1958.

Chung-kuo chin-tai shih ts'ung-shu p'ien-hsieh tsu 中國近代史叢書編寫組, *Hsin-hai ke-ming* 辛亥革命. Shanghai, 1972.

Chung-kuo jen-min cheng-chih hsieh-shang hui-i ch'üan-kuo wei-yüan hui, wen-shih tzu-liao yen-chiu wei-yüan hui (ed.) 中國人民政治協商會議全國委員會, 文史資料研究委員會, *Hsin-hai ke-ming hui-i lu* 辛亥革命回憶錄. 5 vols., Peking, 1963-1965.

Chung-kuo ko-hsüeh yüan li-shih yen-chiu so ti san so 中國科學院歷史研究所第三所, *Yun-nan Kuei-chou hsin-hai ke-ming tzu-liao* 雲南貴州辛亥革命資料. Peking, 1959.

Department of State of Manchukuo 滿州國, *Ta-Ch'ing li-chao shih-lu* 大清歷朝實錄. Tokyo, 1937. Only chap. 25 of the Hsüan-t'ung reign was consulted.

Feng Tzu-yu 馮自由, *Chung-kuo ke-ming yün-tung erh-shih-liu nien tsu-chih shih* 中國革命運動二十六年組織史. Shanghai, 1948.

——, *Ke-ming i-shih* 革命逸史. 5 vols., Shanghai, 1946–47.

Ho Wei-ning 何維凝, *Chung-kuo yen-cheng shih* 中國鹽政史. Taipei, 1966.

Hsiao I-shan 蕭一山, *Ch'ing tai t'ung-shih* 清代通史. 5 vols., Taipei, 1967.

Hsü I-sheng 徐義生 (ed.), *Chung-kuo chin-tai wai-tsai shih t'ung-chi tzu-liao 1853–1927* 中國近代外債史統計資料. Peking, 1962.

Hsü Shih-ch'ang 徐世昌, *Tung-san sheng cheng-lüeh* 東三省政畧. 12 vols., Taipei, 1965.

Hsü Shih-shen 許師愼, *Kuo-fu ke-ming yüan-ch'i hsiang-chu* 國父革命緣起詳註. Taipei, 1954.

Hsü T'ung-hsin 許同莘, *Chang Wen-hsiang kung nien-p'u* 張文襄公年譜. Shanghai, 1947.

Hu O-kung 胡鄂公, *Hsin-hai ke-ming pei-fang shih-lu* 辛亥革命北方實錄. Shanghai, 1948.

Huang Cheng-ming 黃正銘, *Chung-kuo wai-chiao shih* 中國外交史. Taipei, 1959.

Huang Chi-lu 黃季陸, *T'ao Yüan shih-liao* 討袁史料, in Chung-kuo kuo-min tang chung-yang wei-yüan hui tang-shih shih-liao p'ien-tsuan wei-yüan hui 中國國民黨中央委員會黨史史料編纂委員會, *Ke-ming wen-hsien* 革命文獻. 2 vols., Taipei, 1969.

Huang Fu-luan 黃福鑾, *Hua-chiao yü Chung-kuo ke-ming* 華僑與中國革命. Hong Kong, 1954.

Huang I 黃毅, *Yüan-shih tao-kuo chi* 袁氏盜國記, in *CHST*.

Huang Kung-chüeh etc. 黃公覺, *Chung-kuo chih-hsien shih* 中國制憲史. 2 vols., Shanghai, 1937.

Inouye Kaoru-ko denki hensankai 井上馨侯傳記編纂會, *Segai Inouye-ko den* 世外井上侯傳. 5 vols., Tokyo, 1934–35.

Iwanami Shoten 岩波書店, *Nihon Rekishi* 日本歷史. Tokyo, 1963.

Japanese Railroad Ministry, *Nihon tetsudoshi* 日本鐵道史. Tokyo, 1922.

Kajima Morinosuke 鹿島守之助, *Nihon gaikō seisaku no shiteki kōsatsu* 日本外交政策の史的考察. Tokyo, 1958.

——, *Nichi-Ei gaikōshi* 日英外交史. Tokyo, 1957.

——, *Nihon gaikōshi* 日本外交史. Tokyo, 1964.

Kao Lao etc. 高勞, *Ti-chih yün-tung shih-mo chi* 帝制運動始末記. Hong Kong, 1969.

Kao Yin-tsu 高蔭祖, *Chung-hua min-kuo ta-shih chi* 中華民國大事記. Taipei, 1957.

Ko Kung-chen 戈公振, *Chung-kuo pao-hsüeh shih* 中國報業史. Taipei, 1964.

Ku Tun-jou 顧敦鍒, *Chung-kuo i-hui shih* 中國議會史. Taichung, 1962.

Kuo-shih p'ien-chi she 國史編輯社, *Wu P'ei-fu cheng-ch'uan* 吳佩孚正傳, in *CCST*.

Lai-chiang cho-wu (pseud.) 瀨江濁物, *Tüan Ch'i-jui pi-shih* 段祺瑞秘史. 1921.

Lee En-han 李恩涵, 'Chung-Mei shou-hui yüeh-han t'ieh-lu ch'üan chiao-she' 中美收回粵漢鐵路權交涉, in Chung-yang yen-chiu yüan 中央研究院, *Chin-tai shih yen-chiu so chi-k'an* 近代史研究所集刊, I, Taipei, 1969.

Li Chien-nung 李劍農, *Chung-kuo chin pai nien cheng-chih shih* 中國近百年政治史. 2 vols., Taipei, 1957.

Li Chu 黎澍, *Hsin-hai ke-ming chien-hou ti Chung-kuo cheng-chih* 辛亥革命先後的中國政治. Peking, 1961.

Li Nai-han 黎乃涵, *Hsin-hai ke-ming yü Yüan Shih-k'ai* 辛亥革命與袁世凱. Hong Kong, 1948.

Li Shih-yüeh 李世岳, *Chang Chien ho li-hsien p'ai* 張謇和立憲派. Peking, 1962.

Li Shou-k'ung 李守孔, *Min-ch'u chih kuo-hui* 民初之國會. Taipei, 1964.

——, 'Ko sheng tzu-i chü lien-ho hui yü hsin-hai ke-ming' 各省資議局聯合會與辛亥革命, in *CHT*, III.

Li Tse-fun 李則芬, *Chung-Jih kuan-hsi shih* 中日關係史. Taipei, 1970.

Li Tsung-huang etc. 李宗黃, *Yün-nan ch'i-i yung-hu kung-ho wu-shih chou-nien te-k'an* 雲南起義擁護共和五十週年特刊. Taipei, 1965.

Li Yü-shu 李毓澍, *Chung-Jih erh-shih-i t'iao chiao-she* 中日二十一條交涉. 2 vols., Taipei, 1966.

Li Yün-han 李雲漢, 'Huang K'e-ch'iang hsien-sheng nien-p'u kao' 黃克強先生年譜稿, in *CHT*, IV.

Lin Te-ming 林德明, *Yüan Shih-k'ai yü Chao-hsien* 袁世凱與朝鮮, in Chung-yang yen-chiu yüan, *Chin-tai shih yen-chiu so tsun k'an*, no. 26. Taipei, 1970.

Liu Chen-k'ai 劉振鎧, *Chung-kuo hsien-cheng shih-hua* 中國憲政史話. Taipei, 1960.

Liu Hou-sheng 劉厚生, *Chang Chien ch'üan-chi* 張謇全集. Hong Kong, 1965.

Liu Ping-lin 劉秉麟, *Chin-tai Chung-kuo wai-tsai shih-kao* 近代中國外債史稿. Peking, 1962.

Liu Ts'un-hou 劉存厚, *Hu-kuo ch'uan-chün chan-chi* 護國川軍戰記. Taipei, 1966.

Liu Yen 劉彥, *Chung-kuo wai-chiao shih* 中國外交史. Taipei, 1962.

——, *Ti-kuo chü-i ya-pe Chung-kuo shih* 帝國主義壓迫中國史. Shanghai, 1927.

Lo Chia-lun (ed.) 羅家倫, *Ke-ming wen-hsien* 革命文獻. 30 vols., Taipei, 1953–64.

——, *Kuo-fu nien-p'u ch'u-kao* 國父年譜初稿. 2 vols., Taipei, 1959. They have to be used with care because they contain much mistaken information.

Lo Kang 羅剛, *Lo p'ien Kuo-fu nien-p'u chiu-miu* 羅編國父年譜糾繆. Taipei, 1962. This is an attempt to correct the errors contained in the above work.

Lo Kuang 羅光, *Lu Cheng-hsiang ch'uan* 陸徵祥傳. Taipei, 1967.

Lu Hun 爐魂 (pseud.), 'Tui yü Chang Chih-tung ssu-hou chih Hu-nan jen' 對於張之洞死後之湖南人, in *HHKM*, IV.

Nihon kokusai seiji gakukai 日本國際政治學會, *Nihon gaikōshi kenkyu—dai-ichiji sekai daisen* 日本外交史研究——第一次世界大戰. Tokyo, 1962.

Ou Tsung-yu 歐宗輿, *Chung-kuo yen-cheng hsiao-shih* 中國鹽政小史. Shanghai, 1927.

Pai Chiao 白蕉, *Yüan Shih-k'ai yü Chung-hua min-kuo* 袁世凱與中華民國, in *YSH*.

P'an Kung-chan 潘公展, *Ch'en Ch'i-mei* 陳其美. Taipei, 1954.

P'eng Tse-chou 彭澤周, 'Hsin-hai ke-ming yü Jih-pen Hsi-yüan-szu nei-ko' 辛亥革命與日本西園寺內閣, in *CHT*, VI.

Shao Yüan-ch'ung 邵元沖, *Ch'en Ying-shih hsien-sheng ke-ming hsiao-shih* 陳英士先生革命小史. Nanking, 1925.

Shen Yün-lung 沈雲龍, *Hsien-tai cheng-chih jen-wu shu-p'ing* 現代政治人物述評. 2 vols., Taipei, 1959.

——, *Li Yüan-hung p'ing-ch'uan* 黎元洪評傳. Taipei, 1963.

Shih Chün-min 史俊民, *Chung-Jih kuo-chi shih* 中日國際史. Peking, 1919.

Shinobu Seizaburō 信夫清三郎, *Taisho seijishi* 大正政治史. Tokyo, 1968.

Sonoda Ikki 園田一龜, *Kaiketsu Chō saku-rin* 怪傑張作霖. Tokyo, 1923.

Tai Chih-li 戴執禮 (ed.), *Ssu-ch'uan pao-lu yün-tung shih-liao* 四川保路運動史料. Peking, 1959.

T'an Hsi-k'ang 譚錫康, *Ts'ai Sung-po ku-shih* 蔡松波故事. Shanghai, 1924.

T'an T'ien-k'ai 譚天凱, *Shan-tung wen-t'i shih-mo* 山東問題始末. Shanghai, 1935.

Tanaka Giichi denki kankokai 田中義一傳記刊行會, *Tanaka Giichi denki* 田中義一傳記. 2 vols., Tokyo, 1958.

T'ao Chü-yin 陶菊隱, *Liu chün-tzu ch'uan* 六君子傳. Shanghai, 1948.

——, *Pei-yang chün-fa t'ung-chih shih-chih shih-hua* 北洋軍閥統治時期史話. 6 vols., Peking, 1957–1961. A valuable source.

Ts'en Hsüeh-lü 岑學呂, *San-shui Liang Yen-sun hsien-sheng nien-p'u* 三水梁燕孫先生年譜. 2 vols. in *CHST*.

——, *Chung-kuo t'ieh-lu hsien-hsi t'ung-lun* 中國鐵路現勢通論. n.p., 1907.

Tseng K'un-hua 曾鯤華, *Chung-kuo t'ieh-lu shih* 中國鐵路史. Peking, 1924.

Tseng Hsü-pai 曾虛白, *Chung-kuo hsin-wen shih* 中國新聞史, in *Ta-hsüeh hsin-wen hsüeh ts'ung-shu* 大學新聞學叢書. Taipei, 1966.

Tsou Lu 鄒魯, *Chung-kuo kuo-min tang shih-kao* 中國國民黨史稿. 4 vols., Shanghai, 1938.

——, *Kuang-chou san-yüeh erh-shih-chiu ke-ming shih* 廣州三月二十九革命史. Taipei, 1953.

Tung-nan p'ien-chi she 東南編輯社, *T'ang Chi-yao* 唐繼堯 in *CCST*.

Wang Yün-sheng 王芸生, *Liu-shih nien lai Chung-kuo yü Jih-pen* 六十年來中國與日本. 7 vols., Tientsin, 1932–34.

Wen Kung-chih 文公直, *Chung-hua min-kuo ke-ming shih* 中華民國革命史. 2 vols., Shanghai, 1927.

——, *Tsui-chin san-shih nien Chung-kuo chün-shih shih* 最近卅年中國軍事史. 2 vols., in *CHST*.

Wu Hsiang-hsiang 吳相湘, 'Hai-wai hsin chien Chung-kuo hsien-tai shih shih-liao' 海外新見中國現代史史料, in *CHT*, I.

——, *Min-kuo cheng-chih jen-wu* 民國政治人物. Taipei, 1964.

——, 'San-Han Fu-sang so chien Yüan Shih-k'ai kuan-hsi shih-liao' 三韓扶桑所見袁世凱關係史料, in *CHT*, IV.

——, *Sung Chiao-jen* 宋敎仁. Taipei, 1964.

——, 'Yüan Shih-k'ai mou-ch'ü lin-shih ta-tsung-t'ung chih ching-kuo' 袁世凱謀取臨時大總統之經過, in *CHT*, I.

Wu Yü-chang 吳玉章, *Hsin-hai ke-ming* 辛亥革命. Peking, 1961.

Yeh Kung-cho 葉恭綽, *T'ai-p'ing yang hui-i chien-hou Chung-kuo wai-chiao nei-mu chi ch'i yü Liang Shih-i chih kuan-hsi* 太平洋會議前後中國外交內幕及其與梁士詒之關係. Hong Kong, 1970.

——, *Hsia-an hui-kao* 遐庵彙稿. n.p., 1946.

Yen Hsi-shan 閻錫山, *Yen Hsi-shan tsao-nien hui-i lu* 閻錫山早年回憶錄. Taipei, 1968.

Yü En-yang 庾恩暘, *Yün-nan shou-i yung-hu kung-ho shih-mo chi* 雲南首義擁護共和始末記, in *YSH*.

Yu Jun-t'ang etc. 余潤棠, *Chung-kuo tang-tai cheng-tang lun* 中國當代政黨論. Canton, 1948.

Yu Yün-lung 由雲龍, *Hu-kuo shih-kao* 護國史藁. Kunming, 1950.

Yüan Shih-k'ai wei-tsao min-i chi-shih 袁世凱偽造民意紀實. n.p., 1916.

GLOSSARY OF NAMES

Aoki Nobuzumi 清木宣純
Ariga Nagao 有賀長雄
Ariyoshi (? Akira) 有吉明

Canton-Hankow Railway 粵漢鐵路
Canton-Kowloon Railway 廣九鐵路
Chang Chen-wu 張振武
Chang Chien 張謇
Chang Chih-tung 張之洞
Chang Ching-yao 張敬堯
Chang Hsien-p'ei 張先培
Chang Hsün 張勳
Chang Shao-tseng 張紹曾
Chang Tso-lin 張作霖
Chao Ping-chün 趙秉鈞
*Che-chiang ch'üan-sheng t'ieh-lu kung-
   ssu* 浙江全省鐵路公司
Ch'en Ch'i-mei 陳其美
Ch'en Huan 陳宧
Chen-nan-kuan 鎮南關
Cheng-chih hui-i 政治會議
Cheng-fu kung-pao 政府公報
Cheng Hsiao-hsu 鄭孝胥
Ch'eng Te-ch'üan 程德全
Chiang-an 江安
Chiao-t'ung Bank 交通銀行
Chin-wei chün 禁衛軍
Ch'in-lien-chou 欽廉州
Chin-pu tang 進步黨
Ching-men-chou 荊門州
Ch'ing-yüan lien-ho hui 請願聯合會
Chiu Chin 秋瑾
Ch'ou-an hui 籌安會
Chou Hsüeh-hsi 周學熙
Chow Tzu-ch'i 周自齊

Chün-chi ch'u 軍機處
Chün-tzu fu 軍諮府
Chün-wu yüan 軍務院
Chung-hua min-kuo yo-fa 中華民國
   約法

En-ming 恩銘

Fang-ch'eng 防城
Fang Wei 方維
'*Fatshan*' 佛山
Feng Kuo-chang 馮國璋
Fu-pi yün-tung 復辟運動

Gaimusho 外務省
Genro 元老

Haichow 海州
Hara Kei 原敬
Hayashi Tadasu 林董
Hioki Eki 日置益
Ho-k'ou 河口
Hsiangtan 湘潭
Hsiao-chan 小站
Hsiao Feng-hsien 小鳳仙
Hsien-cheng ch'ou-pei hui 憲政籌備會
Hsien-cheng kung hui 憲政公會
Hsien-cheng p'ien-ch'a kuan 憲政編查館
Hsiung Hsi-ling 熊希齡
Hsü Hsi-lin 徐錫麟
Hsü Shih-ch'ang 徐世昌
Hsüan-t'ung 宣統
Hu Han-min 胡漢民
Hu-k'ou 湖口
Hu-kuo yün-tung 護國運動
Hukwang Railways 湖廣鐵路

Huang Fu 黃郛
Huang Hsing 黃興
Hung-hsien 洪憲
Hung Shu-tsu 洪述祖

I Tsung-k'uei 易宗夔
Ijuin Hikokichi 伊集院彥吉
Inouye Kaoru 井上馨
Inouye Katsunosuke 井上勝之助
Ishii Kikujirō 石井菊次郎

K'ang Yu-wei 康有爲
Ko-sheng tzu-i chü lien-ho hui 各省諮
    議局聯合會
K'ao-cha cheng-chih kuan 考察政治館
Kato Komei 加藤高明
Kiao-Tsi Railway 膠濟鐵路
Kokuryukai 黑龍會
Koo, Wellington, Wei-chün 顧維鈞
Ku Chung-shen 顧忠琛
Kuang-hsü 光緒
Kuang-tung yüeh-han t'ieh-lu kung-ssu
    廣東粵漢鐵路公司
Kuo-hui ch'ing-yüan t'ung-chi hui
    國會請願同志會
Kuo-min chüan 國民捐
Kuo-min ta-hui 國民大會
Kuo-t'i 國體

Laichow 萊州
Lanchow 蘭州
Lan T'ien-wei 藍天蔚
Lao Nai-hsüan 勞乃宣
Lao-shan-wan 勞山灣
Lei Fen 雷奮
Li-fa yüan 立法院
Li Hsieh-ho 李燮和
Li Lieh-chün 李烈鈞
Li-ling 醴陵
Li Ting-sing (Li Ting-hsin) 李鼎新
Li Tsung-huang 李宗黃

Li Yüan-hung 黎元洪
Liang Ch'i-ch'ao 梁啓超
Liang-pi 良弼
Liang Shih-i 梁士詔
Liang Tun-yen 梁敦彥
Liao Yü-ch'un 廖宇春
Lin-shih cheng-fu kung-pao 臨時政府
    公報
Liu Cheng-en 劉承恩
Liu Ch'un-lin 劉春霖
Liu chün-tzu 六君子
Liu Shih-pei 劉師培
Liu Tao-i 劉道一
Liu T'ing-shen 劉廷琛
Liu Ts'un-hou 劉存厚
Liu-yang 瀏陽
Lo Chieh 羅傑
Lu Cheng-hsiang 陸徵祥
Lu Tsung-yu 陸宗輿
Lu Yung-t'ing 陸榮廷
Luanchow 灤州
Luchow 瀘州
Lung Chi-kuang 龍濟光
Lung T'i-chien 龍體乾
Lung-yü 隆裕
Lungkow 龍口

Ma Chün-wu 馬君武
Matsui (? Iwane) 松井石根
Min-i 民意
Miyazaki Torazo 宮崎寅藏

Na-chi 納溪
Nan-chi 南溪
Nan-t'ien-pa 藍田壩
Ni Ssu-ch'ung 倪嗣冲
Niang-tzu-kuan 娘子關

Obata Torikichi 小幡酉吉
Odagiri Masunosuke 小田切萬壽之助
Ōkuma Shigenobu 大隈重信

Pei-yang chün 北洋軍
Peking-Hankow Railway 京漢鐵路
Peking-Mukden Railway 京奉鐵路
Peng Chia-chen 彭家珍
P'ing-hsiang 萍鄉
Po Wen-wei 柏文蔚
Prince Ch'ing 慶親王
Prince Ch'un 醇親王
Prince Kung 恭親王
Prince Su (Shan-chi) 肅王(善耆)
P'u-lun 溥淪
P'u Tien-chün 蒲殿俊

Sa-chen-ping 薩鎮冰
Saionji Kimmochi 西園寺公望
Shanghai-Nanking Railway 滬寧鐵路
Shanghai-Soochow-Hangchow Railway 滬杭甬鐵路
Sheng Hsüan-huai 盛宣懷
Shih-chia-chuang 石家莊
Shih-chiu hsin-t'iao 十九信條
Shishi 志士
Shiu-hing (Ch'ao-ch'ing) 肇慶
Shun-t'ien shih-pao 順天時報
Suchow 叙州
Su-fu 叙府
Sun Yat-sen (Sun Wen) 孫逸仙 (孫文)
Sun Yu-yün 孫毓筠
Sung Chiao-jen 宋教仁
Sung Yu-jen 宋育仁
Szechwan-Hankow Railway 川漢鐵路

Ta-Ch'ing Bank 大淸銀行
Tai K'an 戴勘
T'an Yen-k'ai 譚延闓
T'ang Chi-yao 唐繼堯
T'ang Shao-i 唐紹儀
T'ang Shou-ch'ien 湯壽潛
Tatsu Maru 二辰丸
T'ieh-liang 鐵良
T'ieh-lu tsung kung-ssu 鐵路總公司

T'ien-t'an hsien-fa ts'ao-an 天壇憲法草案
Tientsin-Pukow Railway 津浦鐵路
Ts'ai O 蔡鍔
Tsai-hsün 載洵
Tsai-t'ao 載濤
Ts'ai T'ing-kan 蔡廷幹
Tsai-tse 載澤
Ts'an-cheng yüan 參政院
Ts'ao kun 曹錕
Ts'en Ch'un-hsüan 岑春煊
Tseng Ju-cheng 鄭汝成
Tseng Kuang-luan 曾廣鑾
Tsung-she tang 宗社黨
tu-tu 都督
Tuan Ch'i-jui 段祺瑞
Tung-meng hui 同盟會
Tuan-fang 端方
Tzu-cheng yüan 資政院
Tzu-i chü 諮議局
Tz'u-hsi 慈禧
Tzu-yu hsing-tung 自由行動

Uchida Yasuya 內田康哉

Wai-wu pu 外務部
Waichow (Huichow) 惠州
Wang Chih-hsiang 王芝祥
Wang Ching-wei 汪精衛
Wang Ch'ung-hui 王寵惠
Wang Ta-hsieh 汪大燮
Wen-ming Bookstore 文明書店
Wen Tsung-yao 溫宗堯
Wu-chang chün cheng-fu 武昌軍政府
Wu Lu-chen 吳祿貞
Wu P'ei-fu 吳佩孚
Wu Shih-ying 武士英
Wu T'ing-fang 伍庭芳
Wu Wei-te 胡惟德
Wu Ying 胡瑛

INDEX

Shanghai-Ningpo railway: loan agreement 15, 19, 27
Shanghai-Woosung railway 12
Shensi 24, 76, 95, 120 n9
Shantung 64, 75, 76, 98, 112 n4; constitutional movement in 24, 53, 124 n80; foreign powers' occupation in 2, 81, 108 n5, 142 n17
Sheng Hsüan-huai 14, 112 n4, n8, n12, 114 n43; and railway loans 12, 18, 19, 20
Shensi 112 n4
Shensi provincial assembly 25
shishi 40
Shun-t'ien shih-pao 137 n109
Sinkiang 124 n80
Sino-Japanese War 72
Six gentlemen *(Liu chün-tzu)* 131 n6
Society for the Planning of Peace *(Ch'ouan hui)* 76, 85
Soochow-Hangchow-Ningpo railway 12, 15, 27
Stephen, A. G. 72, 73
Straight, Willard 45, 78
Su, Prince (Shan-chi) 11, 49, 52
Sun Yat-sen 62, 102; and the 1911 Revolution 38, 51, 52, 53, 54; relations with Japan 21, 40, 79; relations with Yüan Shih-k'ai 46, 48, 66, 68-70
Sun Yün-yu 131 n6
Sung Chiao-jen 55, 61, 66-68, 127 n18
Sung Yu-jen 76
Szechwan 20, 142 n1; anti-Yüan movements in 71, 91, 93, 94, 95, 96, 138 n128; railway rights in 17, 18, 114 n40
Szechwan railway riot 20, 24
Szechwan Party 96

Ta-Ch'ing Government Bank 18
Tadasu Hayashi 110 n30
Tai K'an 93
T'ai-p'ing Rebellion 1
T'an Yan-k'ai 116 n69
T'ang Chi-yao 91, 93, 99, 138 n125, n128
T'ang Shou-ch'ien 23, 116 n69
T'ang Shao-i 8, 44, 45, 47, 48, 110 n36, 126 n3; and railway loans 12, 20; and the Shanghai peace conference 37-38, 40, 45, 47, 48, 126 n9, n11; as premier of the Republic 55, 56, 57, 63, 66; relations with Yüan Shih-k'ai 27, 28, 64, 65, 77, 94
Tatsu Maru incident 24
Tibet 142 n1

T'ieh-liang 11, 49, 51
T'ieh-lu tsung kung-ssu see Railway Administration
T'ien-t'an hsien-fa ts'ao-an see Draft Constitution of the Altar of Heaven
Tientsin-Pukow railway 15, 53; agreement 13, 15, 16
Times, The 5, 6, 17, 44, 45, 54, 58
Tower, Reginald 8, 110 n32
Townley, Walter 8, 110 n32
Townsend, M. W. 31, 34, 36
Ts'ai O 91, 93, 94, 96, 99, 138 n124, n128
Ts'ai T'ing-kan 46, 49, 50, 121 n35, 124 n87
Tsai-hsün 11
Tsai-t'ao 11
Tsai-tse 11, 49, 50
Ts'an-cheng yüan see Council of State
Ts'ao Ju-lin 138 n126
Ts'ao Kun 91
Tsen Ch'un-hsüan 70
Tseng Ju-cheng 73
Tseng Kuang-luan 118 n83
Tsingtao, Japanese occupation of 80-81
Tsou Lu 128 n24
Tsung-she tang see Imperial Clan Party
Tuan Ch'i-jui 40, 45, 52, 87, 134 n67
Tuan-fang 11, 14, 112 n4
Tung-meng hui 2, 20, 21, 67, 127 n18
Twenty-one Demands 76, 82-85
Tyler, William Ferdinard 72-73
Tyrrell, William G. 6, 104
Tzu-cheng yüan see national assembly
Tz'u-hsi (empress dowager) 10, 22, 27, 31, 52, 53
Tzu-i chü see provincial assemblies

Uchida Yasuya 40, 41, 43, 44, 122 n55
United Kingdom *see* Great Britain
United States of America 40, 115 n45; loans to China 3, 17, 30, 31; relations with China 27, 91, 99, 105, 142 n17, relations with Japan 78, 79, 87; relations with Great Britain 88, 97, 98, 102, 104, 106

Wai-chiao pu see Chinese Foreign Ministry
Wai-wu pu see Ministry of Foreign Affairs
Wang Ch'ing-wei 21, 28, 46, 48
Wang Shih-hsiang 66
Wang Ta-hsieh 13, 14, 20, 112 n2
Warren, Sir Pelham 110 n32